M

Investor Therapy

ALSO BY DR. RICHARD GEIST

The Psychology of Investing
(co-edited by Lawrence E. Lifson)

Investor Therapy

A PSYCHOLOGIST AND INVESTING GURU TELLS YOU HOW TO OUT-PSYCH WALL STREET

Dr. Richard Geist

CROWN
BUSINESS
NEW YORK

Grateful acknowledgment is made to the following for permission to reprint previously published material.

Harcourt, Inc. and Faber and Faber Ltd.: Excerpt from the poem "Burnt Norton" from *Four Quartets* by T.S. Eliot. Copyright © 1936 by Harcourt, Inc. and renewed in 1964 by T.S. Eliot. Reprinted by permission of Harcourt, Inc. Published in Great Britain by Faber and Faber Ltd.

Harvard University Press: Excerpt from the poem "Wonder-is not precisely knowing" from *The Poems of Emily Dickinson* edited by Thomas H. Johnson. (Cambridge, Mass.,: The Belknap Press of Harvard University Press.). Copyright © 1951, 1955, 1979 by the President and Fellows of Harvard College. Reprinted by permission of the publishers and the Trustees of Amherst College.

None of the advice in this book is meant to be, or should be, viewed as specific advice to buy or not buy any identified stock or group of stocks.

Published by Crown Business, New York, New York.
Member of the Crown Publishing Group, a division of Random House, Inc.
www.randomhouse.com

CROWN BUSINESS is a trademark and the Rising Sun colophon is a registered trademark of Random House, Inc.

Printed in the United States of America

Design by Karen Minster

Library of Congress Cataloging-in-Publication Data
Geist, Richard A.
Investor therapy : a psychologist and investing guru tells you how to out-psych Wall Street / Richard Geist.—1st ed.
Includes bibliographical references and index.
1. Investments—Psychological aspects. 2. Stocks—Psychological aspects. I. Title.
HG4515.15.G45 2003
332.6'01'9—dc21
2003002439

ISBN 0-609-60916-5

10 9 8 7 6 5 4 3 2 1

First Edition

FOR SUSAN, WITH LOVE

ACKNOWLEDGMENTS

This book had its beginning in the consultation room. In the late 1980s I was seeing in psychotherapy a number of individuals who talked openly about their investment mistakes. They included both professional and amateur investors, although none of their investment concerns had precipitated a referral to see me. In listening to the stories that were being told around the therapeutic campfire, however, I began to realize that 98 percent of these very competent individuals' errors were psychological rather than financial. In other words, despite having access to similar investment information, the way they used that information, the judgments they made, were rooted in their psychological histories, not their financial knowledge.

That initial experience stimulated me to begin making inquiries outside the consulting room. Interviews with professional investors and individual investors taught me that every investment choice was burdened with psychological baggage that could either help or hinder decision-making. Years of collecting such data structured the form and content of this book. So at the outset I would like to acknowledge the many investors who were willing to share their stories with me. Despite remaining anonymous in the following pages, you are the mainstay of this book, and your examples, both specific and composite, will go a long way to helping other investors understand the psychological underpinnings of their investment decisions.

To these unnamed sources, I need to add the names of several individuals who have made both direct and indirect contributions to this book. Because of the interdisciplinary nature of the psychology of investing, they come from a variety of fields. On the psychological side of the street, my original mentors, Lee Bramson, Erik Erikson, and Robert White, were all instrumental in encouraging me to apply psychological thinking outside the consulting room. On the extremely important application of the relatively new field of Self Psychology to the understanding of investing, Anna Ornstein, both personally and through her writings, was a continual source of inspiration and gave generously of her time when I first began to apply self psychology to my clinical work. I continue to profit and rely on the work of Bob Stolorow and his colleagues, whose papers I cite numerous times through this book. I am also indebted to those teachers who helped me understand the value of clinical work for both patients and investors—Bill Crowell, Bob Eisendrath, and Alan Prager. Haskell Cohen, my psychology doctoral thesis adviser, introduced me to the investment world and has remained a constant friend, critic, and sounding board as we have navigated the ups and downs of the market and life together over these many years.

On the investing side of the street, there are three friends whose psychological insights into the investment world contributed to the writing of this book. Michael Lauer is a bold value investor whose understanding of the psychological aspects of investing surpasses many who make the field their occupation. This book benefited enormously from conversations with him over the years, and from his loyal support and encouragement of my work. Bruce Cowen's generosity in sharing his knowledge of the business world, as well as his friendship and support, has been enormously sustaining. I am deeply indebted to Doug Stahl, whose commitment to me and this project went well beyond the call of friendship. He generously worked behind the scenes with me to polish and enhance the final draft. His editorial and content suggestions were invaluable in improving the expression, clarity, and expansion of many ideas.

I also want to acknowledge the influence of several colleagues who have unwittingly contributed to my ideas by allowing me a glimpse into their thinking processes. Patrick O'Donnell, former chief of equity research at Putnam Investments, was instrumental in allowing me to participate in his introduction of a psychological perspective into a major mutual fund culture, and in the process I benefited from his very atypical institutional perspective as well as his wealth of investment knowledge. At Capital International Asset

Management, J. C. Massar, Maria Khader, and Alisia Coon fostered a welcoming and stimulating atmosphere that enabled me to develop the investment personality questionnaire that is in the appendix to the book; its development contributed to my further understanding of the relationship between personality style and investing. Thanks also to Michael Lipper at the Lipper Group and Barbara Levin at the Forum for Investor Advice for stimulating me to think further about the issues of risk and investing personality. CEOs George Belsey, Michael Lobsinger, and Bob MacDonald unwittingly offered me a virtual course in the often-unacknowledged pressures and pleasures of piloting small companies along the always-rocky road of building shareholder value. Similarly stock brokers Charlie Cox, Kelly Wentzel, and Bob Retz introduced me to the inner workings of the broker's thought processes. Thank you especially to Bob for the many hours of discussion that helped to clarify important concepts expressed in these pages. The book also benefited from my conversations with Chuck Jaffe, Mark Mills, and Chris Pummer, three journalists whose probing questions always force me to rethink my ideas. Larry Isen encouraged me to express some of my original ideas on his website, OTCjournal.com, which resulted in feedback that served to enhance the ideas in this book. Ken Korb, Jim Maselan, and Jeff Rudman were always available to help me understand the legal side of the investing world. Larry Lifson and John Schott, my colleagues and friends at Harvard Medical School, and my co-chair of Harvard's almost annual Psychology of Investing Conference, collaborated in numerous ways that significantly deepened my knowledge of the field. To Michael and Cindy Seligmann and Al Krause, thank you for helping with the launch of a newsletter that became the initial vehicle for expressing many of the ideas presented here.

Special thanks to David Dreman, who is probably the unrecognized father of the psychology of investing and behavioral finance. David was aware of the impact of psychology on investing long before it was recognized by the investment community. His invitation to participate as a member of the Institute of Psychology and Financial Markets and assume a place on the editorial board of the *Journal of Psychology and Financial Markets*—later to become the

Journal of Behavioral Finance—put me in touch with those leading thinkers who remain at the forefront of Behavioral Finance. David's yearly forums on Behavioral Finance and the meetings of the editorial board are constant sources of stimulation that I will always value.

There have been many readers of this manuscript in various stages and drafts. Some were reading my ideas even before the book idea was formulated. All contributed feedback that improved the book. Any failure to heed their comments and criticisms is solely mine. Peter Bernstein, Bruce Cowen, Michael Lauer, Steve Lord, Don McGregor, Patrick O'Donnell, Mal Slavin, and Charles Styron all read parts of this manuscript. And Paul Merriman kindly read the draft from beginning to end.

Esmond Harmsworth, my literary agent, was instrumental in encouraging me to pursue this project. He not only helped to define the scope of the book, but carefully read several versions of the manuscript and added immeasurably to its content and style. My editor, John Mahaney, knew just when to help polish the material and when to allow me to stay true to my style.

Thank you to my family for their love and support in this venture. To my children, I am forever grateful for teaching me the most important lessons and embedding my life with meaning. My sons, David, Mark, and Daniel, through their interests in medicine, psychology, and business, all share aspects of my dual career; and my daughter, Sarah, with her inspiring "spiritedness," was continually tolerant of the time spent on this project. Kristina Wilson, my daughter-in-law, has enriched both the emotional and intellectual life of my family. I would also like to thank Rosalie and Donald Schiff and Corinne Geist for their loving support, and Lester and Dorothy Geist, my parents, for always encouraging me to pursue what was meaningful to me regardless of the barriers.

And this brings me to one final and most important person to acknowledge—my wife, Susan, to whom this book is dedicated. She is not only the love of my life, but a true partner in everything we do. Susan has read every word in this book, and readers will benefit from her sage psychological advice. But beyond that, it is hard to put into words how much I rely on our relationship. There is no one I would rather love, laugh, play, and work with. To the degree that this book explicates not only the psychology of the stock market, but how we make life decisions in times of uncertainty, it emanates from this relationship. For the opportunity to live my life with her, I will be forever grateful.

CONTENTS

When Psychology Meets Finance

In the quiet solitude of a recent sleepless night, as earnings estimates, P/E ratios, inventories, debt to equity, and a myriad of other financial ratios danced before my eyes in a kaleidoscopic image of precise combinations, I emerged from the dark room into the dim shadows of moonlight, tempted to turn on the computer and get online. Although most of my stocks were down, I was particularly worried about one company, LifeUSA, which had dropped about 22 percent below my recommended price. In those days 22 percent was significant—enough so that most of my phone calls that day had been from irritated investors wanting to know whether to sell their stock. I had a fantasy that collecting more data, studying a few more technical indicators, or reading a few more reports might offer some reassuring insight. If only I understood the company better, more comprehensively, more rationally, I imagined that I'd be able to make some productive decisions in the morning. Instead I elected to avoid the market completely and settled into reading Emily Dickinson. In the small circle of flickering light, I came across the following lines:

> *Wonder—is not precisely Knowing*
> *And not precisely Knowing not—*
> *A beautiful but bleak condition*
> *He has not lived who has not felt—*[1]

Dickinson could not have foreseen the information superhighway, but her words—"Wonder is not precisely knowing"—brought me back to reality. The stock market is not just a collection of precise data culled from a computer and processed through the medium of statistical screens. The market is composed of human beings who make decisions based on their individual psychology and those with whom they work, interact, and compete. Our successes and failures in the market, as elsewhere, reflect both human foibles and talents. Each transcends computerized trading and stock-picking programs, as well as all the data we accumulate through our modems, broadband networks, and number-crunching software.

It had been a rough period for LifeUSA, a relatively new insurance company that provided innovative life insurance and annuity products. Sales were weak, and earnings in the first quarter had dropped 71 percent. All the analysts covering the stock had lowered their ratings from buy to hold, which in Wall Street lingo meant sell. Intellectually, rationally, I knew the numbers suggested to most folks that LifeUSA should be sold. Despite the numbers, however, I was psychologically convinced that LifeUSA's depressed stock price was offering a wonderful buying opportunity.

Earlier in my career I would have dismissed that emotional conviction and sold the stock. But several years of tracking my own and other investors' mistakes had taught me something unexpected. If you rely only on the facts and other ostensibly rational information to understand the market, you're an incomplete investor. Uncertainty in the market is too pervasive to be transcended with facts and figures. I came to understand that making sense of the emotions generated by that uncertainty could be useful in guiding investment decisions. For example, one of the things I had learned about my own emotional reactions when buying stocks was that whenever I felt unusually anxious after purchasing a stock, it was a clue that I'd made a good decision; whenever I felt confident, it all too often turned out to be a poor decision. Another emotional guide discerned from my own investing was a repeating pattern in my psychological reaction to management. Whenever I left an interview with the feeling that I would like to work for this CEO, the company managed to struggle through hard times and recover. I also found myself associating images with companies. Over time I learned to tie the personal meaning of similar images with positive or negative company outcomes. These emotional guides were developed over many years. They obviously represented unconscious messages to myself. When recognized as emotional themes, they offered important information that supplemented what was publicly available.

Applying these lessons to LifeUSA, I had felt very anxious after recommending and buying the stock. My conversations with Bob MacDonald, its CEO, left me feeling that I would love to work for him. He was the first breath of creativity I had met in the stodgy insurance business. Each time I talked with him, I had the visceral feeling that management could, in fact, overcome the smug conventions of the insurance industry and implement its unconventional business plan. My visual associations conjured up images of some of my favorite hiking trails in the White Mountains, which I idiosyncratically associated with several successful companies I had picked in the past. I also had a gut feeling that, because of the excitement I sensed about the company, it would eventually become a target for a large acquirer that would share my emotional excitement.

When the emotional side is telling me to do one thing and the near-term facts are indicating the opposite, I always find it useful to search for more supporting information from the "objective" side. The growth of LifeUSA had been spectacular. Starting from revenues of just under $7 million in 1988, the company increased its revenues to almost $1 billion in 1994. Net investment income had increased at a compounded rate of 42 percent per year during the same time frame. The company also earned a profit in every year except its first, and its expenses were below the industry average. Emotionally it also made no sense to me that in 1993, when its total assets were at $974 million and the stock price was moving toward $20 per share, analysts had a buy recommendation on the stock. With projections of $2 billion in assets for 1995 and the stock price at $7, they had the stock on hold (or sell). This combination of emotional and factual indicators swayed me to stick with the company. Five years later LifeUSA was acquired for just over $20 per share.

On this lonely night I was rediscovering what psychology had taught me long ago. To attain a competitive edge, we cannot depend solely on rationally dissecting and figuring out the market or an individual stock as an external entity, or on developing systems that shield us from our emotions. Stock picking is part science, part art, part luck, part intuition, and always uncertain—"not precisely knowing." Because of these inherent subjective elements, successful investing depends on understanding our emotional reactions to the market and its participants. Buried in these emotional responses are both investment errors and investment strengths that remain mostly unconscious unless we devote substantial energy to unearthing them and then leveraging what we learn about ourselves into profitable decision-making. My objective in this book is to help you become a better investor by integrating your emotional understanding of yourself into your investing strategies.

Every investor's dream is to outperform the market. The sad truth, however, is that outperforming is hard to do. Even professionals find it difficult to beat the market. A 1993 study of money-manager performance by Charles Ellis indicates that 75 percent underperformed the S&P 500 between 1970 and 1990.[2] They fared no better in the last decade according to a study by the Lipper Group.[3] That study indicates that during the 1990s fewer than 33 percent of U.S. stock funds managed to outperform their market benchmarks. Informal interviews with individual investors suggest that outperforming the market is at least as difficult for the nonprofessional.

This begs the obvious question of why so many intelligent, competent, creative investors and money managers fail to outperform the market. David Dreman was one of the original thinkers to spearhead research into this question. In his early work, Dreman commented that "to outdo the market we must first have a good idea of the (psychological) forces that time and again victimize even the pros. Once these forces are understood, investors can build defenses and find ways to skirt the pitfalls."[4] Since then there have been many attempts to understand why it is so difficult to outperform the market. On the institutional side, professionals such as Ellis[5] argue that transaction costs lower managers' performance; and competition is so fierce that it obviates a winner. Some economists say the market is so efficient that stock prices reflect all available information, and prices adjust so quickly to this information that any competitive edge is unattainable. Money managers argue that institutions are nothing more than a surrogate for the market and therefore cannot outperform themselves.

On the individual side, investment books are also replete with possible answers to the same question: We sell too early; we hold on too long; we buy concept stocks; we underestimate the severity of an earnings shortfall; we fail to do our homework; we lack a consistent methodological approach to the market; we take too much risk (or we don't take *enough* risk). Behavioral economists have addressed this question with a voluminous literature outlining how our judgments are compromised by cognitive biases when processing complex information.[6] These studies describe a series of cognitive errors that plague investors when making decisions under conditions of risk. These run the gamut from mental accounting, endowment, and overconfidence to representativeness, anchoring, and availability.

Even when investors are aware of their biases, even when they know they tend to sell low and buy high, and even when they scold themselves for investing on tips and rumors or blindly following analysts' recommendations, there is no guarantee of outperforming the market. A study by Fischhoff, for example, warns that most people are unable to alter their behavior.[7] This squares with the maxim in psychotherapy that intellectual insight and awareness of a behavior do not alone lead to change. It appears equally true in the investment world. Knowing that biases exist is the first step in compensating for them, but it is only the first step. What we really need is a systematic understanding of the psychology that underlies these biases, a psychology of investor decision-making. I emphasize this because the one certainty I've found in the market is that the only way to succeed is to understand how our idiosyncratic emotions can undermine or enhance our investment decisions.

To even approach this understanding, however, requires an unusual combination of skills, including the skills that usually come from training in dynamic psychology and experience in the investment world. In the early days of my graduate training in psychology, most investors had little interest in how their emotions affected investment decisions, and most psychologists had no interest in the investing world. It wasn't until the 1990s that participants in the two fields really began to talk with each other. I was fortunate because my first mentor, the renowned psychoanalyst Erik Erikson, strongly encouraged me to apply psychoanalytic thinking to areas outside the consulting room.

And while I spent many years doing clinical work, teaching, and supervising at Children's Hospital and Massachusetts General Hospital in Boston, I was also privately a fascinated student of the stock market or, more accurately, of how individuals made decisions under conditions of risk. This interest was stimulated by the early writings of David Dreman, Claude Rosenberg, and Paul Slovic. But it remained only a personal interest until the early 1990s, when several of us at Harvard Medical School decided to bring together a group of seminal educators and leaders in the fields of investment and psychology to explore the interface between human emotions and financial decision-making. With the support of investment professionals such as Dreman, Rosenberg, Claudia Mott, Martin Pring, and John Train, we held our first conference in March 1995. Since then it has grown into a nearly annual event, and the growing interest by the investment community, behavioral finance researchers, cognitive psychologists, and psychoanalytic thinkers has made the psychology of investing a movement and field of study in its own right.

My involvement in this movement has slowly altered my career. During the past decade, as more individuals have entered the market, technology has provided easy access to information, and the indexing/benchmarking movements have spawned both a stock-market bubble and a crash, we have learned more about the role of emotions in rational decision-making. I've been fortunate to be in the middle of what has become a real cultural transformation. In my role as psychotherapist, consultant to money managers, newsletter publisher, self-trained financial analyst, and consultant to small companies, I've had the opportunity to interview hundreds of investors and managers. From helping to hire financial analysts, to developing investment personality and investment risk questionnaires, to discussing investment errors and successes with a wide cross section of the investment community, to treating in psychotherapy a number of very talented investment professionals and individual investors, I've heard many stories from investors that have assumed a familiar ring.

My experiences with this diverse group of investors taught me that success in the market, particularly since the emergence of the Internet, no longer depends solely on how smart we are, what information we possess, what academic degrees we've earned, how much experience we've gained, or what technical or fundamental systems we use. Rather the key to success is how well we understand and handle our emotions when it comes to our investments.

As I listened carefully to this group of investors, it became clear to me that access to information and financial understanding, long considered the sine qua non for investing success, was meaningless unless the investors who collect the information have a psychological awareness of their own subjectivity and an understanding of how they emotionally react to and interpret the growing plethora of available data. You can possess all the information in the world—all the financial statements, annual reports, analyst reports, and media coverage of investments—but to use it effectively in your own portfolio, you have to know yourself and your emotional makeup. And you can judge how effective an investor you are only by looking at how you have used this information in the past and learn from it.

The information I have collected from investors is very different from the investment psychology information accumulated from surveys, questionnaires, and experimental and quantitative research methods. Those tools have been developed to study investment decision-making from a distance, as if using a telescope to study the stars. Taking a different tack, I have attempted to understand investment decision-making from within the investor's personal perspective. Instead of using questionnaires and conducting laboratory experiments, I have used interview skills acquired in my psychotherapeutic training to investigate from a clinical perspective the more in-depth subjective experiences of investors as they made winning and losing decisions each day in the market.

The type of research we perform often determines the type of data collected. I sensed early on in the course of my work in this field that there was a dearth of data on the subjective experience of investors in the act of making important financial decisions. Little attention was being paid to discovering what investors were actually feeling when they bought and sold stocks. How did they react to success and failure in the market? Why does the herd have such an impact on some investors and not on others? How did investors decide how much risk they should take? How did they develop patience or fail to develop patience? Are there particular psychological characteristics that make for successful investing? These were the questions that framed my qualitative research in my efforts to add a case-study method to the other valuable research already being done in the field.

My work in this field during the past decade has led to a shocking conclusion. I discovered that almost all investors admit privately, at least after some soul-searching, that their successes and mistakes have been shaped by deeper psychological forces that seem to underlie most of the costly judgments and spectacular achievements on both Wall Street and Main Street. Most investors also acknowledged that even more important than knowing how to succeed in the market is knowing how to avoid the common, almost endemic mental errors. In fact, the most frequently requested talk I give to investment groups is titled "The Psychology of Investor Mistakes." There is a pervasive taboo in the investment community against discussing mistakes. Investors have continually told me that they have been taught not to discuss their errors but merely to forget about them and move on. Unfortunately, that prevents us from learning from our mistakes.

This bias is almost universal within the professional investment community, perhaps understandably when you consider that mistakes with other people's money generally lead to job loss and public humiliation. In an interesting experiment devised at one mutual fund to which I was a consultant, this trend was reversed by offering financial bonuses to analysts who, upon recognizing a mistake, were willing to come forward and immediately discuss it with the chief of equity research. Such a policy had a dramatic effect on analysts' willingness to acknowledge, learn from, and reverse their errors quickly. Although I cannot offer you a direct bonus for beginning to think about the psychology underlying your decisions, including your mistakes and successes, your investment rewards from this effort can be substantial, even if you can eliminate just 10 percent of your most common errors.

This book will not help you minimize errors by determining how to combine assessments of profitability, liquidity, return on investment, operating efficiency, and debt ratios to judge a company's chances of success. There are plenty of worldly publications on those mechanics. Instead this book is intended to open doors that can help you understand and process the emotions that drive your investing. This will not make you a *perfect* investor, a brilliant computerlike mind that can swoop in and out of the markets and earn bushels of cash. Although I believe the *human* mind beats the computer at the investing game every time, not even Warren Buffett, Peter Lynch, or George Soros is a perfect investor. Don't try to be. Concentrate instead on your Self—who you are, how you react to success and failure, how you tolerate anxiety, how you respond to the pressures of the herd. Concentrate on getting to know yourself well enough to use your emotions to enhance your performance.

I will try to help you learn how to leverage your emotions rather than exorcise them. This should go a long way to improve your market performance, particularly after you relinquish the goal of becoming a perfect investor. On the contrary, you will realize that you don't need perfect understanding of every company you invest in, and you don't need to act like an unemotional, unintuitive robot to achieve superior market performance. All you need do is to become psychologically good enough.

I have borrowed the term *good enough* from the British psychoanalyst Donald Winnicott's concept of "the good enough mother."[8] What he meant by this phrase is that mothers (and fathers) are not mechanically perfect beings who can always perceive and respond to their infants in precisely the right or requisite manner. Rather they are humans who have their own needs, moods, and weaknesses that occasionally interfere with sustained empathic responsiveness to their children. As Winnicott once stated metaphorically, there are times when "the [parent's] mind has dropped the baby." But in the good enough mother or father, those times are the exceptions since there is a "good enough," but not perfect, ongoing ability to sense and address the offspring's needs.

In my experience the good enough investor is emotionally aware enough of his own psychology to adapt it flexibly to the market. As civilization has matured, markets have become more sophisticated and individuals have attained superior intelligence, but human emotions have remained static. It is the power of human psychology that undermines or facilitates even the most savvy individual investor's decisions. To be aware of your own psychology is to recognize and acknowledge that emotion is part and parcel of investment decision-making and that perfection in the investing game is an illusory concept. Part of this awareness is the realization that much of our investment behavior is shaped by what I will describe as our own unconscious organizing patterns or lenses through which we filter all the data we take in every day. Because organizing lenses are composed of emotional convictions—our longstanding, idiosyncratic ways of seeing the world—investing is by definition a subjective skill. Trying to invest without insight into these emotional convictions is counterproductive because they linger in the background and unconsciously influence our ostensibly rational decisions. The good enough investor has some self-awareness of these patterns and can leverage them to better stock-market performance, for he or she knows that long-term success or failure is related less to the market than to the unique, individual ways we interpret the information the market sends us.

The good enough investor has mastered an investing behavior best suited to his own skills and needs and is in harmony with his personality and lifestyle. Just as we all develop circles of competence and expertise, we also develop emotional styles and preferences that influence our choice of investments. For example, in interviewing money managers and analysts at a large mutual-fund firm, I found that analysts were much more emotionally predisposed to recommend stocks comfortably where they had reams of financial data on the issuers available to formulate financial models and forecasts. Money managers, on the other hand, tended to make stock-picking decisions based on an emotional preference for considering three or four important factors about the issuers. As one manager said, "It does me no good to have thousands of facts about the company. I just want to know the two or three things that other managers don't know." The difference in emotional proclivities is why the system of promoting analysts to money managers often doesn't work, because each profession rewards and punishes different emotional strengths and weaknesses. Similarly, in the individual investing world, if you're more excited about and interested in understanding and pursuing new ideas or innovative technologies, you will have a better fit with emerging growth companies; if you're fascinated by the intricacies of financial ratios and their meaning for the future success of a company, you may have a stronger affinity for large-cap stocks.

The good enough investor understands that risk is a subjective phenomenon related to the psychology of judgment and loss rather than a mathematical equivalent of volatility. For a long time the investment community had convinced investors that if their stock or portfolio bounced around more than the market indexes, they were engaging in high-risk investing. Based on this assumption, financial organizations have developed a plethora of "optimizers" to determine appropriate risk levels for their customers. But these optimizers are based, for the most part, on your assets and liabilities, your investing time frame, and your future cash needs. They generally ignore what I will argue are the most important determinants of risk: the psychological phenomena related to your emotional ability to tolerate the consequences of loss. Personality characteristics like optimism or pessimism, your capacity for modulating tension and stress, your use of denial, and whether you perceive time as moving slowly or quickly become much more meaningful in determining not only your capacity for risk, but also whether you should be acting on your capacity for taking risk. And because your comfort or discomfort with risk is a psychological phenomenon, you will discover that it is not static. It will vary according to the changes in your relationships, the context of your life, and your access to various safety nets.

I first understood the nuances of risk when I was studying the relationship between financial advisers and clients. I came to realize that clients' risk capacities changed according to their perceptions of their relationships with their advisers. Viewing your capacity for risk through a psychological lens can dramatically change your investing strategies and give you new insight into your financial planning.

The successful investor realizes that he is a human investor, not a machine. Thanks to an appreciation of the human condition, the successful investor also realizes that the managers of companies share the same human emotions. Therefore it is possible to interview management in a way that allows you to obtain invaluable subjective data about a company that cannot be discerned from reading annual reports, financial statements, and press releases. Once you understand the subjective nature of how your emotional convictions influence your financial decisions, you will be able to extract from this book various techniques for using this information to understand how management's psychology can often determine the success or failure of a company. Through the use of the psychological methodology called empathy, you will also be able to understand the psychology of other market players. Again, you need not master these techniques. Just know them well enough to outwit those players and achieve superior performance. And by understanding the psychology of other players in the market, instead of always searching for events or rumors to guide your moves, you will develop an emotional flexibility that will help you comfortably anticipate the future and plan responsively rather than merely react to unfolding events.

For years investment books have tried to convince market participants to search for systems or methodologies to eliminate emotion from their investment decisions. Like it or not, however, emotions are endemic to the human condition. When our stocks are crashing, we all feel anxious. We may be able to push that anxiety under the rug, but eventually it will accumulate there, and we will end up tripping. Through interviewing investors for the past ten years, I have learned that it is much more productive to acknowledge and recognize this anxiety, as well as our other investment-related emotions, and to understand ahead of time how they influence our reactions in the stock market. As I will illustrate, one effect of anxiety is to influence the nature of our thought processes so we are more likely to make decisions based on one or two variables (such as price and volume) rather than a whole picture that includes fundamentals, technicals, competition, management, and product and services. This jigsaw-puzzle thinking can have a disastrous effect on our decisions if we are unaware of its consequences. And not surprisingly, the underlying emotions persist despite our best attempts to eliminate them from our awareness or our investment behavior.

Outperforming the market requires years of study and practical experience. Successful investors never stop learning. Instead of approaching this book as a how-to cookbook of get-rich-quick promises, look upon it as a practical set of guidelines for becoming a more psychologically sophisticated and complete investor. When you join me on this journey to becoming a more complete, good enough investor, you will pierce the darkness to learn lessons that may help you reap handsome financial rewards. Mistakes will occur less often, and you will learn how to use psychology to your advantage.

Investor Therapy

ONE

Emotions in the Marketplace

No one can escape the transforming power of the stock market. Investing, once practiced on the periphery of society by a small group of like-minded professionals, has become a cultural phenomenon. More than 50 percent of all households now own stocks in one form or another, double what it was in 1987. Baby-boomers depend on the stock market to put children through college and to retire; financial websites and stock message boards have become the most popular destinations in cyberspace; and the number of household trading online tripled to 6.3 million from 1998 to mid-1999. People browsing the newspaper now turn to the business section before the sports section or comics, and the Federal Reserve's interest-rate decisions are now headline news anxiously awaited by the masses.

Our connections to the stock market have become part of everyday life. Investors now play out in real time and with real money the realities of winning and losing that used to be limited to the fantasies of Monday-morning quarterbacking. Between January 1998 and October 2002, investors made and then lost more money than they ever imagined was possible. While some cashed out with millions, more than $7 trillion was lost in the wake of the technology bubble that closed out the twentieth century. Is it any wonder that investing has triggered such a powerful quest to learn how to win what Charles Ellis once referred to as the "loser's game"?[1]

WE ARE ALL SUBJECTIVE INVESTORS

One of the most important lessons I have learned in my years of consulting with investors is that winning the loser's game requires that we appreciate the highly subjective and personal nature of the investing process. Each minute of the day the stock market generates a vast array of data: market performance numbers, economic statistics, company information, and geopolitical happenings. Thanks to the Internet, all of this data is now at our fingertips. But thanks to human nature, we each react to this market information in our own personal, unique way.

What shapes our perceptions of the market goes far beyond the "real" data we uncover on the Internet, in the newspapers, or on CBS Marketwatch, Yahoo!, MSN, CNN, Fox, or CNBC. We take each bit of information we receive and then interpret it through lenses that organize the data into some personally meaningful interpretation that can be translated into action or the deferral of action. These lenses are formed by our idiosyncratic personalities and emotional makeup. As a result, we all react differently to each piece of new information we glean, garner, or abstract from the marketplace.

One of the enduring findings to emerge from psychological research in the past thirty years is that a primary motivation of all people is the need to make sense of the world around us, to create organization and meaning in our lives. During our formative years, we all unconsciously create principles that help us to organize automatically our many disparate experiences in the world. Our emotions and experiences not only color how we make meaning of the world, they shape the personal, emotional lenses through which we interpret all events, information, and encounters throughout our lives.[2]

Constance Hunting, the poet and critic, perhaps said it best: "Emotion dictates vision. Vision is therefore selective—the eye falls on what fits into the emotional scheme. In grief, for instance, everything reminds of the lost beloved. So the lost beloved becomes the world, and the world is arranged by the griever into a composite portrait of the one who has vanished."[3] This is equally true in the investing world.

Consider, for example, the everyday occurrence of stock picks in the newspaper. An investor scans the Market section of *The Wall Street*

Journal and reads that a well-known analyst has issued a buy recommendation on Pepsico. If you read the financial pages or check out Internet sites on the stock market, you will probably encounter many stock recommendations every day. How you interpret that information has much more to do with you than with the market.

After reading the analyst's enthusiastic recommendation for Pepsico in the *Journal*, our first investor, Ruth, reacts to the story by immediately calling her broker and buying Pepsi stock, even if it means selling her stock in some other company to do so. If we asked Ruth why she had made this decision, she would tell us it seemed like the natural thing to do or that it was the rational, smart thing to do. Ruth may agree with the analyst's theories about the beverage industry and the future demand for Pepsi and Pepsico's other products. Or she may simply assume lots of other investors will read the article and then buy Pepsico, and she might be trying to capitalize on the heightened demand for the stock.

Our second investor, Frederick, reacts very differently, deliberately choosing *not* to buy the stock. Frederick probably assumes that, because this recommendation appeared in the *Journal*, a paper read by millions of people every day, it is already too late to gain any advantage by buying the stock. According to Frederick, by the time he gets around to reading the *Journal*, Pepsico's stock has already felt any bump in the price, and it is simply too late for him to cash in on the rising tide.

Like Frederick, our third and final investor, Susannah, also reacts by not buying the stock, but for different reasons. Susannah is a bit of a cynic, a lesson she learned the hard way after following the recommendations of some star Internet analysts and watching her dot-com portfolio implode. She thinks that the analyst may not be telling the whole truth, that some huge investment bank, perhaps the analyst's employer, is stuck with a huge long position in Pepsico. The demand stimulated by the buy recommendation and ensuing price rise will help the brokerage firm reduce its holdings at the expense of the market. Or Susannah may just be the sort of investor who likes to make decisions based on her own assessment of the facts, not someone else's recommendation. She'll wait until Pepsico's interim results confirm or dispel the analyst's interpretation. Newspaper stock recommendations are almost always irrelevant to Susannah's investment decision-making.

I could give many more examples of how investors react to something as simple as a recommendation in the *Journal*, *Barron's*, or *Investor's Business Daily*, but that is not the key point. There is no right or wrong reaction to a recommendation beyond digesting the information to improve our understanding of the companies in which we invest. What is also important and perhaps even more valuable is for investors to figure out their standard behavior pattern in reacting to this sort of information. What separates Ruth, Frederick, and Susannah is their emotional reaction to reading the *Journal* article. How do they choose their way of interpreting and organizing the data?

My research suggests that each person will automatically organize the information he reads in the *Journal* according to the barely conscious and highly idiosyncratic organizing principles or lenses that he uses to structure his experiences. These principles are really "emotional convictions"[4] that have evolved and acquired their uniqueness through a lifetime of interactions with others. As investors, it is our personal experiences in and out of the market that shape these very subjective but stable windows "that lend form and meaning"[5] to our perceptions.

Ruth's lens is likely to be tinted with experiences in which trusting relationships with admired people provided her with information that proved reliable. Those experiences predispose her to believe she can trust and act on any statement from a well-known, respected analyst. Frederick's lens may be colored with a psychological feeling that he is usually behind the times or likely to miss the boat for new trends. Based on experience, he might believe other people with better connections or positions are likely to acquire and capitalize on information more quickly than he can.

Susannah seems to operate from an emotional conviction that she should never depend on anyone other than herself to make decisions. Her lens may be colored by historical incidents that give her good reasons to mistrust others. If so, the idea that a recommendation in the media could in any way benefit individual investors would now seem naive to her. Perhaps her cynicism took root when friends and contacts gave her information that turned out to help them but hurt her. Susannah concluded that, when it comes to research and facts, it's best for her to rely on herself and not on tips from others. She may therefore have an ingrained belief that any information in a newspaper stock-picking column is unreliable when compared to information gleaned from her own analysis of financial reports.

When we function according to our emotional convictions or organizing beliefs, we often do so unconsciously. We assume that the action of the stock market, rather than our emotional experience, is responsible for investment success or failure. However, long-term success and failure have little to do with the market. Both are related more specifically to the unique, individual way we interpret the information the market throws at us. Market theories, Internet message-board comments, pundit predictions, and individual investment decisions are typically based on these unexplored semiconscious emotional convictions—on feelings, not on facts.

Most of these emotional convictions remain unexplored in the investing community because there is a general resistance to examining our unconscious lest an inward glance distract us from the more reality-oriented task at hand—picking stocks. As Erik Erikson once stated, an individual who focuses on a specific external task "prefers enlightenment away from himself, which is why the best minds have often been least aware of themselves."[6] Although the well-known economist Merton Miller probably never studied the psychoanalyst Erikson, he confirmed this observation with his statement that behavioral finance is "too interesting and thereby distracts us from the pervasive market forces that should be our principal concern."[7] Individual investors comprise some of these best minds. Well educated, creative, and task-oriented, most investors are not trained or disposed to believe that our inner, unrecognized emotional convictions are capable of dramatically impacting what our thought processes analyze and create. In fact, consistent with Miller's observation, most investment theories suggest that the more we keep emotions at bay during the investing process, the more successful we will be.

This resistance to developing an in-depth understanding of investor psychology is in part responsible for economists' unwillingness to acknowledge that investing is a highly emotional, subjective process.

Instead for decades economists have based their decision-making systems on some rarefied models of rationality akin to *Star Trek*'s Mr.
Spock, for whom decisions should be based on pure logic, unencum-
bered by emotions or the ambiguities of human relationships, and
capable of some predetermined standard of perfection.

This philosophical view underlies the efficient market hypothesis
(EMH), which maintains that since stock prices necessarily reflect all
available information, it is nearly impossible for one individual to
know more than the market knows at any give time. The ramifications
of EMH contributed to the development of modern portfolio theory.
Taken to its logical conclusion, it follows from EMH that it is useless
to analyze stocks. If you accept this idea of a perfect market, as the
business schools began teaching, a monkey throwing darts at the stock
tables would have just as much success picking stocks as a well-trained
security analyst.

While the Internet bubble and its subsequent collapse made mon-
keys of many investors, money managers, and security analysts, this
hardly confirms EMH or its progeny. In fact, these events suggest
quite the opposite. As David Dreman has observed,

> The explanation for this phenomenon is relatively simple.
> Investment theory does not consider that psychology plays any
> role in investor decision-making, while in fact, in periods of
> mania and panic, the psychological influences play the leading
> role. Cognitive, social, and group psychology all provide
> numerous experiments that illustrate how psychological factors
> can divert investors from the purely rational decision-making of
> investment theory.[8]

Presumably even Mr. Spock would agree. Hopefully the awarding of
the 2002 Nobel Prize in Economics to Daniel Kahneman, one of the
founding fathers of behavioral finance, will help to put a final nail in
the EMH coffin.

But just as we do not always make rational decisions—especially
under conditions of risk—neither do we always make *irrational* decisions. Contrary to economic assumptions, human emotions are not by
definition irrational. The idea that psychological factors can divert
investors from purely rational decision-making implies that we should

do our best to eliminate these psychological factors (our emotions) when making investment judgments.

I strongly disagree. My clinical research indicates that no matter how much we try to eliminate emotions from the investing process, we will ultimately fail. Why? Because our unconscious emotional convictions (the emotionally tinted lenses through which we see the world) continue to operate and influence our decision-making, no matter how hard we try to deny them. As the Pepsico scenarios indicate, emotional patterns led Ruth, Frederick, and Susannah to make three different, well-thought-out decisions from available data. If asked, all three investors would believe their decisions were "rational" and "logical," no matter how much you challenged them. While Mr. Spock would disagree, it doesn't follow that any of these investors made decisions that were wrong for them.

DEMASIO'S RESEARCH AND
THE CASE OF ELLIOT

There is increasing neuroscientific evidence suggesting that without access to our feelings, it is really impossible to make rational decisions. Antonio Demasio is one of the most recognized proponents of this view. As he pointed out in *Descartes' Error*, ". . . Even after reasoning strategies become established in the formative years, their effective deployment probably depends, to a considerable extent, on a continued ability to experience feelings."[9]

In support of this premise, Demasio describes a patient, Elliot, who underwent surgery for a benign brain tumor in his frontal lobe. Although part of Elliot's frontal lobe tissue was removed with the tumor, the surgery was first thought to be successful. However, Elliot soon experienced a change in personality. His mental and physical capacities remained intact. He exhibited superior intelligence and no neurological dysfunction. But, as described by Demasio, "his ability to reach decisions was impaired, as was his ability to make an effective plan for hours ahead of him . . . especially when the decision involved personal or social matters."

Upon further examination, Damasio found that Elliot was virtually without feeling. He was unable to feel joy, fear, anger, sadness, excitement, or tenderness. Demasio's research indicated that Elliot's irrationality was not the result of too much emotion or any lack of cognitive reasoning. From the study of Elliot and similar patients, Damasio concluded that "reduction in emotion may constitute an equally important source of irrational behavior."

If we place Elliot in an investing context, I think we can accurately predict that he would perform poorly because investing requires both planning and the ability to make subjective decisions. In fact, researchers have found that from the very beginning of life, emotions (or "affects," as psychologists like to call them previous to their becoming experienced feelings) are the primary organizers of our experience.[10] In other words, our feelings not only serve as guideposts for how we experience ourselves, whether excited, sad, pensive, optimistic, pessimistic, anxious, or vulnerable, they also determine the enduring characteristics and spirit of our personality. This has profound implications for investing, although the usefulness of those implications in the investing process seems to have been largely ignored. So let's take a look at some of the functions emotions serve when making investment decisions under conditions of risk.

EMOTIONS IN THE INVESTING PROCESS

Emotions play a complex role in the investing process, but one that we can break down into five parts. To do well in the market, you must learn to *use* your emotions, not be *led* by or eliminate them. These are the five key ways in which you can use them:

Emotions Help Us Evaluate Our Options. Investing requires us to assign certain values to different options. If we all had access to perfect information and interpreted it the same way, we'd all have identical investment accounts. The fact that we don't, despite all the research tools and resources now available on the Internet, has more to do with emotion than with different degrees of access to information.

In estimating earnings based on available past results, many economists would argue that the analysis is straightforward. When analyzing most companies, professional analysts and individual investors generally have access to several years of historical data on which to

base their estimates. But as we know all too well, even audited earnings numbers can sometimes be massaged, and interim unaudited
numbers are subject to numerous fudge factors, enabling management
to boost their companies' stock prices at least in the near term. Also,
historical financials, no matter how accurate, don't include pro forma
data reflecting a company's recent acquisitions or divestitures. And
particularly in evolving industries, past performance may be a poor
indicator of current results, let alone future performance.

According to David Dreman's research, the professional analyst's
average error rate for earnings estimates is 41.5 percent, and that's
based on their judgment two weeks before companies make their earnings announcement.[11] Imagine how difficult it is to value a company
when there is no history and we are dealing with a developing firm in
a new industry where the company has no revenues, let alone earnings.
So as precise and objective as we may assume earnings to be, estimating them is very difficult. Forecasting them based on prospects for a
new technology or undeveloped market is even more so. As Warren
Buffett once said, "Indeed, some important American fortunes have
been created by the monetization of accounting mirages."[12] Although
the numbers can be misleading and at best can tell us only part of the
story, I'm convinced that feelings, when guided by objective data, tend
to point us in the right direction, particularly when there is uncertainty in the future. They help us to assign values to different alternatives.

Emotions Are Vital Signals. A good case can be made that emotions,
rather than disrupting the investing process, can serve as signals to the
self, enabling us to distill the facts and figures. Over the course of
many months or years, if we keep careful track of our emotions when
making investment decisions, we will find that certain feelings can be
better than others in guiding our decision-making. To take a simple
example, you probably have difficulty sleeping after making certain
investment decisions. Most folks just pass this phenomenon off as a
normal part of the investing game. But if you begin to keep track of
what happens to the investments each time you have difficulty sleeping, you may find a pattern that indicates a logical road to explore. It
may turn out that each time you can't sleep, your stock winds up mov-

ing sharply in one direction or the other. Thus, for some of us, not being able to sleep sends a signal that we've missed something important about our investment, and it motivates us to review carefully the variables that went into making our original decision. For others, not being able to sleep will indicate a pattern of excitement that suggests we made the right decision to buy a stock, and it can be experienced as an affirming response to our decision. But it is only by paying close attention to the patterns of feelings that accompany investment decisions that useful information can be garnered.

This is why it's important to become familiar with your well-ingrained organizing lenses or emotional convictions. Once you know how you react to information like the *Journal* pick of Pepsico, you will know the direction in which your emotional intuition tends to lead you. And then, by looking at your history, you can decide whether your "hunches" are worth following.

If you're a Frederick, it's worthwhile for you to look at what happens to the stocks that you *don't* buy. You should first recognize that your intuition will tell you it's too late to take advantage of newspaper stock picks. Well, is it? I hope the Fredericks of the world will take the time to look at stocks like Pepsico the morning after the stock is recommended in the *Journal*. Did the stock have a nice healthy bounce or did it, in fact, go down? This essential process forces you to check out your intuition and discern over time if it's worth following.

Emotions Help Us Tolerate Market Volatility. Experiencing our emotions can help us to deal with losses in the market and, more important, to move on and recover from them. Professional analysts are correct in their decisions about 60 percent of the time. Individual investors are correct in their stock picks about 40 percent of the time, if they're lucky. The fact is, we're probably all going to be wrong a high percentage of the time.

Mistakes and losses—and gains as well—cause us all to feel a variety of disruptive feelings. We must be able to tolerate the anxiety and depression arising from our failures. We must also avoid letting the excitement that accompanies our successes go to our head. And to deal with these feelings, we need to have access to our emotions.

Allowing ourselves to feel badly about an investment mistake prevents that mistake from becoming traumatic; it circumvents the tendency of most of us to beat ourselves up for making a wrong decision; and it allows us to move on. My research suggests that investors who deny or suppress feelings around a loss tend to behave as if they must make up for the loss by holding their stock until "they get back to even again." Those who allow themselves to experience their feelings are much quicker to cut their losses and try to make up their money with a different choice of stocks. As with any loss, there can be no moving on in life without a period of mourning. This requires the sadness, disappointment, disillusionment, or depression to be experienced and tolerated.

The same principles apply when we make unrealistic gains in the marketplace. Investors who don't process the euphoric feelings that accompany these dizzying gains tend to hold on to their stocks far too long. They become emotionally involved in their companies, expand upon the virtues of their companies at cocktail parties, and boast about their success to anyone who will listen. Remember the investors who made so much from Priceline or Amazon and forgot their gains were just on paper? Investors who processed their emotions and acknowledged their grandiose feelings, unlike the cocktail party braggarts, realized that they needed to sell when the stocks became overvalued, according to whatever measures they used.

Emotions Help You Figure Out the Best Way for You to Invest. Only when you let yourself experience your feelings during the investment process can you find a stylistic fit between your personality and your investing methodology. Those who experience intense anxiety if their stocks are volatile probably should not invest a significant portion of their portfolio in technology stocks. Those who feel an intense excitement over emerging products and services that have the potential to alter the way people live or do business will probably enjoy investing in the micro-cap market. Those who naturally strive to hit home runs are much more likely to feel better with less diversification than those players who feel most secure when they hit a single or a double.

Life has become much too complicated for investors to understand all segments of the market. In my opinion, it is much more important to find a market niche that matches your personality than it is to be a value or a growth investor, a fundamentalist, or a technician. And the only way to find that niche is to recognize the emotions that are evoked by each segment of the market. For example, I know that my interest is piqued and I am motivated to perform more thorough research on a micro-cap or small-cap company, a technology company, or a biotech company than I'd be able to perform on a consumer durable or a big oil company. And my emotional reaction to the tobacco companies has prevented me from ever recommending or buying their stocks. Thus more of my recommendations fall into the former than the latter category, not because they are better companies, but because they have a better fit with my emotional style.

Emotions Can Free You from Following the Herd. Ben Graham, the dean of security analysts, once told a wonderful story, repeated by Warren Buffett:

> An oil prospector, moving to his heavenly reward, was met by St. Peter with bad news. "You're qualified for residence," said St. Peter, "but, as you can see, the compound reserved for oil men is packed. There's no way to squeeze you in." After thinking for a moment, the prospector asked if he might say just four words to the present occupants. That seemed harmless to St. Peter, so the prospector cupped his hands and yelled, "Oil discovered in hell." Immediately the gate to the compound opened and all of the oil men marched out to head for the nether regions. Impressed, St. Peter invited the prospector to move in and make himself comfortable. The prospector paused. "No," he said, "I think I'll go along with the rest of the boys. There might be some truth to that rumor after all."[13]

Allowing yourself to experience feelings helps you to organize your self-experience. It lets you be the same person all of the time, grounded in your own beliefs and convictions, a person more naturally resistant to herd mentality. When feelings are suppressed and avoided, we are much less likely to remain the same person in the midst of change and controversy and, paradoxically, much more likely to substitute rumors from the herd for our own stable and solid personality. Most likely it would be the investor who eliminated emotional insight from his investing style who ran smack into the technology bubble and who failed to distinguish between the herd's stampede and the real news affecting his stocks.

EMOTIONS IMPLY SUBJECTIVITY

Successful investing requires us to acknowledge that emotions predispose us to function subjectively all the time. Once we acknowledge this, we can gain an understanding of how our emotions influence our behavior and then use those emotions as guideposts for future decisions. The best method for accomplishing this is to become familiar with our subjective lenses and to learn how they influence our investment decisions. As Comte once suggested, "the intellect should be the servant of the heart, but not its slave."[14] To be a successful investor, we must draw on our capacity to reflect comfortably on our emotional organizing patterns as they emerge from repetitive investment decisions. Let's take a look at a few common examples of these organizing lenses.

Pattern: When something good happens, something bad is sure to follow. On my recommendation, Allen, a money manager, bought Mitek Surgical (MYTK), a small-cap designer and marketer of surgical anchors for attaching soft tissue to bone. His entry price was $20 per share. The stock soon increased to $24. Several months later, the company announced a change in its distribution system from an outside sales force to the development of an in-house sales group. A significant charge against earnings was taken to retrain the sales force, and MYTK management predicted lower earnings in the coming quarters. The stock was battered back to $13 when Allen called to discuss the situation.

From previous conversations, Allen was aware that one of his organizing principles dictates that when something good happens, something bad is sure to follow. Therefore, as the stock had already gone to $24 (something good) and then retreated (something bad), he was automatically inclined to take his loss and move on. Indeed Allen could recount many examples of premature sell decisions based on the same organizing pattern. Once he became aware of the fact that he filtered external data through very subjective lenses that reshaped the meaning of the ostensibly objective information, Allen could step back and reconsider his inclination to sell. Doing so, he realized that his initial reaction to sell Mitek was based on a very idiosyncratic emotional conviction tending to distort the fundamental data that had prompted him to buy the stock in the first place. Allen decided to keep the stock. I didn't hear from him again until six months later, when J&J bought MYTK for approximately $30 per share. He was glad he had listened to his self and had recognized his pattern in time.

Pattern: Taking profits prevents losses. Jennifer bought Express Scripts, a pharmaceutical benefit-management company, just after it came public at $13.50. The stock quickly climbed to $30 per share. At this point Jennifer was ecstatic that she had more than doubled her money, but she found herself becoming anxious. "I'm so excited," she reported. "I've doubled my money already. Everybody says you can't go wrong taking some profits, so I think I'll sell." Before carefully reviewing Express Scripts's fundamentals, which she had almost obsessively studied before buying the stock, Jennifer sold her position and then rationalized it with that old Wall Street maxim that you can never lose money by taking profits. As if to confirm her prophecy, ESRX plunged quickly to $20 on profit taking.

The problem with old Wall Street maxims, however, is that they are usually based on unexamined, unconscious organizing principles that reflect a specific and subjective way of viewing the world. In this case, ESRX bottomed out at $19 and then climbed straight to $68 in the next eighteen months before splitting two for one. Jennifer missed a 400 percent profit by acting on her subjective organizing pattern, which caused her to sell automatically when she achieved a 100 percent gain. To use a Warren Buffett analogy, if the Boston Red Sox were to act on this organizing pattern, they would go out and sell their star pitcher, Pedro Martinez, to another team for a large profit on their original investment rather than let him continue to help win games for them.

Pattern: Action leads to success, and passivity leads to failure. Many investors share an unwitting assumption that as long as they are buying and selling continually, they will make money. They become frustrated over and over again if one of their stocks has not moved very much in the few months following its purchase. These investors are highly influenced by our cultural tradition of emphasizing doing over being and thus activity over patience.

Historically the general market averages gains of about 10.7 percent per year, with small-cap stocks averaging around 12.5 percent per annum. If you can average between 15 percent and 20 percent per year, you will be performing on a par with the elite of investment professionals. When stocks don't move for months at a time, however, these investors frequently feel the need to act, to trade one company for another one that looks like it has immediate potential for a strong move. They forget that holding a stock for three years and achieving a 200 percent gain during the third year will certainly make them wealthier than a 25 percent gain each year, while also saving money in transaction costs and taxes in nonretirement accounts. For those who operate through the organizing pattern "action leads to success, and passivity leads to failure," however, the 25 percent gain each year on an actively traded portfolio will provide great satisfaction in the short term. Sitting patiently with a company that has been carefully researched and continues to possess solid fundamentals goes against the unconscious organizing assumption that activity leads to success.

Pattern: When it rains, it pours, or bad news will always be followed by more bad news. This unconscious way of organizing the world also has its conscious expression in a Wall Street maxim called the Cockroach Theory, which suggests that when you find one cockroach in the kitchen, others are sure to follow (e.g., one bad quarter of earnings is sure to be followed by more).

To return to our example from the introduction, after LifeUSA reported significantly lower earnings in the first quarter of 1994 compared to the year-earlier quarter, some analysts with strong buy recommendations on the company immediately changed their rating to hold, and the stock dropped precipitously. The fundamentals of the company had not changed, but many investors sold their shares on the unwitting assumption that one poor quarter would be followed by subsequent ones—an assumption reinforced by analysts who were operating on their own unconscious assumptions about the company. The stock dropped from about $11 per share to $6.88 before climbing 50 percent, where it remained for a short time. Eventually the company was bought out for about $23 per share. Although the Cockroach Theory is sometimes correct, it's often dead wrong. That's because it makes us ignore fundamentals in favor of an underlying pessimistic lens that transforms them into a subjective "bad news Bears" story often having no correlation with reality.

Pattern: Always measure time on a calendar year. The investment community measures performance by timetables generally dovetailing with filing requirements for annual reports on Form 10-K, quarterly reports on Form 10-Q, or their equivalents for foreign issuers and mutual funds. Because these reports track performance on calendar years and quarters for most companies, and because our income tax filings are also based on the calendar year, we are predisposed to organize our investment decisions and successes or failures, as well as many other life decisions, on a calendar basis. The rigidity and inherently artificial nature of this organizing principle can distort and often undermine our decision-making.

For example, in the second quarter of 1995, it was widely reported in the media that small caps were lagging behind their larger brethren and that switching to large caps would be prudent. But if we had changed the calendar year calculation and looked at the progress of small caps from the end of second quarter 1994 to the end of second quarter 1995, they would have consistently outperformed the major market indices. In the first quarter of 1995, however, they were slightly behind the S&P 500. Depending on how one measures time, we could interpret the data to suggest either an end to the small-cap bull market or just the beginning of a major new surge for the small caps.

DISCIPLINED SUBJECTIVITY

If investing is such a subjective and emotional process, you must be wondering how it is ever possible to succeed in the market, to say nothing of using psychology to increase the odds of success. To make that leap, we must take the idea of subjectivity one step further to disciplined subjectivity,[15] a concept borrowed from psychoanalytic practice.

In the days when I spent more time seeing patients and supervising other therapists, there were many arguments in the psychoanalytic community between those who believed that psychotherapy was an art form that had general but vague parameters for guiding its practice and those who conceived of it as a science. The latter insisted that there was a set of rules or correct procedures and techniques that should be followed and used with every patient, since a system or discipline was required for reducing the influence of our individual subjectivity. This also provided "default settings to which we could return in the face of uncertainty,"[16] making new therapists feel good about their therapeutic interventions because it was clear that most new therapists (and some experienced therapists) didn't have the slightest idea of what they were doing. Whatever structured system they used became a scientific substitute for their inability to use their own personality as a primary tool in their profession. Although these systems made everyone feel good about their approach, they eliminated the therapists' motivation to think about what they were doing or how their personalities influenced work with different types of patients. It also deprived them (and their patients) of the benefit of their intuition. To borrow one of psychoanalyst Donna Orange's apt analogies, it was a bit like purchasing a picture frame and then searching for a piece of art to go with the frame.[17]

Investing and psychotherapy have much in common. Roy Neuberger, the savvy businessman who founded Neuberger & Berman, has been investing for some sixty-eight years. His autobiography delineates ten principles for successful investing, the first of which is Know Thyself: "Your personal strengths will help determine your success as an investor. Before you begin studying companies for investment, study yourself."[18] Good advice for both psychotherapists and investors.

At the heart of good investing is a core of disciplined subjectivity. This core includes our *intuition*, the ostensibly *objective data* we collect on our companies, our *theoretical framework*, and our *investing experience*.

Intuition is a cognitive process in which our thoughts take on a life of their own with little conscious awareness until we suddenly have an idea, gut feeling, or course of action that feels right. Because we are not aware of the thought processes, intuition can at times be extremely accurate and at other times completely wrong.

The objective data we collect includes financial statements and operating information in periodic reports filed by publicly held companies with the Securities and Exchange Commission. It also includes the subsequent interpretation of that material by analysts, often in the form of standardized financial ratios that give us clues about future performance. Some technicians also rely on objective market data, usually in the form of stock charts reflecting daily market action of each stock.

Our theoretical framework refers to our analytical preference. These include fundamental analysis, technical analysis, top-down investing, and bottom-up stock picking.

Our investing experience refers to how much we have learned from our past investment decision-making. To be meaningful, investing experience has more to do with self observation than with duration.

Let's take a look at how these four pillars are supported by self-awareness in practice. As warnings began to mount about the technology bubble at the end of the last century, I recommended, or more accurately, re-recommended a speculative company, Zi Corporation, which I had been following for several years. The company had an uneventful history, although if you read the stock message boards, many investors and the press felt that it had failed to live up to expectations, and they had equal skepticism about its future. This jaundiced view was reflected in its stock price, which had bounced as high as $8, fallen as low as $1, and finally settled in the $2 range during August 1999. But examining my reasons for recommending the stock should demonstrate why the disciplined subjective approach to investing is preferable to restricting our data to only "objective" systems, tools, or methods.

Zi was a vertically integrated technology company focused on developing and delivering intelligent interface solutions and services to both the wireless and consumer Internet space worldwide. The company's core product, eZiText, was an intuitive and predictive text-input and language technology that enabled people to use short messaging, e-mail, e-commerce, and other applications on Internet and information appliances such as mobile phones, TV-set-top boxes, computers, and network computers where only a limited key pad was available. What was intuitively exciting to me about the company was that they were finding new ways for consumers to interact with their devices (cell phones, set-top boxes) to access information and communicate with one another.

Zi's technology had its roots in enabling people who are literate in character-based languages (primarily Asian) to use technology. In the Western world, language utilizes a phonetic alphabet. Typewriters and keyboards enable language processing because we type in the same form as we write; what we see on a computer screen is exactly the same as what we type (input) on the keyboard. Therefore we can easily develop software that works the way our language works. In contrast, character-based languages such as Chinese, Japanese, and Korean use ideographs instead of an alphabet. These pictures or symbols are used to represent a thing or an idea, but not particular words or phrases. This difference means that features related to language processing that we take for granted in the West—spelling and grammar checking, text retrieval, and alphabetizing—are implemented in a different manner in the character-based languages. This cultural difference makes it difficult to match our technology to their languages. The challenge which Zi had successfully met was to design products to fit the language and the culture.

Various algorithms using linguistic data (frequency of use, word association, and dictionaries) enabled the use of smart or predictive text input process with a variety of world languages. At the time, Zi's input system had the capacity to work not only with the Asian languages, but also with French, German, Italian, Spanish, English, Greek, Turkish, and some Scandinavian languages (eventually Zi developed the capacity to be used with nearly every language in the world). The underlying architecture and design of the input system was language independent and could be used on almost any platform. In fact, because the input system required only a small number of physical or virtual keys, it could work on a variety of consumer devices such as keypads on mobile phones or on remote controls for TV-set-top boxes, touch screens, and a home row on a standard computer keyboard.

Zi's technology was very seductive, particularly if you believed that the mobile phone market would eventually become a huge industry. But what captured my interest at this point were two events. In addition to entering into licensing agreements with several small companies, Zi had entered into a licensing agreement with Ericsson Mobile Communications AB (Ericsson) to develop and integrate Zi input technology into Ericsson products. Objectively, the relationship with Ericsson validated for me the value of Zi's technology, as companies as large as Ericsson typically do not enter into such agreements without in-depth due diligence.

Secondly, Zi had entered into a joint venture with China Huayu Limited, a subsidiary of the Ministry of Education in China. China Huayu was a computer manufacturing subsidiary responsible for the distribution of all products—computers, set-top boxes, books, content, etc.—into the school system. The president of China Huayu had stated that the company was committed to using Zi's input software on every applicable product that China Huayu and its affiliates manufactured, sold, or distributed in China. Zi now had one of the most powerful ministries in China endorsing its technology, but I knew that, despite promises, doing business in China was a very difficult and long process even for well-established companies.

In checking out their technology, I found out that Zi had acquired the rights to and ownership of the character-based language technology underlying three separate license agreements (known as the Jiejing licenses), of which the company had been the exclusive worldwide licensee since November 1993. Zi had also been aggressive in protecting its patents, filing a patent infringement suit against its major competitor, Tegic Communications, a Seattle, Washington, company that would eventually be bought out by AOL. While this aggressive approach to patent protection was admirable, I knew it could cost the company millions of dollars and years of time and energy that could hold back its business before the suit was finally settled.

In addition to Tegic, Zi's other competitors were Motorola and Nokia, both of whom had their own proprietary input systems. But Zi appeared to me to be the only company that had the capacity for true word prediction. In addition, manufacturing was shifting to Asia, where Zi had established strong relationships.

Zi's industry seemed to have positive potential. According to China Telecom, China's mobile-phone networks had 26 million subscribers, a figure that had grown more than 100 percent per year for the past seven years. A Hambrecht & Quist report had stated, "for the next 12–18 months the real investment opportunities lie not with the manufacturers of Internet appliances, but with infrastructure software and service providers. These companies provide network operators and businesses with the enabling infrastructure solutions that would make universal access a reality." Zi was also in the process of changing their original Asian focus to a more global presence.

So far so good, but then I turned to the company's financials. For the previous fiscal year, Zi had reported only $1.6 million in revenues and a net loss of $2.3 million, or $0.08 per share. I had followed this company for three years, but they still had not ramped up revenue or become profitable. They had cut operating costs significantly from $10.9 million in 1997 to $2.6 million in 1998, which helped to lower the operating loss to $2.5 million from $12.7 million. Assets at the end of 1998 were $1.8 million and liabilities were $634,000. The current ratio was 2.8. Cash was just over $1 million with no long-term debt, and shareholders' equity was $2.6 million. Insiders owned about 23 percent of the company.

Trying to make accurate projections for the ensuing years was extremely difficult because I had no accurate information on how the market would receive the Ericsson phones or whether the Chinese government would actually move to put computers in the schools (and if so, when). If all went well, which it never does with small development stage companies on the verge of a transition into a major high-tech sales and marketing company, I expected the 1999 year to show revenues of $3 to $4 million with a very small loss. I thought that Zi would then ramp up revenues significantly in 2000 and become profitable. As it turned out, my projections, like most analyst projections, were on the optimistic side.

I was also aware of Zi's investment risks at the time. While being a very intriguing and potentially lucrative invesment, the company had been involved in several deals that had not materialized, so they were in a position where they had to demonstrate to the investment community that they could close deals successfully. Because there was no history of significant revenues or earnings, my forecasts were being made primarily on the basis of estimating how much market share the company would be able to capture with its new products and what kind of licensing fees seemed reasonable from original equipment manufacturers (OEMs). I also knew that doing business in Asia involved risks arising from foreign government policies and regulations. The success of the company would also depend on finalizing OEM agreements with significant players in the Asian Pacific, European, and U.S. markets. I had no guarantee that these agreements would come to fruition. In addition, I believed the company would have to raise money to fund their burn rate.

At this stage of my due diligence, I felt Zi was a potentially lucrative investment, but it was clearly high-risk if I looked at only the ostensibly objective data. Analyzing these "objective" aspects of Zi alone could have dissuaded me from buying or recommending the stock. The facts were that Zi was in a development stage, had somewhat shaky financials, could face difficulty breaking into a new market and doing business in China, and had received negative press for not meeting its projections for several years; these were all rational reasons for moving on to other prospects. And although I was convinced the technology was sound, I also recalled all the superior technologies that had never been accepted in the marketplace.

My own emotions and subjective lenses, however, played an important role in finalizing a decision. Emotionally, I found myself worrying about the company's future when trying to fall asleep at night. I knew from experience that this anxiety about a company tended, idiosyncratically for me, to be a positive rather than a negative signal. A slight edge of anxiety had led to successful investments in the past, whereas a confident feeling and lack of anxiety had typically been associated with losing investments. I also experienced a strong fit between my style of investing in young, growing companies and the course that Zi had set for itself, and therefore knew I could tolerate the ups and downs that would inevitably follow.

Despite the emerging technology bubble, I believed that we were just entering the beginning of a new technology boom that would include mobile phones and their accompanying software as a prominent investment space. In addition, my own subjective lenses included the belief that most micro-cap successes depended on management's capabilities. After learning some important lessons the hard way, I believed I had a grasp of some of the psychological elements that made for superior management, as discussed in Chapter Seven. I also had learned that to invest in micro-caps you had to be able to assess the investors who were backing the company. Without a source of ongoing capital, even the best technologies were unlikely to make it to the marketplace.

In Zi's case, my assessment of management was at odds with the negative spin on the Internet message boards. I had first met CEO Michael Lobsinger in Boston in 1996 when he was doing a road show for the company. He was what I have come to call an outsider—a person who has more belief in his own skills, research, and judgment than in ostensible authorities in the field. This is essential for successful entrepreneurs. What struck me most about Michael in this first meeting was his story about his interactions with some large U.S. companies. He had taken Zi's technology to several well established, multi-national firms to demonstrate that by using Zi's input system, Chinese speaking people would not have to learn English in order to use a computer or to send text messages on their cell phones. Their response to this idea was an arrogant belief that anyone wanting to use a computer would have to learn to speak English first. In essence they were saying, "If they want to buy our product, they'll learn our language." It was Michael's contrary vision that China would insist on maintaining its cultural traditions when interfacing language and technology that piqued my curiosity in his company. And, in fact, it was Lobsinger's contrary vision that led to Zi's successful relationship with the Chinese government in the ensuing years.

Not only did I agree with his vision for the future, I was impressed with the fact that he perceived all the doors that were closed in his face not as defeat, but as an opportunity. As he told me, "You are not going to teach an entire population from ninety-year-olds down to two-year-olds another langauge just so they could use a computer. I knew that was not going to happen. So it became a point of honor and a belief that I was right, and the largest companies approaching China were wrong."

As I came to know Michael over the next few years, it became clear that he was putting together a team that would eat, drink, and sleep growing the business, no matter what the obstacles. Despite not achieving the projected revenues, they never took their eye off the ball. They knew they were going to be attacked by others, but the more their adversaries told them they could not succeed, the more motivated they became to do what others said could not be done. As Lobsinger said, "An entrepreneur can't have fears, you can't keep saying 'Oh my god, I'm doing the wrong thing' just because somebody criticizes you on the Internet." I also noticed that this was a company that could be flexible. When goals and opportunites changed, it was able to change with them. Rational thinkers often view these sorts of corporate shifts as symptomatic of difficulties rather than as opportunistic adaptations but I knew intuitively that windows of opportunity only remain open for short periods of time, and if a company is too busy worrying about shareholder criticisms, it can fail to take advantage of managing the opportunities effectively.

Zi was also a company that appreciated the value of relationships—political, financial, and cultural. I noticed they were often willing to sacrifice immediate financial gains to reap rewards in the future. Management knew that their road to success would involve going up hills and through valleys, around corners, through tunnels, and over bridges—that there would be no straight line to success, but that you could never afford to take your eye off of the eventual destination. This gave me confidence that his company was a finisher. Even when I felt critical of company strategies and annoyed by what felt like over-enthusiasm and strategic or hiring errors, it was clear to me that management could acknowledge and correct their mistakes. They were aware of their imperfections, but felt the important issue was not their mistakes, but how they eventually handled and fixed their errors. I was also convinced that the company backers were psychologically and financially sophisticated and committed to the company's survival.

While it may seem totally irrelevant to many investors who don't use their feelings as part of their investment decision-making, I felt Zi was blessed with luck. One of their reasons for survival was having run into the right backers and the right contacts in China. Part of that fortune was due to the CEO's abilities, part to being in the right places at the right times. Luck plays a much larger role in success than the investment community will ever acknowledge, and one of my organizing lenses includes an emotional bias that when a company gets lucky once, its chance for future luck increases. None of these feelings alone resulted in buying Zi's stock, but all of them together swayed me to trust my instincts, particularly my emotional evaluation of management, predisposing me to focus on the "objective" facts that supported those instincts. In that way, my feelings became, as Damasio's work suggests, "indispensable for rationality."

As it turned out, my decision did pan out as the stock rose from a low of $1 to $40 per share. With a stop loss of $25, most investors made significant money on their investment. Zi then crashed in the tech debacle, but continues to ramp up its business to become a major player in the interface solutions marketplace.

Employing only traditional valuation tools, I probably would not have bought or recommended Zi. But with the use of disciplined subjectivity—publicly available information (objective facts), intuition, experience, and the understanding of my own personal organizing lenses—the buy decision took on a broader and more comprehensive nature. It enabled me to assess not only the company's financial and business model, but also to examine nontraditional data such as management's emotional ability to succeed, my psychological fit with the company, my intuitive feel for the company's vision, and the past results of similiar investments. Such an expanded organizing lens allows us to make more in-depth decisions by viewing a company from multiple perspectives.

SO WHAT'S AN INVESTOR TO DO?

We are all emotional people; and, as I have found in my research, whether we like it or not, emotion affects our investing decisions. In fact feelings can help or hinder our investing performance. That's why disciplined subjectivity becomes so important. It alone enables us to listen to our emotions and learn from them, to gain perspective, to understand why we react to things the way we do, and to discover the patterns and the emotional convictions that guide our investment thinking. As you read this book, think about your unique emotional makeup. Which of your emotional convictions drive your decision-making? Once you discover those patterns, you will be able to distinguish between the emotional triggers that are destructive and those that are helpful.

Aspire to become a self-aware human investor. Forget about trying to be a perfect, machinelike investor. As you abandon the search for perfection, try to concentrate instead on becoming what I call good enough. A good enough investor recognizes emotions but does not let them into the driver's seat. As signals they are supremely useful and can set you apart from the crowd. As drivers they cause havoc. And since this balance is a little precarious at times, it is important to remember that sometimes you will let your emotions make the wrong decisions for you—like those times you feel an urgent need to sell a stock and forget to look at the fundamentals that contributed to your purchase in the first place. At other times your emotions will be sending you important signals that you would be wise to heed but will unfortunately ignore or discount. But if you can listen to your feelings and succeed enough of the time, the rewards will be unmistakable. Just by getting in touch with your emotions, your errors will lessen significantly, and your performance in the market will benefit.

TWO

Watching Out for Mr. Market

While you probably didn't buy this book to read about the psychology of human development, a short side trip into an integral aspect of personality development—our sense of self—will help to highlight some of the emotional underpinnings of investor mistakes in hopes of helping you avoid them.

A SHORT PRIMER ON OUR SENSE OF SELF

Psychologists refer to our sense of self as the core of our personality.[1] While difficult to define precisely, *sense of self* generally refers to the subjective way we feel about and perceive ourselves. A strong sense of self translates to a feeling of wholeness (all our parts feel glued together), vitality, aliveness, well-being, and solid self-esteem. A weak sense of self refers to a feeling of emptiness, depletion, inadequacy, anxiety, low self-esteem, and a sense of falling apart.

We all have good days, when we feel strong, alive, and whole, as well as bad days, when our self-esteem is low and we feel inadequate and insecure. Superficial behavior can often camouflage our sense of self, making it difficult for others to figure out by observation alone how we experience our selves. But when our sense of self is solid, we feel it on a gut level. We experience a sense of wholeness and aliveness, or, as my daughter likes to call it, a feeling of "spiritedness." We also feel more resistant to the bumps and bruises of everyday life and can recover quickly from disappointments. For the metaphysically inclined, we feel continuous over time and through space. In other words, if we moved across the country to a new job, we would feel like the same person in California that we were in Massachusetts. When our sense of self is solid, we feel relatively independent, as the need for support from those around us fades more into the background. On these good days, we feel as though our mind and body function smoothly together. And on the *really* good days, we feel capable of pursuing our ambitions, ideals, and relationships in a creative, personally meaningful way, regardless of the obstacles.

The evolution of a strong sense of self is fostered by growing up in an environment where significant others are empathically attuned to our needs. Although less critical after the formative years, our need for empathic responsiveness continues throughout adulthood, however abstractly. As a result, because we depend in part on relationships with significant others at all stages, the experience of our selves as empowered, self-confident, and vital can be enhanced or disrupted throughout life. We can also gain self-esteem through repeated positive experiences with aspects of the nonhuman world that symbolize the presence of others, like sports, art, politics, nature, music, and, for many of us, the stock market.

Several decades of research suggests that our sense of self is maintained through three important support systems: mirroring, idealizing, and partnering. These are key concepts that I will refer to again and again in this book.

• Mirroring refers to the experience of having our skills, talents, and vitality confirmed and validated. It is much more complicated and deeper than just receiving a compliment or a pat on the back. Mirroring refers to experiencing another's appreciation for our inner being, an affirmation of who we really are. Thus, we don't need to have our boss standing at the door each day telling us what a good job we're doing, but we do need to have an ongoing feeling that our work is valued and that we are contributing to our company or profession. We also need occasional affirmation or positive feedback from the world at large, including employers, clients, and professional peers, as well as family and friends.

- Idealizing refers to the sense of security and self-confidence evoked when we are allowed to share in the knowledge, power, repute, or calmness, organization, and ideals of others. When we begin a new job for a well-respected company, for example, our sense of self is bolstered by virtue of becoming a part of the admired organization. When we work for a politician we respect and admire, the association enhances our self-esteem. Idealization can take a more simple form, too. Whenever we feel connected with someone we look up to or whose opinion we value, we experience heightened self-esteem if he turns out to be right (*I feel good about myself because I am connected to such a smart friend*, we think).

- Partnering refers to experiencing the sustaining effect of human sameness—a sense of "we-ness" that fosters a feeling of belonging to an important group that shares the use of similar skills, objectives, or shared beliefs. Our need for partnering motivates us to seek out groups or individuals who share the same philosophies and biases. It causes us to choose partners who have an essential alikeness even though they may have different interests and enjoy dissimilar activities.

Years of psychological research have proven that just as we all need oxygen to sustain our physical selves, we are hard wired to need and seek out attachments and experiences that provide the psychological ingredients needed to maintain and strengthen our sense of self.[2] In most instances these attachments involve relationships with other people. But, as indicated previously, the same function can also be served by nonhuman environments—institutions, ideas, books, nature, music, and the stock market. Think, for example, of how a walk in the woods or listening to music can provide calmness and soothing when we are upset, or how being associated with a well-known institution can make us feel more confident and important.

When these attachments and experiences fail us, however, our sense of self feels injured. Self-esteem suffers when we receive negative feedback from the world, like a poor evaluation at work or a pink slip. We feel inadequate when we join a company or a group that turns out to be harming others, competing unfairly, or functioning inefficiently.

We feel that all our good work went to waste. And if we feel isolated and estranged from the larger human community, our self-esteem takes a direct and proportionate hit.

THE INFLUENCE OF MR. MARKET

In a variety of ways, investors use the stock market to serve all three functions of mirroring, idealizing, and partnering. Some of these applications are productive, but many are unproductive or even counterproductive.

For example, when we select individual stocks, we hold up our skills and judgment for mirroring, confirmation, and validation. Thus, when we achieve investment success, we experience pride in our decision-making skills. Conversely, when we fail, most of us experience a lack of mirroring, even a sense of humiliation if our mistakes are exposed to public or private scrutiny. This is one reason that many Wall Street analysts would rather fail by recommending stocks that everyone else recommends than pick unknown or unloved stocks and lose.

When we buy or sell stocks according to others' recommendations, we are joining them in a sense of power and knowledge, particularly if the recommendations anticipate significant market moves in under-followed companies before the crowd joins in. The success of the shared judgment leaves us feeling uplifted—buoyed by our connection with the admired other who originated the recommendation. This is the reason that comments by talking heads on television can move stock prices, even if only for a day or two.

When we follow recommendations that fail, however, we feel let down and suspicious. We begin to devalue the adviser, or security analysts in general, or cancel a newsletter subscription. The devaluation not only fuels our pessimism, but also defensively protects us against mobilizing hope too quickly again. It is this devaluation that evokes the feeling that nothing will get better anytime soon. It is, in part, this devaluation, when it becomes widespread, that causes bear markets to continue well below objective valuation levels.

When we select stocks according to our need for sameness, we emphasize our connection with like-minded others. We are "value investors," "growth investors," "technicians," "fundamentalists," or "new economy investors." We become part of a group defined by skills, tools, or belief systems passed from one generation of investors to the next. But if we tie our sense of self too closely with a group, we can become complacently expectant that the group will maintain its structural integrity and supportive ambience.

Because investors establish ties with the stock market and its participants, upon whom they come to rely for the maintenance of their self-esteem, their relationship with the market or its constituents is analogous to patients' beginning connections with their therapists. Mr. Investor develops what I like to call a self-sustaining fantasy in relation to the anonymous Mr. Market, who, like any good therapist, represents hope, which is built into the market through a never-ending array of profitable possibilities. In other words, we look to Mr. Market to answer our emotional needs. It is this quality of hopefulness that encourages investors to engage in self-sustaining mirroring, idealizing, and partnering fantasies.

Unlike an empathic therapist, however, Mr. Market can be dysfunctional or at least unpredictable, failing to remain attuned to investor fantasies. In fact, Mr. Market can be downright cold, outrageously rude, and apt to betray our expectations to the point of making us feel foolish. This applies not just when a favored stock goes into free fall, but also when a company we shunned, like Yahoo!, announces positive news, sending its stock, to our amazement, into orbit. Like Loren Eiseley's "irrational, restive ghost that can whisper disastrous messages into the ear of reason,"[3] Mr. Market's propensity for empathic failures has the constant potential to continually disrupt our sense of self.

From numerous consultations with professional and individual investors, I have become convinced that psychological forces originating in the market's disruption of our sense of self, more than any other factors, are what victimize even the most intelligent and creative people who function exceptionally under any other conditions of risk. Let's try to capture a deeper understanding of how these disruptions presage investor mistakes.

THE PHENOMENON OF ANXIETY

Anxiety is the most insidious cause of mistakes on Wall Street as well
as Main Street. It elicits early-childhood fears, superstitions, and conflicts that undermine rational thinking and distort day-to-day decisions; it causes a regression from logical, rational, cognitive thought
process to emotional, intuitive, impulsive reactions; it pits investors
against one another and company management. And it can wreak all
this havoc without our even realizing anything out of the ordinary is
occurring.

We may not know it when we see it, but don't despair. We can still
feel it. Anxiety is a universal feeling of unpleasant tension that can be
experienced in a variety of cognitive, emotional, and physical ways.
Cognitively we may experience difficulty in concentrating or thinking
clearly or in remembering what is usually recalled naturally. Because it
distorts rational reasoning processes, it may also confound our
attempts to communicate clearly. Emotionally we may feel a vague
sense of apprehension and uncertainty, low self-esteem, helplessness,
impending doom, and diminished energy or vitality. Perceptually we
often experience anxiety in dreams. A common anxiety dream may
involve having to take an examination for which we're not prepared,
or being late or missing the test only to wake up relieved that "it was
just a dream." Sometimes we concretize anxiety in a dream through
vivid imagery such as a structure falling apart or through dreams of
physical illness. Physically we may experience a sinking feeling in our
stomach, rapid heartbeat, trembling, tremors, perspiration, changes in
breathing rhythms, and awkward posture, gait, or speech. All of these
symptoms can range from mild to severe, at times reaching the point
of terror and panic where the anxiety overwhelms our coping mechanisms.

To paraphrase Erikson, fear and anxiety are overlapping emotional
states. Fear, however, is a state of apprehension that is focused on an
appraisable, realistic danger for which we can rationally formulate a
plan of action. Anxiety, on the other hand, causes us either to exaggerate the existing danger, thus evoking irrational responses, or to
deny a danger that we should realistically fear. It may often be difficult if not impossible to differentiate between fear and anxiety

because they tend to occur simultaneously. Even so, learning to make the differentiation is one key to avoiding mistakes. As Erikson wrote in his classic book *Childhood and Society*, "To be able to be aware of fear . . . without giving in to anxiety; to train our fear in the face of anxiety to remain an accurate measure and warning of that which man must fear—this is the necessary condition for a judicious frame of mind."[4]

Because the market has an upward bias to it (historically trending higher two-thirds of the time), hopeful complacency (the opposite of anxiety) is inherent in the attitudes of most investors and money managers. We expect to make smart market decisions. We expect to be rewarded for following a market guru's advice and to experience a certain "we-ness" where other market participants will agree with our decisions. Reinforcing this fantasy is the external reality that on a day-to-day basis the stock market is relatively quiescent. Major advances and declines tend to occur suddenly in short, unexpected bursts (thus the argument for continually being in the market rather than trying to time it). These rhythms reflect the flow of life—"the concentration of major events in short bursts interspersed with long periods of relative stability,"[5] as Stephen Jay Gould put it.

We take for granted that over the long run stocks will help us make money and hedge against inflation. This deep enmeshment with the market is deceptively unconscious. To obtain some perspective, consider the more dramatic complacency we feel about our dependency on oxygen. We don't scurry around worrying that there will not be enough oxygen for our next breath; rather we assume its existence and subjectively feel as though we are quite independent of our molecular surroundings. Only when there is a dearth of oxygen do we experience sudden anxiety as our complacent state is severely threatened. The equivalent of oxygen depletion in the market is downside volatility. Any sudden market turmoil destroys our normally complacent market expectations and creates anxiety. The suddenness and unpredictability of downside volatility, either in the market or in individual equities, are the two factors that seem to create the most significant investor anxiety.

Anxiety causes two psychological phenomena that hamper our investing decisions: jigsaw-puzzle thinking and cognitive regression.

JIGSAW-PUZZLE THINKING

A common reaction to volatility-induced anxiety is what I like to call jigsaw-puzzle thinking. It can be described clinically as a reduction in the cohesiveness of our rational thought processes that makes it difficult to think clearly. One investor described it as analogous to a ball of mercury being dropped. What he meant by this is that jigsaw-puzzle thinking causes us to experience the world in bits and pieces where one incomplete piece of information is substituted for the whole picture. As we attempt to correct this insidious cognitive disorientation, what appears to be a rational decision often turns out to be flawed, based on the elevation of an isolated variable to unrealistic proportions.

Consider John, another investor who had a comprehensive grasp of Express Scripts (Nasdaq: ESRX), whose stock, as you may remember, had climbed steadily from its $13.50 initial public offering (IPO) price to $30 per share. A profit-taking correction had ensued, and the downside volatility left John feeling anxious and injured. John had also heard rumors that the company was not going to meet its latest earnings projections: "I should have sold at $30; I knew it." Hardly an unfamiliar lament. But at this point, his jigsaw-puzzle thinking caused him to see only one piece of the puzzle, the volume of shares being sold. By the time the stock price retreated to $20, John was on the phone with his broker every hour to check the volume and price. At $19.50, he anxiously sold out. Several weeks later, as the stock price returned to $29, John could not understand how he had overlooked the business fundamentals of ESRX: "They would have told me clearly not to sell." ESRX eventually appreciated above $100 presplit.

While many would cynically say that John simply got nervous and bailed out because of his anxiety, that would be a facile explanation. John's experience illustrates a phenomenon that receives short shrift in the investment literature—a dangerous way in which anxiety affects our thinking processes and investment skills.

We all tend to think holistically. That is, when we attempt to understand a company, we look at it from many perspectives—fundamental, technical, management, product, services, competition, and industry.

Combining these perspectives gives us a picture of the whole company and how it functions. When we feel anxious, however, jigsaw-puzzle thinking takes over. We start to see just individual pieces, not the whole image. Instead of maintaining a more comprehensive perspective, we let our thinking become fragmented, focusing only on bits and pieces. When we are experiencing jigsaw-puzzle thinking, we substitute one incomplete piece of information—such as price or volume—for the whole picture.

As in John's choosing to sell Express Scripts based on an isolated sell-off, what appears to be a rational decision will often turn out flawed if based on the elevation of one transitory variable such as stock price or volume to unrealistic proportions. Only after the anxiety is alleviated do we return to thinking about the whole picture, in this case to our overall knowledge of the company and its true prospects. But if we sold out precipitously, the resulting regret will serve no purpose unless we learn from the experience not to act on anxiety. While we can never eliminate anxiety from the investing process, by knowing ahead of time what happens when we become anxious, we can virtually eliminate the type of mistake that caused John to sell ESRX if we anticipate the occurrence and impact of jigsaw-puzzle thinking.

ANXIETY: COGNITIVE REGRESSION

Another important and related consequence of anxiety is what psychologists call cognitive regression—a retreat to a mode of thinking in which words and thoughts are connected by emotions rather than logic. For example, if I asked you to say the first word that comes into your head when I say the word *mother*, your association would probably not include the dictionary definition of mother ("a woman who has borne a child"). That's because *mother* is an emotionally loaded word. When we experience anxiety, we retreat from thinking in our usual logical, rational, ordered way to thinking in a manner that is more magical, dreamlike, and emotional. In this altered state we are much more susceptible to false rumors, tips, and gossip. This accounts for John's vulnerability to the rumors about ESRX's earnings shortfall. This also helps explain why both touters and short-sellers can take advantage of Internet stock message boards by creating enough anxiety to make investors more susceptible to positive or negative rumors about a company.

THE DISRUPTION OF IDEALIZING TIES

Most investors and even money managers turn to experts for advice on the market. We all have a normal tendency to look up to others, to borrow strength and knowledge when in need of a lift, to walk in the shadow of our heroes. This proclivity to idealize others is part of the human condition. It fuels politics, makes teaching and learning possible, and organizes groups around their ideals. In the stock-market arena, it helps sell newspapers, adds to the popularity of certain websites and newsletters, and draws us to particular companies or CEOs. It also contributes to our slight overvaluation of both the human side of the market (economists, brokers, analysts, money managers, newsletter editors) and the nonhuman side of the market (information, technicals, fundamental ratios). And it partially explains the myth attached to stories about innovative companies and their leaders, adding to the allure of their stocks.

While these idealizing connections may animate otherwise tedious research tasks, they can also foster several common mistakes by investors. When in a bullish trend, the market comes to represent an ideal, and its leaders become symbols for that ideal. As investors, we feel an emotional tie to both, like being part of a winning team on the way to the playoffs or a political campaign on the way to victory. But when the market goes against us, our connection with this ideal becomes disrupted. We are left in a position of a child whose hero has traumatically let him down. It is as if we have traveled the yellow brick road to the Emerald City only to discover that Oz is a mere mortal. As the connections with admired others are temporarily interrupted, depletion and suspicion occur quickly. We feel betrayed and profoundly disappointed; the world (in this case the stock market) becomes a dangerous place. We fire our broker and swear never to watch CNBC again. We may even get caught in more paranoid fantasies of another 1929-like depression and total loss of capital.

It is in this psychological vacuum that we are most likely to act without the guiding ideals that have provided a consistent framework for our investment decisions. We may become disappointed in a company management team that we had previously admired. If we act in the mist of this psychological void, investment errors are all but inevitable.

Gerry, for example, was a savvy investor who admired the management style of the CEO of a large technology company he followed. His positive feelings for the company leader allowed him to have faith in the stock through good times and bad. Indeed the faith had paid off with substantial returns over a three-year period. When the CEO suddenly resigned for personal reasons unrelated to the business, Gerry felt confused and tempted to sell his stock. Although the CEO had assembled a superior management team likely to implement an easy transition, Gerry's loss of his fantasy connection with the CEO left him feeling pessimistic about the company's future. On the day following the CEO's departure, Gerry sat in front of his computer screen watching each tick in price. The stock was up most of the day but for thirty minutes suddenly dipped below its previous closing price. Gerry immediately sent in a market order to sell his shares. By the end of the day, the stock price was up several points. Management made a smooth transition to a new CEO, and the company continued to outperform the market.

There is a well-known phenomenon in psychotherapy where patients who come away from a therapy session having experienced a temporary disappointment in their therapist get into their car and drive the wrong way home. They usually return to their next appointment describing how, despite several years of turning right at the end of the street, they turned left and didn't realize it until several blocks later. Similarly, in the investment world a perceived loss of connection with an idealized other frequently causes a cognitive disorientation in investors that leads to incoherent decisions—including selling or buying stocks impulsively, placing confusing messages on Internet stock boards, experiencing sleepless nights characterized by somewhat paranoid thoughts about losing all one's money, and so on. Only after connections to admired others are reestablished do the cognitive errors begin to disappear.

IDEALIZATION OF THE SYSTEM

Every investment book and adviser recommends the rigorous adherence to an investing methodology, philosophy, or system, and many of them work for different people. At least in private, most advisers admit that the real purpose of any of these systems is to eliminate emotion from investment decisions. On an institutional level, computer-trading programs embody this approach to investing. On an individual level, the myriad available trading systems have one thing in common. They encourage decision-making purified of the offending emotions that can distort individual judgment. On either level, however, these systems can pose an unintended threat to sound decision-making if they come to be idealized by their users.

These computerized systems serve as a shield between our wealth and our emotions.[6] In this sense they represent one of many mechanisms we use to keep our emotions from dominating us—for example, "count to ten before expressing anger" or "look before you leap." Within the investment field, as in life in general, the idealization of technology has the potential to cause more mistakes than it prevents, particularly if the technology is used as a shield rather than as a source of information and data. Computers offer every investor the same information. To attain a competitive edge, we must assimilate the nuances of investment situations. These will always remain outside the realm of computer data.

Institutions support the use of computer technology as a shield by assuming it will perform the decision-making process faster and more efficiently. The assumption is partially correct. But many institutional investors, in fact, make decisions about investing billions of dollars faster than they would make a home-buying decision for themselves.

My experience with this aspect of the idealization phenomenon is that, without the mediation of psychological insight, it facilitates many more investor mistakes than it prevents. Much like the individual who believes that with conscious effort he can overcome powerful unconscious forces, at some point any system breaks down, and we find ourselves overruled by emotion at our most important decision points. Or because of the slight cognitive disorientation resulting from an injury to our sense of self, the system is used incorrectly. Or we keep our system but change it slightly to react to current events, unwittingly creating an entirely new "system" that no longer works.

Making matters worse, when an investor fails to maintain the ideal of unemotional, rational decision-making, the failure becomes the source of continual self-blame and condemnation. This in turn tends to further distort investment choices. While sticking to a good system is fine, it can be used successfully over time only if we have already mastered the emotional vicissitudes that contribute to mistakes in the first place.

THE DISRUPTION OF MIRRORING TIES

As I indicated previously, one of the self-sustaining fantasies that investors bring to the market reflects our mirroring needs—the wish to have Mr. Market validate a healthy sense of self-esteem and well-being by confirming our investment judgments and skills. Stan illustrates the downside of this phenomenon. Although most of Stan's portfolio was in a diversified selection of funds and stocks, he held concentrated positions in a few companies. His largest position was in ANB, a stock he had chosen after cultivating a friendship with management. This position was unusual for Stan because of its size, which went well beyond the percentage of his portfolio usually allocated to a single stock. Moreover, much of his position was in a margin account. As Stan commented, "I know these guys [management] real well and have every confidence that if they tell me good things are happening, I should own a lot of their stock."

For several months the stock appreciated slowly from Stan's entry level. But in the sixth month the stock began to languish when none of the anticipated developments materialized. Even when ANB suddenly began to tumble, Stan remained confident. "Everything's okay," he reassured me. "They'd let me know if something were wrong." Stan repeated this theme until the stock was 40 percent below his buy price.

At that point, ANB put out a press release saying that its licensing agreements had been delayed due to a technological glitch in its product. Earnings would be well below their expectations, but the glitch was being corrected and management expected the company to be back on track within a quarter or two. Stan called the CEO and was furious. He felt injured and betrayed. "I've been telling all my friends to buy this stock and expected the least you would do was warn me if things weren't going well. You made me look really stupid in front of my friends." Stan told me about the conversation and then said, "I'm going to sell my stock and tell all my friends to sell, and I'm going to put a message on Raging Bull [a stock message board] telling everyone what a fraud this management is."

Stan then sold his shares at a steep loss, only to watch the stock skyrocket two quarters later as the delayed license deals were completed. Not only did Stan lose money when he sold the stock, he stubbornly refused to buy it back on the way up "just to send a message to management that they can't treat me that way." As this demonstrates, a severe injury to our self-esteem can wreak havoc with both our buy and sell decisions.

When the normal four-year-old jumps off the couch and says, "Look at me, I can fly," he is asking for an adult to appreciate his unique growth and development. When we attempt to "beat the market," particularly in obscure or more speculative stocks, we are engaged in the adult equivalent. We want to exhibit our investing prowess, but when the market goes against us, we frequently respond as if our personhood has been insulted.

One typical reaction to this injury that underlies many investor mistakes is the angry blaming of others. It's not unlike the wicked queen in Snow White, who asks, "Mirror, mirror, on the wall, who's the fairest of them all?" When the market mirror fails to confirm an investor's self-esteem, the mirror is at risk of being smashed into fragments. Anger in these situations serves to revitalize a crumbling sense of power and efficacy. It makes us feel powerful and strong again, even if at the same time it undermines our ability to think clearly about our investment decisions. The real problem with letting our investment prowess drive our self-esteem is that it corrupts our ability to think carefully about the companies we own. Instead we tend to obsess about whether the company, or the market, is affirming our prowess as a stock-picker.

When we feel injured by Mr. Market or one of its companies, we often experience a sense of emptiness and depletion, which we try to overcome by increasing our excitement and stimulation. This nearly always means investing in a higher-risk situation for which we're not prepared. Although our conscious goal is to make up for the previous loss, our unconscious actions often betray our need for stimulation. Stan reacted to the poor performance of his ANB investment by immediately investing in a high-risk startup with huge upside potential. Stan was clearly looking for stimulation to overcome the depression from his loss on ANB. But he neglected to do any in-depth due diligence on the startup, and the company failed shortly thereafter. That is another problem with using the market to mirror our self-esteem. When it's disrupted, the resulting need for stimulation can distort our usual capacity for seeing things clearly from multiple perspectives; our only goal becomes getting even. In this vengeful state, the choice of the next investment will almost always lack the careful consideration that initially guided the first.

GRANDIOSITY

Dealing with Mr. Market's mirroring validation of success is a much more pleasurable experience than the fallout from failure, but it still puts the investor at risk for erroneous judgment. When investors are hot, making several investment choices that perform exceedingly well, there is a natural stimulation of grandiose feelings. It's normal human nature. Defined as a strong belief in our greatness, abilities, knowledge, or character, grandiosity's ideational content is most often expressed by both children and adults (and in myths) through dreams and fantasies of flying. But within the investment world, variations of flying fantasies not only accompany achievements, but can also contribute to major mistakes and monetary losses.

The myth of Daedalus highlights the difference between grandiosity that carries us spinning out of control and that more controlled grandiosity that helps us achieve our ambitions and ideals. Daedalus had built a labyrinth for Minos, king of Crete, and wished to return to his home in Greece upon its completion. But he was so useful as an engineer and inventor that Minos refused to let him go, ordering a strict watch on all vessels to block egress by sea. Compelled to stay in Crete against his will and unable to escape by sea, Daedalus turned to the air. "Minos may control the land and sea," he said, "but not the regions of the air. I will try that way." So he fabricated wings for himself and his young son, Icarus, out of feathers and wax and "gave the whole gentle curvature a shape like the wings of a bird." When preparing for the escape, Daedalus warned Icarus to "keep at a moderate height, for if you fly too low the damp will clog your wings, and if too high the heat will melt them."[7]

As the two took flight, plowmen and shepherds on the ground watched them, astonished at the sight, and concluded that because they were flying, the pair must be gods. Suddenly Icarus, exulting in his newfound ability to fly, soared upward toward the heavens. The proximity of the sun softened the wax holding his feathered wings together, and Icarus plunged helplessly into the sea. Daedalus arrived safely in Sicily, where he built a temple to Apollo and hung up his wings as an offering to the god.

This story about narcissistic grandiosity and its effects on two individuals gives metaphorical life to a basic psychological truth. On the one hand, it demonstrates how painful it can be to fall from the heights of unrestrained grandiosity; on the other hand, we learn how grandiosity in the service of realistic ambitions and ideals can lead to innovation and achievement.

Marian Tolpin, a Chicago psychoanalyst, has suggested that the roots of our flying fantasies arise "in connection with the infant's sensations of being lifted and then carried around by the parent at a time when mind–body experiences are so closely intertwined."[8] Later experiences obviously add idiosyncratic meaning to the flying fantasies, but within our culture we seem to continually return to this idea. We are "carried away," we feel "uplifted," we sing about "fly me to the moon and let me dance among the stars," and we "follow every rainbow."

The phenomenon of unrestrained grandiosity is curiously a neglected aspect of the psychology of investing. But its ramifications can be experienced in many different arenas. One of the most evocative illustrations comes from a story called "The World's Smartest Man" by Bennett W. Goodspeed.[9] Picture the world's smartest man together with the president of the United States, a priest, and a hippie all dealing with their final moments before an inevitable plane crash. Although there are four men on board, there are only three parachutes. Naturally the president takes the first parachute and bales out. The world's smartest man claims the second parachute, believing he is "an irreplaceable asset of humanity." The priest then turns to the hippie and offers, "I have lived my life, and now it is in God's hands; you take the last parachute." The hippie replies, "No sweat, Padre, we both are safe; the world's smartest man jumped out with my knapsack on his back!"

With a cooperative market, brilliant investors feel like the world's smartest man before his exit. Invincible as Icarus, the master stockpicker can do no wrong, make no mistakes. Risk is for the faint of heart and need not even be considered. But the sense of invulnerability that flows from the brilliant investor's grandiose fantasies often proves false when the market turns volatile and uncooperative.

In his autobiography, Winston Churchill described a scene when, as a teenager, he was being chased by a cousin and younger brother. As he crossed a bridge leading over a ravine, he found himself trapped by his pursuers: "But in a flash there came across me a great project. . . . In a second, I had plunged, throwing out my arms to embrace the summit of the fir tree below."[10] Churchill remained unconscious for three days and then in bed for three months. Clearly his flying fantasy was not yet under the control of his more rational thought processes. Fortunately for Western civilization, his grandiose penchant for extricating himself from difficult situations as an adult was more controlled by his rational ego.

Thus, while grandiosity can lead even brilliant investors to regressive thinking and error proneness, at least they're in good company with the likes of Icarus, the world's smartest man, Winston Churchill, and countless others. As Tolpin pointed out, we all share a drive to "refind the [early] feeling of being uplifted," seeking the "high" of that pleasurable flying fantasy we experienced as children.[11] Thanks to the market's mirroring validation, successful investors are particularly vulnerable to this siren call, which is particularly dangerous because of its penchant for obscuring investment risks. Only those few investors who have learned to contain their grandiosity can expect to balance those risks and maintain their outstanding performance with consistency and longevity.

THE DISRUPTION OF PARTNERING TIES

Thinking of ourselves as investors is partly a social role, often acting as a self-sustaining experience. We belong to a group of like-minded others who relate to the stock market and understand its dynamics. We enjoy a shared sense of satisfaction when we interact with others who invest in the companies we follow and are knowledgeable about their business. We become part of the market group.

Each of us has an inherent need for sameness—a need to be in the sustaining presence of like-minded others. Just as infants need to be surrounded by familiar sights, sounds, and smells, adults need a sense of partnering or "we-ness" to help sustain their sense of self. The phenomenon of we-ness provides group cohesion and defines group boundaries. Group formation based on partnering needs fosters cooperative efforts in the deployment of its members' skills and talents in the service of the group's objectives.

When group memberships are disrupted and the individual is left feeling alone, isolated, and unrelated, the stranded members will usually make frantic efforts to rejoin a community. In their emergency attempt to restore partnering connections, the pressure of groupthink increases. Consider the Mexican devaluation of the peso in the mid-1990s. Many professionals who perceived themselves as knowledgeable international investors were surprised and humiliated by the Mexican government's actions. As they began to sell Telmex shares, the Main Streeters who fancied themselves part of the international investor community reacted to their anxiety by reorganizing themselves around the group leaders. Despite the historical lessons that these devaluations have been generally good for long-term stock prices, these investors as a group let anxiety overrun rationality.

When our healthy sense of group belonging is disrupted, the fear of aloneness and isolation evokes an urgent wish to reinstate the lost sense of we-ness. The reconstitution of our sense of self becomes far more important than any rational knowledge about specific investments. It is in the service of these types of actions designed to restore the equilibrium of our injured sense of self that the origins of group-think errors can best be discerned.

Although there are no official statistics on investor mistakes, my interviews of both professional and lay investors suggest they are doing extremely well if they choose four or five out of ten stocks correctly. Similarly, professional money managers and analysts are probably at the top of their game when they choose six out of ten stocks correctly. Of course, neither pros nor private investors will admit their mistakes publicly or come totally clean even with insiders; but for ballpark numbers, I think we're close in concluding that success rates for serious investors are generally about equal to a good high-school baseball player's batting average.

The kind of knowledge we need for investing is not absolute, as in learning a system or simple formula that can then be applied to all, or even most, situations. Investing is a lot like bringing up a child. We are guided by an overall philosophy of child-rearing, which we consciously or otherwise apply through a trial-and-error process that may work to one degree or another at some stages of development and fail miserably at others. We also know that an intellectual understanding of child-development theory is not enough. We must be participants in the process, practicing what we know and revising our theory and practice as our feedback requires. So it is in the stock market. We must constantly be self-reflective and aware of the patterns of organization that unconsciously influence our fantasy relationship with Mr. Market.

FREEING OUR EMOTIONS
FROM MR. MARKET

The good news is that once we become aware of how wicked old Mr. Market plays with our self-esteem, we can learn to sever the link between our sense of self and the gyrations of the S&P 500. This is what emotionally sophisticated investors do. We learn the ways the market disrupts our mirroring, idealizing, and partnering needs, and we force ourselves to examine the ways we usually react when this happens. Once we know the emotional and cognitive patterns that follow market action, we can learn to reduce their influence and even avoid their disruptive effects on our investment behavior altogether. While easier said than done, here are some guidelines:

• Before making any investment decisions, check your anxiety level. We all experience anxiety in different situations and through idiosyncratic symptoms. Get to know your symptoms, write them down, and keep a log of what is happening between you and the market when you begin to experience these symptoms. Even more important, try not to buy or sell stock when you feel more anxious than usual.

• If you begin to make decisions based on only one or two variables rather than a comprehensive picture of a company, stop and reconsider your decision-making process. Whenever you buy a stock, write down six reasons why you are making the purchase. When you find yourself wanting to sell based on one or two variables, go back to your original list and review the other variables before you sell.

• When you feel anxious, realize you will be vulnerable to tips and rumors. Avoid getting caught up in either negative or positive stories. Under no circumstances should you act on anything you read on a stock message board or hear at a cocktail party or private conversation with a friend who has a "hot tip" or "inside" information. If you are tempted to act on these rumors, wait twenty-four hours before buying or selling, and then review your anxiety symptoms.

• If you feel overly confident about your investing, be especially careful with your subsequent investment choices. When you've made a series of brilliant investment choices, try to write down everything that could go wrong with your picks and with the market. Purposefully look for investment advice that will make you worry about the market.

• Don't make investment decisions when you feel disappointed in an admired other, whether it's company management, an investment adviser, or a personal friend or colleague who has let you down. At these times you are vulnerable to turning left when you should be turning right.

• Try not to let your self-esteem be dependent on market success or failure. As a successful investor with a strong sense of self-esteem, you don't have to worry about what anyone else thinks, good or bad, of your investment performance.

THREE

Building Castles in the Sand

Every investment in the stock market involves unknowable and unpredictable outcomes. Within the investment community, risk is a fact of life. It varies only by degree. Efforts to quantify and manage risk have centered on the concept of "uncertainty." For most of us, uncertainty is a very subjective concept. But for the academicians, economists, and mathematicians who dominated the investment field for many years, uncertainty was translated into a statistic that could be objectively measured as volatility of potential returns. The translation was codified in modern portfolio theory (MPT), which focuses on objective and purportedly scientific definitions and measurements of risk, as well as far less scientific methods for managing investment risk.

For most individual investors, however, risk remains a subjectively experienced emotional state. And most of us acknowledge that our psychological response to making investment decisions under conditions of uncertainty can have a dramatic influence on our performance.[1] Perhaps because human emotions will always be more complex than the thorniest mathematical equations or the most arcane economic theories, however, the impact of emotions on risk-taking has received much less attention than MPT and its progeny.

The first rule to remember when trying to understand risk is that we're all different, and our emotional responses to risk will vary accordingly. As Loren Eiseley once said, "There is a difference in our human outlook, depending on whether we have been born upon level plains, where one step reasonably leads to another, or whether, by contrast, we have spent our lives amidst glacial crevasses and precipitous descents. In the case of the mountaineer, one step does not always lead rationally to another save by a desperate leap over a chasm or by an even more hesitant tiptoeing across precarious snow bridges."[2]

These differing landscapes of the mind create contrasting lenses through which we view the world. One would have us believe that the world is rational, predictable, and based on historical patterns. The other reminds us that however scientifically we evaluate and order past events, there is always a deeply rooted unexpectedness and not quite ordered universe lurking behind our ostensible consistency. Nowhere is this contrast more apparent than in our attempt to define investment risk—that slippery topic whose parameters encompass both objective measurement and gut-wrenching emotion. So let's turn to the subjective aspects of risk, discuss the emotional factors that influence our capacity for taking risks, and examine some of the ways successful investors deal with the concept and the reality of risk.

DEFINITIONS OF RISK

The most widely accepted measure of risk within the investment community is volatility of returns. Academicians assess volatility in several ways. Standard deviation measures volatility in absolute terms, that is, how much a portfolio varies from its own arithmetic mean returns; beta and R2 measures volatility in relative terms, that is, how much change you should expect in a stock price relative to the change in a major market index. Betas are then used to measure the ostensible risk of portfolios. For example, if Xco's stock or your portfolio consistently drops (or rises) 20 percent more than the market, Xco's stock becomes by definition a riskier investment. With no free lunch on Wall Street, there's a corollary to the effect that the higher the risk, the higher your potential returns should be. These two rules of thumb remain accepted wisdom on the Street despite arguments from value investors for ignoring risk–reward equations in stocks that are undervalued based on low P/Es, price to book, or other criteria on the theory that these stocks offer more opportunity for appreciation with less risk than the equations suggest.

Because of the equation of risk with volatility, some investors place great faith in the idea of risk-adjusted performance, a concept developed by Nobel Prize–winning economist William Sharpe. He argued that it doesn't make any sense to look only at how much money our portfolio made; we must also look at how much risk we took to achieve the gain. Essentially risk-adjusted performance penalizes volatility, no matter how successful the eventual outcome of the investment.

Count me in with the value investors on this score. For several reasons, the risk = volatility equation has always struck me as absurd. First, return on investment can never be knowable before an investment decision, and even after the results are in, an investor still cannot judge how risky the investment actually was. If you are a long-term investor, volatility should decrease rather than increase the risk of your investments because it offers you the opportunity to buy more stock at lower prices. Second, if your stock drops precipitously relative to the market, the risk = volatility equation suggests that it is now a higher-risk situation than when you bought it. This is akin to saying that if you are looking to buy a house and the owners lower the price, it becomes a higher-risk investment than if you paid the original asking price.

Consider an investor who made a long-term investment in the Titan Corporation (NYSE: TTN) at $19 per share. The stock moved to $28 and then retreated to slightly below $19. Do you sell Titan because it has become high risk, or do you buy more because Mr. Market has offered you an unusual opportunity to take advantage of a misperception of its fundamentals? Contrary to conventional economic theory, assuming you understand the economics of Titan's business and they remain positive, then Titan's lower price should also make it a much lower-risk investment at $19 than it was at $28. If you believe this example, then risk must be redefined as a subjective phenomenon related to the psychology of judgment rather than a mathematical equivalent of volatility.

In fact, some investment professionals have suggested that the risk = volatility equation is too limiting and that we need a broader risk paradigm. For example, Robert Jeffrey suggested that risk is a function not only of volatility, but also of our present and future liabilities, meaning the amount of cash we need to meet future obligations.[3] Peter Bernstein added the notion that liquidity, specific risk, and life of an investment also contribute to the definition of risk "because the cost and difficulty of changing our minds increases as we go from the instant liquidity of dollar bills to the inescapable buy and hold caused by the specific risks of the machine and the factory."[4] Taking into account both the asset and liability side of the equation, the holding period, and the ability to change our minds certainly enhances our understanding of risk, but it still fails to deal with the fact that investors, like all other humans, think subjectively, not rationally, when making decisions under conditions of uncertainty. This simple psychological fact means that risk, by definition, contains important subjective elements not typically considered or evaluated by economists or the investment community.

Risk can be defined subjectively as the emotional reaction to our idiosyncratic perception of the chance, probability, fear, amount, or consequence of loss. From an emotional perspective, risk is the psychological reaction to potential loss. It is often equated with uncertainty because all investments in instruments that trade in the capital markets involve decisions about an unpredictable future. Investment results are uncertain because they are contingent on the relatively unpredictable performance of a company and its management, the behavior of others in the marketplace, the randomness of world events, and our psychological reactions to each of these phenomena. Uncertainty generates anxiety, a diffuse tension state that frequently elicits either the illusion of excessive danger or the denial of a danger that we should fear.

Objective risk exists as a mathematical reality. And we can employ a variety of well-known techniques to lower the "chance" of loss. These include dollar cost averaging, hedging, low expenses, minimum turnover, diversification, careful asset allocation, buying with a margin of safety, a consistent sell discipline, careful fundamental evaluation of prospective investments, and ongoing fundamental tracking of companies in which we've invested. But no matter how much we choose to emphasize and lower objective risk, we must still deal with the subjective reality of our emotional responses to risk. It is the psychological impact of loss on rational decision-making that makes most attempts to categorize investments according to an objective, schematic risk profile so misguided. However much we may acknowledge that there is some "objective" knowledge of risk that the investment community can quantify and disseminate, for the majority of investors risk remains predominantly a subjective phenomenon intimately related to loss and experienced not in the external world of stocks and bonds but in the internal and subjective world of our conscious and subconscious processes.[5] Concepts like volatility become relevant in this context only to the extent that they create anxiety, which can cause us to sell out at precisely the wrong time.

THE PSYCHOLOGICAL CAPACITY
FOR ASSUMING RISK

The investment literature delineates two major risks for all of us when we buy and sell stocks. First is systematic risk, which we cannot avoid when participating in the stock market. It includes factors endemic to the market such as interest rates, inflation, and credit crunches. If, for example, we experience a recession, company revenues and earnings generally trend downward, changing the psychological expectations of investors and encouraging lower perceived fair valuations reflected in stock prices. Systematic risk is, by definition, market risk.

Second is unsystematic or corporate risk, which is unique to individual companies or industries above and beyond generalized market risk as a whole. It refers to the vagaries of future performance by specific management teams, products, services, and industries. It also includes the uncertainties of how these performance unknowns may idiosyncratically affect individual securities in a portfolio. Corporate risk can also be affected by changes in a company's capital structure (for example, debt versus equity financing) and the life stage of the company (for example, startup, emerging growth, or mature). The dangers are execution of an individual company's business plan and, ultimately, whether it will go out of business.

Company risk, theoretically and mathematically, can be reduced by diversification, by owning at least ten to fifteen stocks in different industries. Nevertheless, as Bernstein has correctly pointed out, diversification does not provide a guarantee against loss, only against losing everything at once.[6] Market risk, on the other hand, cannot be eliminated or substantially reduced. It remains the price we pay for investment rewards. Systematic and unsystematic risk share one important characteristic. Each remains an external factor unrelated to our sub-jective perception of risk. And external factors have never seemed ter-ribly useful in helping us answer a fundamental question: How much and what kind of risk are we prepared to take when investing in the stock market?

Only part of the answer can be gleaned from factual data like age, income, savings, future need for cash, and investing time horizon. While these are the kinds of questions any good financial planner would be sure to ask, they all focus on capital loss—whether we will have cash to pay necessary expenses in the future. From my discus-sions and interviews with many investors over the years, I have increasingly come to believe that at least as important are influences related to the psychological aspects of risk. These include the stresses inherent in actively playing the market, idiosyncratic personality (internal) factors, the context in which we are investing, and our cog-nitive style. All of these factors are inchoate but nevertheless con-tribute not only to our capacity for risk, but also to our actual behavior when facing the consequences of risk, which may or may not corre-spond to our risk tolerance.

NORMAL MARKET STRESS
INFLUENCES RISK CAPACITY

Whether managing their own portfolios or other people's money, investors report similar inherent stresses in the investing process. The pressures of being in the market can unwittingly disrupt nearly all attempts to gauge objective risk and can be grouped under the broad concept of "cumulative stress."[7] Cumulative stress derives from the continuous psychological strains that we experience when trying to invest our money under uncertain conditions. None of the pressures that contribute to cumulative stress are traumatic or abnormal. In fact, these pressures are not even necessarily observable by an outsider watching us invest. But they are still powerful, as they accumulate silently over time, become embedded in our personality, and bias us toward vulnerability, thus silently affecting our risk tolerances. If this concept of cumulative stress has value, it lies in helping us examine the interplay between specific pressures that exist as a result of merely participating in the market and our psychological tendency to seek out or avoid risk. Let's turn, then, to some of the normal pressures reported by investors, both private and professional.

UNCERTAINTY AND AMBIGUITY: SELF-CRITICISM

Most active investors and money managers do not believe in the efficient market hypothesis or the random walk theory. Almost by definition, they believe that the market is inefficient enough to take advantage of discrepancies between intrinsic value and stock price and that they have access to the information that enables them to judge these discrepancies. As an active investor, you are probably well educated, knowledgeable, and intelligent. It is this intellectual rigor and academic or street learning that promotes self-confidence in your advisory, money-management, or investing skills.

Unfortunately no matter how much we know, no matter how much sophisticated technological and logistical support we receive, no matter how many novel ways we learn to organize and analyze information, there is no way to digest all the available macroeconomic data, let alone all the corporate fundamentals and technical charts, to say nothing of all the nuances of trying to assess the quality of management. We can never know everything there is to know because we function under the aegis of what the physicists call the "uncertainty principle." Stephen Hawking describes this phenomenon of quantum mechanics as not being able to "measure both the position and the speed of a particle to great accuracy; the more accurately you measure the position, the less accurately you can measure the speed, and vice versa."[8] So even if it were possible to read all the annual 10-K and quarterly 10-Q reports, follow all the Wall Street research, keep track of international currency markets and economic, political, and social events, and then follow all the "proven" technical indicators, there surely would not be enough time to actually think about and carefully digest all the information available on any one investment, let alone an entire portfolio. This fact of market life was sadly brought home to both individual and professional investors in the wake of the Enron accounting scandal and its questionable accounting progeny in early 2002.

The proliferation of readily available information, coupled with the complexity of all the technical variables used to measure and analyze the market and its participants, creates a continuous low-level pressure to know everything, read everything, and keep on top of everything that is going on in the world that could possibly influence our individual investments or the stock market in general. While some research has suggested that the technological advances providing the means to address this situation can lead to overconfidence, interviews with investors strongly indicate an ironically different consequence. From my observations, the pressures of the Information Age predispose us to continual self-criticism and emotional depletion for missing a market signal or significant company event, for not having been prescient about the public's response to a new product, for not predicting interest-rate directions accurately, and so on. Most investors acknowledge the inability of any individual to be omniscient on the market, but they still experience an internal burden to accumulate and synthesize more raw data than the human mind can possibly process. Over time, this can easily lead to an often unrecognized low-grade feeling of depletion (burnout), self-criticism, and self-doubt.

The fluid continuum between overconfidence and self-criticism contributes to readily changing capacities for assuming risk. And more important, it may create a disconnection between those capacities and our actual behavior at any given time. When we feel intelligent and successful, we are psychologically much more likely to perceive ourselves as able to discern and handle manageable risk than when we become depleted and humbled by the market.[9]

LIFE IN THE GOLDFISH BOWL: SHAME

Investors operate in a public arena dominated by those with myopic time horizons. On the professional side, their quarterly performance records are often closely followed by clients, competitors, employers, and pension-fund consultants, whose recommendations can have devastating effects on assets under management. Their ability to perform relative to market benchmarks is judged continuously. While individual investors (and buy-side managers) are not exposed to nearly as complete public scrutiny, we privately experience the same kind of pressure in the form of self-consciousness. We are also susceptible to criticism from within our own firms and families; and we frequently compare ourselves to our friends, neighbors, and colleagues on a short-term basis. Thus our buy and sell actions create a long-term atmosphere of both public and private scrutiny.

This fishbowl existence predisposes us to feelings of shame in two areas. First, because most investors are talented individuals with confidence in their ability to perform well, we often experience ourselves as exposed to the vagaries of negative and humiliating responses when our investment decisions appear flawed, however temporarily. Much like the lecturer whose attempt to tell a joke in front of a large audience is met with deafening silence, investors experience either private or public scorn for decisions that do not pan out immediately.

Second, because active investors truly believe they can beat the market, we are frequently exposed to frustration of our own internal goals and aspirations. The nameless mortification and dejection inherent in failing to achieve our ambitions and ideals is captured by the word *shame*. Shame is the hallmark of a "self that has fallen short of its goal."[10] Because it is so difficult to maintain a high batting average when picking stocks, we all suffer under the continual pressure of failing to live up to our expectations. Those of us who tend to feel shame more intensely are less likely to want to expose ourselves to risk, since it increases the possibility of failure, which in turn will lead to humiliation. Because the extent to which we feel prone to shame can vary with the relationships we are in, however, our risk capacities can readily change over time and in differing relational contexts.

REAL LIVES, REAL MONEY, REAL ANXIETY

Many investors, and certainly most money managers, live their work twenty-four hours a day. Managers toil long hours and are frequently away from family visiting companies. Even on vacations, they rarely forget about the market. Managers usually can distance themselves from feelings of direct responsibility for other people's money. As one manager said, "I don't think of it as my neighbor's money; it's all a game for me that I love and play well." Still, the fact that they are responsible for huge sums tends to remain a subconscious burden in the paradoxical life of individuals who generally love both the cerebral and practical aspects of the investing process. Particularly during market downturns, sleepless nights and workaholic styles are common for most money managers, and they tend to experience a low-grade anxiety orbiting around thoughts of failure, money loss, job loss, and client loss.

Similarly, while individual investors generally spend less time on their portfolios, often working long hours in an unrelated profession, they still spend many off hours studying the market. It is nearly impossible to distance ourselves from our investments when we feel responsible for managing our family's money and making sure there will be enough savings for retirement or our children's education. Thus, to a large extent, the same anxieties that afflict money managers also touch individual investors, who experience those tensions as jolts to self-esteem on top of the potential for monetary loss and failure.

The stress inherent in managing real money influences our risk capacity through the creation of anxiety. Whether anxiety stimulates us to be more risk-prone or risk-averse depends on our idiosyncratic personalities. James, an active trader, told me, "When I become anxious about whether I'll have enough for retirement, I'll often make big bets to try to get it all at once. It's like I take too much risk." On the other hand, Fred, a long-term investor, told me, "If I feel anxious about making enough money to put my kids through college, all I can think of when I buy a stock is the possibility of losing money, so I often hesitate to invest in a company even if I know it well. I get the feeling, if I buy it, the stock will go down." Anxiety affects James's and Fred's risk levels in diametrically opposed ways, but their concerns illustrate that our capacity for risk and our subsequent action are always influenced by anxiety in one way or another. The more we understand how anxiety affects our specific capacities and behavior, the greater our chances of countering its negative impact.

COMPETITION

Most money managers and individual investors work in an atmosphere characterized by an ongoing lack of emotional attunement. Within the professional arena, because of its competitive nature, there is little emphasis placed on understanding another's experience and responding to it with a positive and warm tone. Although surrounded by others, money managers tend to experience their professional environment as lonely, despite their protestations about the positive aspects of independence. Managers often experience others more as competitors searching for their mistakes than as fellow travelers or colleagues. As the well-known fund manager Ken Heebner once told the press, "You only want to talk to me when I'm losing money."

Individual investors are also a competitive group. They are always looking for tips and systems to help them outperform their friends and fellow investors. As investment club member Ann once told me about one of her fellow club members, "John and I often talk about our investments and give each other ideas to be helpful, but I often find myself feeling secretly glad when my ideas succeed and his fail." Competitive aggression in itself is not unhealthy. On the contrary, it's a normal and positive reaction to obstacles that hinder the attainment of a person's aims in the world. Much of the energy we use to make money and achieve other goals is derived from competitive aggression. Competition is often a constructive force both in the work world and in human relationships. But competitive aggression can also become a driving force, divorced from the benignly opposing instincts that make us supportive and responsive even when faced with active opposition or competition from others. When competitive aggression takes on this obsessive twist, it is often accompanied by an insidious fear of helplessness and powerlessness. We frequently respond to this threat with anger, which serves to make us feel empowered.

Where competitive aggression becomes a driving force in our investing, restoring and maintaining self-esteem by beating out someone else can become our primary focus. This can make us more prone to take large risks in hopes of competitive victory, which overshadows our usual risk tolerances, and this often results in major investment blunders even by very successful investors. In retrospect, we can see that many successful dot-com investors were so focused on the competitive landscape that they forgot to notice the deteriorating fundamentals and prospects of their investments.

EFFICACY: LOSS OF CONTROL
AND COMPETENCE

We all feel enhanced self-esteem when we experience our selves as effective agents in influencing others. Psychologists call this phenomenon efficacy, but however you name or conceptualize it, the experience of having an impact on our surroundings serves as a basic foundation of our sense of self. It is as if we can say to ourselves, I have an impact, therefore I am somebody. The converse can have an equal but opposite impact on our sense of self.

Money managers and individual investors can experience a loss of efficacy, for example, when they have no impact on a stock or bond movement after buying, when a sound investment decision is destroyed by chance economic or political events, or when they fail to convince others that a particular investment choice is a good one. In a January 1994 *Wall Street Journal* article on front running by fund managers, Bill Hays suggested that if managers had their money at risk, they might have more appreciation for what it's like for individual shareholders to have money at risk. In a different context, Steve Somes of Boston State Street Research stated that "investing is not only their [managers'] profession, it's their hobby....They love the markets and that love is what separates the really good managers from the rest." The love of having an impact in the market is what motivates many investors. And our need for efficacy is what makes passive index funds anathema to most active investors. But it also is what makes maintaining our self-esteem in difficult market environments so arduous.

When our sense of efficacy is injured, it tends to lower our self-esteem and self-confidence. Social psychological research tells us that those with low self-esteem are likely to rely more on the judgments of others than on their own research and ideas.[11] This takes us to another paradox of risk. When we begin to rely on the herd for our information and decisions, we underestimate the amount of risk we are taking because the influence of the group lulls us into feeling comfortable with behavior supported by groupthink. In most cases, however, following the herd means unwittingly taking huge risks masked by a false sense of being risk-averse, smart investors. More about the herd later.

THE RESULTS OF CUMULATIVE STRESS

Cumulative stress resulting from the subtle but ongoing and combined pressures of uncertainty, exposure, anxiety, competition, and loss of efficacy creates an underlying vulnerability in all investors' sense of self. This tends to distort our perception of our risk tolerances. These misperceptions may be too high or too low, but they rarely reflect a good fit between our personality and our capacity for assuming risk. This is an occupational hazard, part of the price we pay for being active investors. It's also part of the reason why traditional economic theories miss the mark by assuming that investors are naturally rational when participating in the market. As long as we function in the market's pressure cooker, we'll remain vulnerable to risk distortion. But that doesn't mean the distortion must remain unrecognized. There are behavioral symptoms that should serve as warning signs that cumulative stress is beginning to interfere with risk perception and investment decision-making.

Stimulating activities used to overcome feelings of depletion and deadness. Particularly noticeable is a need to create pseudo-excitement, a frenzied lifestyle in the business or social sphere. Gambling, working too much, investing in high-risk situations, and churning or overtrading accounts are common characteristics. In this situation, any tendency to hyper-trade should signal a need to be more risk-averse.

Searching for shortcut methods to counteract feelings of powerlessness and helplessness. We resort to this as a way of demonstrating to ourselves that we have absolute control over others or the markets. This attempt to circumvent the painstakingly slow investing process generally leads to an unusual susceptibility to rumors, hot tips, and Internet stock promotions. This tends to produce a feeling of high risk-seeking capacity at exactly the time we should be feeling risk-averse.

Narcissistic rage resulting from perceived injuries to our sense of self in a competitive atmosphere. This often takes the form of a wish to get even, to destroy the injuring party. When combined with the search for shortcut methods to quick profits, we often see activities that temporarily bolster our self-esteem at the cost of our longer-term net worth.

Arrogant grandiosity. This is often a reaction to feelings of humiliation or shame. It is frequently accompanied by a sense of magical omnipotence that undermines reasonable decision-making. Arrogant grandiosity is particularly prevalent in institutional settings that promote a rock-star mentality, placing one or two ostensibly brilliant money managers in the spotlight, at least until their bubbles eventually burst. On an individual level, arrogant grandiosity masks our limitations or short-circuits any attempt to analyze our mistakes. In these situations, risk becomes subordinated to an irrational and sometimes insatiable hunger for short-term rewards.

Persistent anxiety. As anxiety slowly builds up, it can lead imperceptibly to jigsaw-puzzle thinking, resulting in decisions based on one or two variables rather than a whole picture. Because of its apparent simplification of a complex set of variables, this phenomenon lends a false sense of confidence that increases risk-seeking behavior.

If any of these symptoms sound familiar, it may be time to take stock of the accumulating stress in your investment practices, readjust your assessment of risk, and adopt a risk-management regime that fits your style and financial objectives.

PERSONALITY FACTORS

In addition to the inherent stresses that accumulate during the investing process and influence our capacity for risk, personality (internal) factors, external contextual factors, and cognitive styles also influence our risk perception and behaviors. To make matters worse, all of these factors and the ways they interact constantly change throughout our lives. Let's try to put them in perspective, starting with the internal factors.

Recently I designed an Investment Personality Questionnaire for Capital International Asset Management, which was subsequently tested on five hundred investors.[12] While the scoring system for the questionnaire is proprietary, some of the internal factors it addresses to assess an investor's capacity for risk include our self-image and general worldview; our subjective perception of our own investment knowledge, experience, and enthusiasm; our capacity to cope with stress, use emotions to our advantage, and maintain realistic denial when needed; our perception of time; our capacity for dealing with shame; our capacity for realistic action, and our psychological capacity to deal with the potential for loss and its consequences.

These are admittedly complicated factors to measure, which may explain why it is much easier to simply define risk as volatility of returns and be done with it. But taking the easy way out by foregoing an emotional evaluation of risk also means sacrificing an enormous amount of rich information about yourself and what makes you tick as an investor.

For example, consider the case of Barbara, an investor who is hopeful and confident about the future and whose self-esteem is resistant to the bumps and bruises of everyday life. Barbara once told me, "I'm a fairly optimistic and confident person, and I recover quickly when I fail at something, so it just seems natural for me to actively invest in the small-cap market. I feel confident I can evaluate companies, and I am optimistic that if I wait long enough, my decisions will pan out." In this brief remark, Barbara is touching on several important risk measures. She is hopeful and optimistic about the future, and she copes well with stressful feelings or events rather than being overwhelmed by them. This is an important internal factor, because my research suggests that investors who perceive themselves as more skeptical about the future and more self-doubting in stressful situations seem to have less capacity for assuming risk. Measured on this one variable, Barbara has a high tolerance for taking risks in the market. But does that mean she should be acting in a risk-prone manner? Because of her strong sense of self, Barbara was clearly able to maintain her independent judgments in the face of strong pressure from others, but her optimism was a double-edged sword. On the one hand, optimism is necessary for risk-taking actions. On the other hand, as research by Barber and Odean indicates, those who maintain an "optimism bias" overestimate the control they have over their investments, and they are likely to mistakenly believe they are better than average.[13] So Barbara's optimism must be controlled by a capacity for ongoing reality checks and corrective action. As she offhandedly mentioned, "The thing about me is I have to be careful sometimes that I don't get carried away with my enthusiasm over technologies and forget about the vulnerabilities in the business plans of some of the companies I like." In other words, Barbara may at times have difficulty containing her ebullience when acting on her psychological capacity for risk-seeking.

Because risk is intimately related to loss, our capacity for assuming risk is also contingent on our psychological ability to deal with the potential for and consequences of loss. This is affected by a number of internal factors, including our history of real and emotional losses, our anxiety level when confronting loss, and the times of the year marking the anniversary of our major losses. Barbara had experienced a difficult divorce the year before our interview. She was still feeling shell-shocked and confused about why she hadn't seen her marriage falling apart until it was too late. She knew she was depressed but felt she had to deny her feelings in order to function in her life. When one of her more aggressive sector funds began to collapse, Barbara described how she denied that anything was wrong and, despite her adviser's pleas, refused to sell part of her holdings. It was only after the monetary damage had been done that she realized her need to deny and avoid the feelings of loss in other areas of her life had prevented her from facing the upheaval in her portfolio.

While Barbara's capacity for risk was high on the optimism, self-esteem, and the experience and enthusiasm scale, her current issues involving loss called for caution when it came to investing aggressively in the market until she had dealt with her marital loss. Risk depends partially on our capacity to cope with stress, use emotions to our advantage, and maintain realistic denial when needed. Risk capacity will vary with fluctuations in our emotional strength. At any given time, it will depend on whether we can calmly and comfortably deal with stressful feelings or events or deny the importance of stressful emotions or feel overwhelmed by them. Contrary to traditional economics, emotions (particularly emotions surrounding loss) and how we cope with them are intricately involved in every assessment of risk.[14] Barbara's comment on this phenomenon showed the awakening of insight: "I seem to make the worst decisions on anniversaries that bring back my marriage difficulties. Maybe I should avoid being so aggressive at those times."

Barbara clearly had the capacity for being a risk-prone investor, but recent events in her life, coupled with her tendency to become carried away with the excitement of a new technology while downplaying the hurdles to implementing the business plan for its commercialization, suggested that tempering her actions even in the face of her capacity to tolerate risks may contribute to her investing success more than continually acting on that capacity.

One method of becoming familiar with your capacity to assume risk and your ability to act on that capacity is to review a series of questions aimed at furthering your self-understanding:

- Am I generally an optimistic or pessimistic person?
- How quickly do I bounce back from situations where I feel emotionally injured and hurt?
- Do I feel a passion for investing, or does it feel more like a burden?
- Am I able to calm myself down when I feel stressed out?
- Do I generally perceive time as passing slowly or quickly?
- Does my worry about feeling shame stop me from looking at my mistakes?
- Have I dealt with the emotional and real losses in my life, and at what time of year have they occurred?
- Does my sense of denial interfere with my acting realistically when I deal with money?

The answers to these psychological questions may feel somewhat imprecise compared to mathematical formulas that measure variance or volatility. But to borrow from Warren Buffett's phraseology, it is probably better to be generally right about our psychological capacity to assume risk than to be mathematically right about beta and precisely wrong about our psychology.

CONTEXTUAL RISK FACTORS

One of the most often overlooked factors in attempts to measure risk is that we perceive it differently in disparate contexts. As a result, both the concept and tolerance for risk fluctuates over the course of an individual's lifetime. In addition, research suggests that our risk-seeking capacity may vary from one area of life to another. The Olympic skiers hurtling down a mountain at eighty-five miles per hour are taking huge risks with their bodies but probably perceive that risk very differently than those who are watching on television. Yet these same athletes may perceive conservative investing as a high-risk activity. The many members of the investment community who were murdered in the World Trade Center attack perceived little risk in working every day 1,100 feet above the ground, but after September 11, everyone saw things differently.

Imagine for a minute that you are a hiker lost in the woods, trying to find your way back to civilization. You become hyper-vigilant. Every sound becomes a potential danger or possible clue to escape. You try to discern oncoming weather patterns, worry about darkness overtaking you, or wonder whether someone missing you has sent out a search party. You listen for helicopters above. You begin to plan how you are going to survive the night, whether you have enough warm clothes, whether you should stay put or keep moving. Compare these feelings with the serenity of hiking in the same woods on a beautiful fall day under normal conditions, knowing exactly where you are and enjoying the changing foliage, listening to the birds, feeling the crackling leaves underfoot, observing how fast the clouds are moving, and being conscious of your muscles coordinating a steady push toward your destination. The experience of context causes a totally different perception and capacity to assume risk. Because you perceive the environment so differently in disparate contexts, you are likely to think of your risk capacity very differently.

When lost in the woods, depending on your mood, you may be terrified to take on any significant risk, or you may feel that failing to take on extra risk will worsen a dangerous situation. On the other hand, when you are sure of yourself, knowing where you are, and enjoying your immersion in the woods, you may not even notice that risky choices exist; the chances of anything dire happening feel remote. Being alert to danger is the furthest thing from your mind. While perhaps oversimplified, this example shows that not only will your capacity for risk be different in each scenario, but your actual level of risky behavior will also change in each context.

Since psychological perception of risk influences risk-seeking and risk-aversion, perhaps your investor self is wondering about some of the contexts that influence our perception of market risk and capacity for managing it.

Relationships. It is no secret that investors with a strong sense of self experience themselves as more independent-minded than those with low self-esteem and low confidence. Because people often seek out relationships that function to strengthen their sense of self, the nature of our relationships can alter our capacity for risk. For example, a client who has a strong, trusting, and supportive relationship with a financial adviser frequently has more risk-seeking capacity than a client who is less sure of his relationship with his adviser. It follows that a change in advisers can significantly alter an investor's capacity for risk and perception of that capacity. Lois, an investor who was dissatisfied with her advisor because "he wasn't interested in hand holding during volatile markets," sought out a financial planner who felt that "the relationship was the most important part of the business."

Lois began to notice a distinct difference in her investing style. "Before, I didn't want to be in any stock or fund that was volatile. But now that I know I can call Shirley whenever I'm nervous, and I know she'll calm me down and help me stick to my plan, I'm becoming comfortable with more aggressive investments, which I need if I'm going to be able to retire."

This is just one example of the influence that relationships exert on risk capacity. Support from family and significant others or the loss of significant relationships also can enhance or play havoc with our ability to take on financial risk.

Investing Style. At different periods of our lives, we may assume very different investing styles. These disparate approaches to the market can be influenced by psychological changes, available time, interest in the market, losses, changes in family constellations, and so on. For example, at one phase of life, before becoming experienced with investments or interested in market information, we may follow the advice of the popular magazines, which are geared to informationless trading and emphasize diversification and index funds as a valid investment strategy. But as life events add to our maturity, we may move from disinterest in the markets to a passion for investing. This may stimulate us to revisit our former emphasis on diversification.

In August 1934, John Maynard Keynes wrote to his business associate, F. C. Scott:

> As time goes on, I get more and more convinced that the right method in investment is to put fairly large sums into enterprises which one thinks one knows something about and in the management of which one thoroughly believes. It is a mistake to think that one limits one's risk by spreading too much between enterprises about which one knows little and has no reason for special confidence. . . . One's knowledge and experience are definitely limited and there are seldom more than two or three enterprises at any given time in which I personally feel myself entitled to put full confidence.[15]

Warren Buffett, who quoted Keynes's letter in one of his annual reports (which should serve as a brilliant course in investing strategy), follows Keynes's philosophy:

> The strategy we've adopted precludes our following standard diversification dogma. Many pundits would therefore say the strategy must be riskier than that employed by more conventional investors. We disagree. We believe that a policy of portfolio concentration may well decrease risk if it raises, as it should, both the intensity with which an investor thinks about a business and the comfort level he must feel with its economic characteristics before buying into it.[16]

As our investment style matures along the lines suggested by Keynes and Buffett, our capacity for risk may also increase to accept higher concentration levels. Or our risk capacity may decrease for other psychological reasons. In either case, our risk capacity cannot be assumed to correlate to some mythical age requirement that says as we grow older and head toward retirement we should become more risk-averse. The truth is that there are many investors who should become more risk-seeking as they get closer to retirement because their idiosyncratic psychology and life context allow them to feel more comfortable with greater risk.

Safety Nets. Another contextual determinant of risk capacity is our changing safety nets. I've often thought that investing in turbulent times is a little like hiking in the alpine zone of the White Mountains. The Mt. Washington area offers an intriguing juxtaposition of rapidly changing weather patterns. You feel exposed to harsh and dangerous weather one moment but experience a peculiar sense of being part of several million years of evolution telescoped into a few moments of warm tranquility and peace several minutes later. After enough years of hiking in that alpine zone, one learns to take hats, gloves, jacket, and long underwear along with shorts and T-shirts, even in August.

Investing is a long way from mountain hiking, but its rhythms have a similar cadence, especially in volatile markets. One minute we feel surrounded by ominous clouds, and the next minute everything feels right with the world and investing seems deceptively easy. How much risk you can assume in the mountains depends not just on the season, but also on the competence of your hiking companions, your knowledge of the terrain, and your equipment. How much risk you can assume in the market also depends on your safety nets. These include your knowledge of your individual holdings, your trust in those who recommended them or the management that controls them, the supportive relationships in your life, and the inner resources (your psychological equipment) currently available to tolerate sudden disruptions or threats to their business. The important point is that these are not static qualities. Since they're constantly in flux, knowing your current safety nets is as important as carefully choosing your stocks.

COGNITIVE STYLES

In addition to internal psychological lenses and available safety nets, I believe that our styles of thinking and perceiving also help determine how we make market decisions under conditions of risk. In this sense, our cognitive style represents an important psychological structure that shapes both adaptive and maladaptive approaches to the market.

We often come to know people by their cognitive style. Patterns of perceiving and thinking tend to maintain an inherent consistency over time, changing very slowly and demonstrating similar recognizable patterns through a variety of disparate behaviors. They are part of our adaptive equipment. And they influence our methods for discerning the world, coping with emotions, making decisions, and storing events in our memories. How we perceive what is happening in the market has important roots in the filters that these cognitive styles impose on our organizing lenses.

Nearly forty years ago, David Shapiro wrote a book called *Neurotic Styles*. He summarized his premise as follows:

It is only when we understand the style and the general tendency of the individual's mind and interest that we can reconstruct the subjective meaning of the content of an item of behavior or thought. The same mental context or behavior will have different significance to different individuals, and different contents will have closely similar significance. Without this understanding, we run the risk . . . of seeing only textbook meanings, possibly correct but far removed from the sense and tone of an individual's experience.[17]

The "sense and tone" of the investor's experience—his or her cognitive style—is partially responsible for motivating investments in particular stocks or sectors of the market. It also influences the investor's capacity for assuming the corresponding levels of risk. Let's take a look, then, at some different cognitive styles and how they influence our assumptions about risk. In beginning to examine these styles, however, you should not assume they represent pathology; rather we are recognizing the fact that the illustrated ways of thinking and per-

ceiving do exist to varying degrees, and most of us lean toward one or
the other.

Preoccupation with Detail. Those investors whose cognitive style
emphasizes a preoccupation with details are often able to ferret out
important and relevant facts or statements in periodic reports that
most others overlook. At the same time, they can also be more prone
to missing the subjective nature of the whole picture. Investors who
focus on details are often interested in and at home with technical
analysis or with the mathematical models of fundamental analysis.
They are more comfortable with the apparent precision of mathematical principles and formulas than with the vagueness they attribute to
hunches and general impressions. A detail-oriented investor will be
more inclined to perceive the "facts" from hard data and weigh their
importance, for example, than to seek out impressions of management. When an investor with this orientation believes he knows all the
details about a specific investment, he is likely to feel confident in his
choices and assume a high-risk approach is warranted. The only problem is the detail junkie's tendency to miss the forest for the trees. In
many instances, it is the general picture that contains the best clues to
a risky investment.

Recently I sat in on a conference with management where a number of analysts were asking questions about the company's numbers—
inventory buildup, revenue projections, turnover, and so on. The
analysts came out of the meeting with the facts but seemed to miss the
general flavor of the meeting, characterized by the constant interruption by the CEO of his management team whenever they began to
speak. Despite engaging very successfully on their balance sheet and
income-statement inquiries, they were missing the subjective happenings at the margins. So they missed the risk they were taking by investing in a disjointed management team.

Investors too caught up in details without enough focus on general
impressions tend to gravitate to specific occupational arenas within
the investment field. Many financial analysts and technicians lean in
this direction. Obviously the top analysts and technicians have the
capacity for both, but as a rule these groups are more analytically
focused and comfortable with details. Projections either fit or don't fit

with their carefully constructed models. Often financial indicators become more important than emerging events, which may explain why many analysts don't change projections until the indicators have changed and, all too frequently, after the stock price has dropped. For the detail-oriented investor, integrating new, subjective information that is not based on "objective" fact is like pulling teeth. It is much more natural, even if sometimes self-defeating, for them to rely on isolated facts without considering the whole picture in deciding to change direction. The preoccupation with detail also seems to nurture memories that, despite a high capacity for historical minutiae, are woefully inadequate to help predict the future.

The Impressionistic Thinker. Unlike the detailed thinker, the impressionistic investor relies on an overall reaction to a company or management or earnings picture rather than formulating a detailed, factual, and sharply defined picture. If you ask an impressionistic investor to describe a company product, you will receive a global, diffuse, gee-whiz kind of response that captures the essence and excitement of the product but not its details. These investors are comfortable with subjective impressions and hunches about a company's prospects. But these hunches are rarely modified by facts, and their owners often fail to delve into the details to support their subjective ideas with reality. On the other hand, they tend to be more visionary, capable of seeing how a new service or product could appeal to selected groups in society several years down the road.

These types of thinkers, in their extreme, are also more influenced by others' beliefs and tend to respond favorably to the latest authoritative opinions. They are subject to the influence of media headlines because they lack the detailed facts to support their impressions. A well-done road show is likely to capture their attention more than the prospect of wading through hundreds of pages of SEC documents. Impressionistic thinkers are easily surprised when things go wrong and often feel deceived because they did not discern what to others was an obvious and observable fact. They are easily seduced by management with a good story but no business. These extreme, concept-oriented investors are often the participants on the Internet message boards who write, "This looks like a great stock. Does anyone know anything about the company?" On the positive side, many who use impressionistic thinking and intuition are among the most visionary and creative investors. Those who combine their vision with some analysis tend to gravitate to small-cap and development-stage companies, willing to make large bets on a few companies and frequently succeeding. Impressionistic thinkers have high risk-seeking capacities that are largely determined by their intuitive judgments.

The Suspicious Thinker. The financial markets are filled with suspicious thinkers. The Internet message boards are crammed with lovely examples of this cognitive style. The suspicious thinker comes to the financial markets with rigid preconceived notions about a company's product, stock price, or management. His rigidified ideas are typically negative, and he often presents himself as out to expose a scam or let others know that a company's books are "cooked." Any data that do not confirm his underlying preconceived suppositions are ignored and dismissed as hearsay or propaganda. Suspicious thinkers attempt to convince others that they are merely seeking the underlying truth about a company; but in most cases this turns out to be nothing more than the prejudice they started out with. All too often, their preconceived biases are imposed on the facts encountered in their exploration.

The suspicious thinker, because he knows ahead of time what he will find, experiences an arrogance that allows him to feel morally superior to anyone who might have other facts to contribute. Additional information is quickly dismissed as if it represented a ludicrous suggestion by a naive investor. At the same time, the suspicious thinker is usually highly intelligent and acutely perceptive, even if he does use these qualities more to confirm biases than to pursue original thought. It is this characteristic that leads many suspicious thinkers to make rationally brilliant mistakes. As Shapiro once stated, "The suspicious person can be at the same time absolutely right in his perception and absolutely wrong in his judgment."[18] In other words, he correctly perceives a fragment of reality but so ignores its context and the sway of his bias that he has no basis for reasonable judgment.

The suspicious thinker cannot tolerate any uncertainty, contradictory opinion, or new evidence that threatens his premise. Therefore he will often try to execute an investment strategy that confirms his original bias. In fact, uncertainty is so threatening that elaborate due diligence often enables him to access information ahead of other investors, although he is so narrowly focused that his information usually proves to be meaningless.

It is not surprising that those who see their mission in life as exposing the shams of the investment world engage in this type of thinking. They tend to be conservative, risk-averse investors who are very careful thinkers. But by insisting on having complete information to dissect, they have difficulty accepting the fact that no one has all the answers and that investment decisions must be made without complete information.

The Impulsive Thinker. Investors who act and think impulsively tend to respond to an initial situation that is exciting, interesting, and colorful, full of intriguing promise. They also tend to downplay the supporting role of cognitive functions like planning, organizing, reflecting, decentered awareness, and concentration. They are market players with a narrow horizon, eschewing long-term results for short-term profits. They also have the capacity to size up an immediate situation more effectively than some of their long-term colleagues. Because impulsive thinkers are more emotional in their decision-making, they often counter their lack of objectivity by developing systems designed to contain emotion. This is particularly true for short-term traders, although the best ones, in addition to being able to evaluate an immediate opportunity, also have developed long-term plans, goals, and interests to guide their short-term approach.

The cognitive style of impulsive thinkers predisposes them to act on whims. This can make them vulnerable to cold calls and media recommendations unsupported by any of their own homework. Because they do not assume responsibility for their actions and often think in very concrete rather than abstract terms, they are quick to blame brokers or analysts for making poor recommendations.

IMPLICATIONS OF
CHANGING DEFINITIONS

If we change the definition of risk to encompass not only volatility, but also certain properties inherent in the market, personality characteristics of the investor, the context in which he or she is investing, and the investor's cognitive style, then, as mentioned before, we begin to ask different and novel sorts of questions: Do I experience time as passing slowly or quickly? Do I have any unresolved real or emotional losses? What is my tolerance for sudden change? What is my enthusiasm and interest in the market? What is my propensity for shame? Can I tolerate uncertainty without undue anxiety and denial? Do I have more faith in my own judgment than in that of others? How does my cognitive style influence the type of investments that attract me? What relationships do I maintain that are supportive of my investing style? How are my current safety nets different than they were last year? What cognitive style is most comfortable for me?

When we view risk as an important psychological phenomenon that structures our subjective way of interpreting external reality, many of the traditional concepts that are taken for granted on Wall Street begin to change. This change is reinforced by how successful investors perceive risk, for these investors report a very untraditional view of risk that corresponds to our view that, at its most fundamental level, risk is a psychological phenomenon related to subjective perceptions of loss and judgment. Consider the following psychological characteristics of risk reported by these investors.

First, rather than viewing risk as either chance or consequence of loss, they seem to experience it as decoupled from the concept of loss. Decisions become turning points for better or worse, part of the multiplicity of choices that compose our everyday lives. Their approach brings to mind a statement by Keynes that "most of our decisions to do something positive can only be taken as a result of animal spirits . . . and not as the outcome of a weighted average of quantitative benefits multiplied by qualitative probabilities."[19]

Second, the intellectual challenge for these successful investors seems to replace the common concern with loss. Every decision becomes a challenge to assess not only the correct time to buy, but also the quality of management or the products and services being offered by a company. Investing choices become less like decisions and more like the feel of an ideal tennis shot or a perfect gymnastic move. These investors seem to subscribe to Freud's idea that "the voice of the intellect is a soft one, but it does not rest till it has gained a hearing. Finally, after a countless succession of rebuffs, it succeeds."[20] It is this confidence in their own intellect that allows them to hold on to an imperturbable optimism. This intense belief in their intellectual capacities turns decision-making into an art that is enjoyed for its own sake and can survive the rebuff of occasional failure.

Third, part of what allows a focus on decision-making rather than loss is the successful investors' capacity to remain slightly aloof from market fluctuations. They employ a particular kind of psychological distance or even denial when studying the media headlines, markets, and stock prices, enabling them to draw on a concurrent overriding belief in their ability to assess the intrinsic value of a company and the quality of its management. (They might say, for example, "So what if the market dropped three hundred points? My company is still worth what it was yesterday.") Their capacity for the right amount of denial is key. Too much denial prevents an accurate assessment of reality; too little leads to undue anxieties about loss.

Fourth, nearly all of the investors who have the capacity to decouple the idea of loss from risk seem to establish very strong bonds with kindred spirits while they are engaged in their creative investing. They have a safety net of human relationships in place to support their view of risk.

Finally, investors who decouple risk from loss appear to think of themselves as outsiders. They do not experience themselves as adapted for this world and have a history going back to childhood of remembering being different from the groups to which they belonged. These investors were not traditional loners; they had friends. But they experienced themselves as not quite fitting in. Thoreau's notion of walking to a different drummer is applicable here, but with a twist. These investors have come to terms with having taken the road less traveled so that remaining an outsider has become a prized part of their identity.

FOUR

In the Company of Strangers

Most investors seem to share an ingrained instinct to follow the crowd, presumably because by definition it represents strength in numbers. This may serve some ecological law of nature for overpopulated herds of lemmings. But financial markets aren't guided by the laws of nature, and human beings aren't lemmings. The laws of market supply and demand may reinforce investors' herd mentality in the short run, since strong buy-side pressure for a highly touted stock will tend to boost its trading price, at least temporarily. And the short-sellers clearly thrive on the converse to this market dynamic. But investment performance in the longer term is another story.

In the foreword to the 1980 edition of Charles MacKay's 1848 book *Extraordinary Popular Delusions and the Madness of Crowds*, Andrew Tobias quotes Bernard Baruch:

> Have you ever seen in some wood, on a sunny quiet day, a cloud of flying midges—thousands of them—hovering, apparently motionless in a sunbeam? . . . Yes? . . . Well, did you ever see the whole flight—each mite apparently preserving its distance from all others—suddenly move, say three feet, to one side or the other? Well, what made them do that? A breeze? I said a quiet day. But try to recall—did you ever see them move directly back again in the same unison? Well, what made them do that? Great human mass movements are slower of inception but much more effective.[1]

WHAT MAKES THEM DO THAT?

One of the most fascinating psychological features of markets is herd mentality. No other investment phenomenon is as well documented or familiar yet as pervasive or destructive. Surprisingly, though, our awareness of herding pitfalls seems to have scant power of persuasion against its continuing influence. Although we are familiar with boom and bust cycles, although we read and write about herd mentality continually, and although we "know" intellectually that acting contrary to groupthink could save us enormous monetary pain, the irrational allure of crowds seems to have a life of its own. Sound judgment and even healthy self-esteem do not prevent investors from walking blindly with the herd, they do not prevent the financial media from encouraging and participating in herd behavior, and they do not prevent companies from being swept along unproductively with the stampeding masses.

This chapter reviews some of the underlying dynamics of this "repetition compulsion" and attempts to explain why, even though we're intimately familiar with herd mentality, it continues to work its dark magic on us so consistently. What is it about our psyches that makes us so vulnerable to crowd behavior and so susceptible to its charms? Can we ever escape it? And should we even try?

Ever since Gustav Le Bon wrote his small volume *The Crowd*, investors have been aware that individuals who tend to act rationally and sensibly when alone will frequently relinquish any semblance of rationality and well-reasoned, albeit illusory, beliefs when under the influence of crowds.[2] The emotional contagion that characterizes group action came to be called herd mentality or crowd behavior. Perhaps symptomatic of its allure, even the terms *crowd behavior* and *herd mentality* have become facile rationalizations for speculative manias and daunting crashes within the investment community. Despite our familiarity with the phenomenon, the psychological dynamics underlying groupthink have never really been adequately explained. Perhaps this is because we tend to focus our research either on the aberrations of the individual investor or the vagaries of the market.

Writing about babies and parents, Donald Winnicott once said, "There is no such thing as a baby—meaning that if you set out to describe a baby, you will find you are describing a baby and someone.

A baby cannot exist alone, but is essentially part of a relationship."[3] What Winnicott meant was that the baby and the parent formed a contextual unit. The baby's psychic processes were inseparable from the parental functions, and you could not study one without understanding the other.

In the context of investing, I will risk an analogous remark: There is no such thing as an investor in a vacuum. If you try to describe an investor, you will ultimately confront the fact that there is a market. Just as a baby and a mother or father form an indivisible unit, so herd mentality is a property not of investors alone, but of the investor-market system. This "intersubjective" system[4] brings into sharp relief the fact that investors' inner experiences, the unconscious dynamics that organize and motivate behavior, are always embedded in the larger context of the market, creating a complex, mutually reciprocal influence. The resulting herd behavior exists continuously, while the classic market bubbles and panics are merely two extremes of herd mentality. In other words, investors deviate severely from their normal standard of valuation analysis only when there is an economic, social, or cultural situation that favors the emergence of specific emotional convictions. As Stolorow and Atwood argued, "The organization of experience can . . . be seen as codetermined both by preexisting principles (our organizing patterns) *and* by an ongoing context that favors one or another of them over others."[5]

THE INTERNET BUBBLE

By the late fall of 1998, a relatively new company called Amazon.com had become the darling of individual investors. If you had bought the stock at $9 per share (pre-split) in May 1997 and patiently watched the price move up to $600 toward early winter of 1999, and then had the good sense to sell your shares, you might well be headed toward retirement. Within eighteen months of its IPO, Amazon became the Internet's leading online shopping site, capturing the loyalty, hearts, minds, and pocketbooks of millions of book-lovers. Despite losing $0.53 per share on $357 million of revenue in 1998, the company boasted a market cap (number of shares times stock price) of $17.8 billion. With only 5 percent of the stock in their collective mitts, institutional investors were initially perplexed by the staggering rise. Market gurus who predicted Amazon's demise at several junctures during the stock's 6,000 percent appreciation were equally puzzled.

How could a company that was losing money eclipse in eighteen months the combined market cap of competitors like Barnes & Noble and Borders, who took decades to build their businesses? Some old-time investors argued that Amazon represented "a speculative bubble of manic proportions," a wild enthusiastic folly that would soon come tumbling down to humble those irresponsible New Age investors who didn't understand that what goes up unrealistically must eventually come crashing down. As one portfolio manager told *Investor's Business Daily*, the Internet reminded him of "the tulip bulb craze of the 1600s in Holland. . . . If you're buying stocks selling at sixty to hundred times sales, all you've really got is a lottery ticket. Maybe one or two of the companies will be winners. But they all can't win." And after all, once Amazon reached $600 per share (pre-split), it did retreat about 90 percent. In ordinary times, such warnings might have swayed many investors.

But these were not ordinary times, and to understand why investors were so captivated by Amazon and its cousins, we must understand the cultural factors that influenced their emotional convictions. Never in history had we discerned a confluence of so many synergistic factors: 1) an increasingly educated investor; 2) an economy sparked more by intangibles than products and fueled more by prospects than reality; 3) a huge population of baby-boomers who both needed and loved the stock market and who had turned investing into a cultural phenomenon tantamount to the Super Bowl or the Olympics; 4) enormous liquidity through the $11.4 trillion of inheritance that began flowing into baby-boomers' pockets; 5) the benefits of globalization encouraged by new communications technologies for transcending geographical boundaries by sending electronic signals across the planet in a fraction of a second; 6) the novelty and excitement of shopping in your bathrobe; and 7) the visible impact of technology on lifestyles that, for better or worse, were becoming increasingly wired.

Amazon was able to take advantage of these trends, capitalizing on the networked society by creating a global, educational, interactive community, providing high-quality customer services, and making it easy and enticing to buy online. At the same time, the company was a beneficiary of the incipient change in the valuation measures that were creeping into the new economy, measures that emphasized competitive advantage periods and market share over P/E multiples, earnings per share, and other fundamentals used by traditional investors. Amazon literally became one of the phenomena around which certain investors shared their vision of the future.

The individuals who shared Amazon's vision were able, however fleetingly, to take advantage of the shifting rules of the new economy. They had a feel for what elements worked in a networked society— information and knowledge, the value of community and connections, free services, open standards, and increasing opportunities. These savvy investors seemed prescient in their ability to reformulate an understanding of risk, respond counterintuitively to herd mentality, play the market-timing game, and develop new methods to value emerging technology companies. More important, they were also able to surmount the psychological hurdles inhibiting other investors from buying Amazon and her ilk at an early stage. The stunning success of the first-wave tech investors raised the possibility that, contrary to the warnings of old-time value investors, we were not in a speculative bubble; maybe, just maybe, the new wave said, we were entering a period where an entirely different psychology of investing would be required for success in the stock market.

A very experienced and successful broker friend put the issue succinctly when he complained, "You know, I haven't made my clients any money in two years while these Internet stocks have gone through the roof; I just don't understand the new psychology out there. I don't understand how to value or buy those kind of stocks, and I'm afraid to do it. Everything I was taught about investing seems to be changing." Indeed for a short time, market participants deviated from what was considered rational behavior and bought stocks that were trading at thousands of times above valuations dictated by once-sacrosanct fundamentals.

During the Internet bubble, this behavior was not limited to the average investor. Professional money mangers, venture capitalists, and analysts often encouraged their followers to bid up Internet stocks to levels that were ludicrous by any traditional standards. As David

Dreman suggested in a commentary on this bubble, "This demonstrates that analysts and money managers, despite their rigorous training in establishing reasonable valuation levels for stocks, can in exciting periods of technological or other scientific evolution, almost completely disregard time-tested standards of stock evaluation."[7] Dreman also pointed out how fundamental analysis was totally abandoned during the Internet bubble. From the time it started to burst in November 1999, the average price decline of the leading Internet stocks through mid-March 2001 was 66.44 percent.[8] Many of the wilder stocks declined 80 percent to 90 percent.[9]

AFTER THE BUBBLE BURSTS

Just as the herd's grandiosity knew no bounds at the top of the Internet bubble, its fear and pessimism promoted extraordinary despair following the crash. The Nasdaq tumbled from the 5,000 level all the way down to 1,100. Economists were telling us that the U.S. as well as the rest of the developed nations were facing a servere recession. In the first half of 2001, semiconductor sales dropped 75 percent. And while inventories declined, high-tech shipments plummeted three times faster. As a result, aging inventories that should have dwindled were actually increasing. Consumer spending was lackluster, and layoffs following the horrendous terrorist attack on September 11, 2001, were reaching seven figures. One of the few CEOs with a reputation for telling it like it is, Scott McNealy of Sun Microsystems, when asked if the economy was bottoming out, was quoted in First Union's June 8, 2001, weekly economic report as saying, "I see a bottom every time I change my one-year-old's diaper. That's the only sure bottom I know. Anyone who is trying to predict doesn't know."

Even the Fed, despite its traditional role as cheerleader for this economy, didn't seem very upbeat. Vice-Chairman Roger Ferguson was quoted in the press as saying, "I expect a period of some weakness. I haven't been specific about how long." Early announcements of higher-than-expected negative earnings for the second and third quarters of 2000 merely served to confirm McNealy's beliefs. By October 2001 the economic data confirmed just how miserable the economy remained. Nonfarm payrolls posted their largest decline in almost

twenty years, with pink slips eliminating 415,000 jobs. The unemployment rate rose 0.5 percentage points, the largest rise since winter
1986. The National Association of Purchasing Management new
orders survey posted one of the worst declines in its seventy-year history. As the economy unraveled, pessimism was rampant, reinforced
by the Damocles sword of imminent further terrorist attacks. As
investors obsessed over the economy and the demise of the fast buck,
only a handful of the pundits were reminding us that the economy and
the stock market do not have to be synchronized. Just as there were
obvious signs that the market was overvalued in March 2000, there
were significant indications that the market was becoming undervalued in September 2001.

Jonathan R. Laing wrote an article in the September 17, 2001, issue
of *Barron's*, in which he cited a Ned Davis research project that examined twenty-eight crises over the past sixty years. Davis had found a
similar response to each crisis. Immediately following these crises, the
market had traded down by 7.1 percent, then rallied from the end of
the reaction period, moving ahead by an average of 3.8 percent a
month later, 6.8 percent three months later, and 12.5 percent six
months later. A high reward-to-risk ratio occurred only when fear had
investors frozen in their tracks. Davis concluded that in the majority
of cases this pattern occurred when a major catastrophe forced us all
to focus excessively on the short term.

Psychologically most of the contrarian market indicators were
screamingly bullish in the fall of 2001. The psychological panic at that
time was palpable in contrarian market-timing charts like the equity
put-call ratio and the ARMS index, which purport to gauge the
amount of fear and panic in the market. Based on Davis's research,
once these indicators move beyond a certain level of fear, the chance of
another bull run is high. At the same time, the Smart Money index was
extraordinarily bullish. It compares what money managers (the "smart
money") are doing in the last hour of the day with what retail investors
(the "dumb money") are doing in the first thirty minutes of the day.
These money managers may have been talking pessimistically, but they
were certainly buying lots of equities for their managed accounts.

The most controversial market parameter at the time was valuation. There were many smart investors who believed that the market

had farther to fall and that stocks remained overvalued because both the trailing and forward P/E ratios on the S&P 500 remained high by historical standards. In fact, the S&P 500's trailing twelve-month earnings of $36.79 yielded a market multiple of 29.9. And the forward P/E on the S&P was 20.13. The long-term average is about 13. But since P/E ratios are not absolute numbers, you must compare these multiples with inflation rates and the yield on the ten-year treasury note. In both cases, I saw only positive comparisons.

At the same time, the yield on the ten-year note was 4.34 percent. Compared to the earnings yield on the S&P 500, we were in the enviable position of having more value in large-cap stocks than bonds. In addition nearly $1.8 trillion was languishing in money-market funds (shortly to reach $2.5 trillion). It was only a matter of time before this money would be shifted in the direction of stocks with good fundamentals. At that point, it should have been obvious to all that the market would eventually resume its bullish trend. In addition, the S&P 500, when compared with the ten-year treasury note, had dropped to 49 percent undervalued level, suggesting plenty of room for an upside advance.[10]

On the monetary front, the Fed continued to cooperate with investors, printing money at historically high rates in their panicky attempt to avoid a recession. Whenever the Fed floods the monetary system, the excess cash almost always flows into the stock market. The prospect of that inflow, combined with extremely low interest rates, the likelihood of continued interest rate cuts, a major tax cut, a deflationary environment, and a major stimulus package being pushed through Congress, should have brought confidence if not sheer joy to investors. After all it seemed obvious we were experiencing the most favorable monetary policy for stocks in decades.

So why was it so difficult for the average investor to pierce the veil of gloom to see one of the best long-term buying opportunities in a lifetime? Successful investing requires us to go beyond our usual, well-entrenched ways of seeing the world and to develop alternative lenses that can enlarge and enhance our perspective, even when "accepted wisdom" is constantly reinforced by the herd. There are times we must take off the myopic lenses prescribed by the crowd in bearish markets and look farther down the road. At those times the harder it is to expand our organizing lenses to see beyond a grim external reality, the more imperative it may be to do so.

If we had mastered that art at the beginning of the Internet boom, we would not have allowed the collapse of the Internet bubble to push us to the sidelines of the new economy and deny its existence, as so many investors were prone to do. The initial stage of the Internet Age took the form of an expansive playground. Within this playground entrepreneurs began using their newfound technological competencies in the service of what they imagined to be visionary truths of the future. Individual investors, especially baby-boomers who were in a phase of life that fostered the drive to create, whether it be children, products, or wealth, began to embrace this world of visionary truths as a belief system based on a factual reality. The interaction between the two groups tied them together in a community that was sharing one of the most phenomenal world transformations ever recorded. Not having the technological skills of their entrepreneurial counterparts, investors had their own object—money, which they could endow with symbolic meaning and use in the service of their own mental images of a visionary future within the investment community.

We only have to think of the mobile wireless boom as a classic example of this phenomenon. Bill Gates and Paul Allen envisioned a world of data flowing freely into your cell phones, laptops, and palm pilots without regard for sovereign boundaries, time zones, or location. These entrepreneurs invested in Metricom, a mobile wireless company, and brought a host of believing followers with them. Metricom ran all the way to $109.50 and then collapsed to $1.38. Were Gates and Allen wrong in their playful vision? I don't think so. Mobile wireless is going to be a huge industry, but when we kid ourselves into treating visions as present reality rather than future prospects, we get caught up in a world of illusion.

This illusionary landscape confounded analysts. They were caught in a no-man's-land between investment-banking firms, entrepreneurs, investors, and their fellow analysts. To anticipate the future, they must have the capacity for visionary make-believe, but to retain any legitimacy with the investment community, they must be rooted in reality. If they are to keep their jobs, they must bring in or support investment-banking deals. But to retain their bona fides within the analyst community, they must have similar opinions. Most important, if you manage a mutual fund and must beat a benchmark such as the S&P 500 to keep your job or earn a bonus, you must buy or sell what every other manager is buying or selling regardless of valuation parameters. Reality and make-believe sometimes come together, as when Paul Johnson made his career by going out on a limb and becoming the first analyst to recommend Cisco in 1990. More often, though, reality and make-believe don't come together.

Erikson wrote, "True make-believe may play with facts, but it cannot lie, while false reality may, up to a point, seem to mask facts, but it never tells the truth."[11] I once asked him how you tell the difference between true make-believe and false reality, to which he replied simply, "You can't until it's over." Too often what happens is that, somewhere on the playground, emotions become so intense that playfulness gets disrupted before the make-believe systems have a chance to demonstrate whether they are real or false. We go through what seems like an agonizingly long period before the playfulness returns to the market. In this period the analysts, entrepreneurs, and venture capitalists are all denigrated and dismissed with an "I told you so" attitude, and there is a distinct sense of superiority that emanates from those who had been wrong for the previous eight years but had suddenly found their shining moment in the sun. Stock prices plummet and everyone agrees that a return to traditional methods of valuation is in order. What everyone forgets is that in the present we don't know whether the drop in stock prices is true make-believe or false reality. If you take a five-to-ten-year outlook, I'm betting on the latter.

What is important to remember about the Internet bubble may not be what the herd tells you—that tech stocks became overvalued and eventually came to an unfortunate and panicky end. This is common knowledge and is more of a personal psychological issue for investors to deal with, especially by asking why you were carried along with the herd in the Metricoms of the world when you knew everything was overvalued. What is equally important to understand as the herd plunges deeper into pessimism is the positive aspects of the Internet bubble. Unlike analogous bubbles (such as the Dutch Tulip bulbs), the Internet bubble was not fictitious. Underlying the stock run up, there was a technological revolution. It was fueled by a human competence and innovation that will reverberate though the century and, in my view, will become its lasting heritage despite the collapse of many individual companies. Here are some of the reasons for my optimism:

- It fostered an entrepreneurial spirit and creative imagination that will spur further innovations for the foreseeable future.
- It renewed a communal spirit among segments of society that had been splintered and mired in a kind of social anomie.
- It broke down barriers to global communication and cooperation at new levels and proportions.
- It changed the world of genetics and medicine forever.
- It introduced an element of playfulness into the investing communities, allowing both entrepreneurs and investors to dare to dream big.
- It changed the hierarchy between corporations and their customers.
- It brought a generation of new investors into the market for the long term.
- It created a networked society that not only fosters community, but also the open development of new systems and processes that will define the shape of our economy going forward.
- It created new employment opportunities and spawned a generation of knowledge workers.
- It made more learning tools available to more people around the planet than was even imaginable before.

I don't want to trivialize the estimated $7 trillion lost in the collapse of Internet and related tech stocks. Many of these companies and their stocks will never bounce back. But we must, if we are to avoid groupthink, distinguish between the benefits stimulated by the Internet bubble and the failure of individual companies within that bubble. Putting aside those analysts who were solely promoting their own firms' investment-banking business, analysts confused the benefits of the Internet bubble with the viability of the companies supporting or exploiting it. In the long run they will be proven to have been generally right, while being all-too-often specifically wrong. When you hear and read about the folly of the Internet bubble and its leaders, remember that it could not contribute to such progress if it were not grounded in a playful creativity that will continue to fuel technology's role in transforming our society. Only with a deeper understanding of that creativity will investors free themselves from the herd mentality to take advantage of the next wave of technological innovation.

But let's turn now from the external context to the internal emotional convictions that contribute to herd mentality. Scott Nearing was not an investor, but he was perhaps one of the most contrarian thinkers of the twentieth century. Independent, indomitable, and opinionated, Scott and his wife, Helen, decided it was better to be poor but fulfilled in the country than poor and confined in the city. They moved to Vermont, and then to Maine, and inspired a back-to-the-land movement, which captured the imagination of an entire generation. Scott died just after his hundredth birthday. Among his papers was the following note:

> The majority will always be for caution, hesitation, and the status quo—always against creation and innovation. The innovator—he who leaves the beaten track—must therefore always be a minoritarian—always be an object of opposition, scorn, hatred. It is part of the price he must pay for ecstasy that accompanies creative thinking and acting.[12]

Scott would have been a good investor, especially at turning points in the market, when all the headlines pull the herd in the wrong direction, when the market has ways of fooling most of the people most of the time, and when creative thinking requires standing alone. But there are numerous psychological factors that prevent us from taking Scott's counterintuitive stance. Let's take a look at some of the social and psychological factors that ensure the herd mentality's permanence in the investment landscape.

EVOLUTIONARY BIOLOGY

My colleagues Mal Slavin and Dan Kriegman, in an intriguing series of papers, point out that not only has evolution fostered the adaptation of our physical bodies to our environment via natural selection, but, equally important, it has shaped our psychological adaptation to our surroundings. For example, we seem to have built into our psyche a predisposition to care for our young—a tendency that can be securely elicited by a baby at birth. According to Slavin and Kriegman, "important universal psychological features that currently exist were favored by natural selection because they represented functional designs that in evolutionary times were advantageous; that is, they increased the inclusive fitness of individuals who possessed such psychological organization. . . . Inclusive fitness refers not only to the individual's capacity to survive, but to the survival and success of one's offspring and relatives."[13]

From an evolutionary standpoint, we come from a time when living and functioning in herds was in the best interest of survival—not only for the individual, but also for the group, often composed of relatives and offspring. Given this developmental history, I believe that the deeply ingrained psychological tendency to function in herds, especially under conditions of risk, was in evolutionary time an adaptive, protective mechanism that has remained a built-in part of our psyche. Not only is this tendency elicited when we face perceived threats, it also is readily evoked when we perceive large groups forming around us. Rekindled evolutionary propensities toward herd behavior are not based only on self-destructive motivations or guilt-induced, self-defeating behaviors, as so many mental-health practitioners would like us to believe. Rather they are inherently adaptive. Keeping this in mind is particularly useful because it helps us understand why investing does not come naturally to so many people. Successful investing requires us to go against a long and powerful evolutionary history of psychological adaptation that has not "selected" us for the rigors of the investment task. In Darwinian terms, investing is an unnatural act.[14]

IMPACT OF THE NETWORKED SOCIETY

The networked society complicates the issue of herd mentality since it encourages electronically created and connected environments. These new communication processes are restructuring how we do business, how we form social organizations, how we relate to one another, how we understand ourselves, and how we invest. As Kevin Kelley suggested,

> Communication is so close to culture and society itself that the effects of technologizing it are beyond the scale of a mere industrial sector cycle. Communication, and its ally computers, is a special case in economic history. Not because it happens to be the fashionable leading business sector of our day, but because its cultural, technological, and conceptual impacts reverberate at the root of our lives.[15]

Psychologically, communication networks imply the random, inexorable intertwining of many people, machines, and organizations. The technologizing of communications exacerbates the reciprocal influence of both the individual's way of organizing his world and the mercurial, frequently unpredictable structures of the market and the economy. In new-era jargon, we now communicate in cyberspace, or "spaces instead of places."[16] Cyberspace allows information to be communicated among millions of people at once on a single website. Instead of having a one-on-one conversation with a broker or financial adviser, or watching an interactive television show such as CNBC's *Buy, Sell, or Hold*, we have multiple conversations simultaneously with a selected group of investors, all interested (for better or for worse) in a particular company or mutual fund. This has three important implications.

First, in the new economic era we will continuously perceive large groups forming around us, thus exacerbating the pull toward crowd behavior. Whenever investors feel uncertain, they turn to the Internet, an electronic space that provides information (erroneous or not) to support any view they want confirmed. As reliance on this new aid to decision-making increases, crowd behavior is exacerbated.

Second, the pressures of the herd increase geometrically when there is a live community voting for decisions in real time. As a result, investors will have an increasingly difficult time resisting the influence of the herd at major turning points in the market. If you turn to a stock message board just before making a trade—even when you've done intensive research—it can be extremely difficult to resist the impact of the most recent ten messages discouraging you from buying your stock.

Third, in between turning points, when in the past the herd has often been correct, major whipsawing of small investors can be expected. Internet message boards are full of innuendo, hype, puff, and paranoia, to say nothing of intentional misinformation. This means that investors will be easily influenced to act contrary to the herd at times when they are safer remaining a part of the group, and they will be pushed to remain part of the group when they should assume a contrarian stance. They will be influenced in and out of positions with a kind of volatility not seen before on such a mass scale.

Another way of thinking about the effects of cyberspace on investing is to consider psychology's three traditional areas of experience: the external world, our inner world, and the boundary that separates them. The external world refers to our perception of our surrounding environment; our inner world refers to our fantasies, daydreams, and emotional reactions; and the boundary that separates inner from outer is our skin.[17] Individuals become disoriented and upset when the skin fails to maintain the boundary between inner and outer. For example, when I provided consulting to an orthopedic surgical service, we saw several bungled cases of compound fractures, where the bone breaks through the skin. They had been mishandled by well-trained doctors who were so unnerved by bone breaking through its boundary that they pushed the bone back into its proper place too quickly and without regard for proper procedures. The Internet, because of its borderless state and its anonymity, breaks down traditional boundaries so completely that investors can hardly differentiate sometimes between fantasy and reality.

When my friend Jane called me after I suggested she buy SureBeam at $1.60 per share, she told me she had checked out the message board and found postings that were critical of the company. She had also found some unfavorable media coverage of SureBeam: "I wouldn't want to buy a stock that so many people think is a poor choice. I don't understand how you could have recommended it." Upon questioning, I found that Jane had done no research herself, nor had she contacted the company. Jane never bought the stock. Within three weeks, it appreciated 100 percent. But in cyberspace—which is mostly a creation of our mind—there is no "skin" to separate our fantasies from our realities. Whenever such a dearth of boundaries exists, investor decision-making becomes vulnerable to crowd behavior—to being influenced by the latest rumors and misinformation, or facts and accurate information, touted instantaneously by the least qualified people with the most public platforms for delivering their spin.

THE IMPACT OF INDIVIDUAL PSYCHOLOGY

In addition to the impact of social change on herd mentality, our psyche plays a large role in consistently reinforcing herding behavior. As humans, we are hard wired to seek connections to others. But there is an inherent conflict, and a need for balance, between our individual motivations and those of the group. At times the needs of the group are in the foreground; at other times our individual needs take precedence. When investing under conditions of risk, we experience enormous pressures that silently challenge or stress our sense of self. When our sense of self feels temporarily strained, a harmonious and adaptive balance between herd mentality and individual expression becomes weighted in the direction of the herd in what too often is bound to be an abortive attempt to meet the needs of the self.

For example, when unable to mobilize ways for modulating tension states and self-soothing (in other words, to calm down), an individual investor is much more likely, in the face of a volatile market, to seek guidance and direction from people he looks up to. Ordinarily the capacity to reach out to admired authorities is a healthy response. That's what makes teaching and learning possible. It's also what sells newspapers and makes certain politicians or cultural figures popular. But when our sense of self is sufficiently strained, the connection with others can be more akin to relationships of political or rock-star groupies following cult leaders blindly into oblivion. In high-stress environments, our need to be connected to heroes can be counterproductive and even dangerous. It becomes a weakness that politicians or stock commentators can exploit through TV or the Internet to move public opinion or markets at least temporarily with a few superficial sound bites.

While it is common investment lore that our sense of self is truly stressed only in down markets, my experience suggests that strong bull markets also place significant strains on investors. When the market is going up, individual investors are afraid of missing the boat or, more honestly, of not doing as well as the Joneses. In fact there is often as much self-criticism for failing to beat the indexes or a neighbor's boasted stock gains in a bull market as self-abuse for failure to outmaneuver a bear market. So, turning to authority figures, especially well-known analysts and TV or radio personalities, also relieves the strain on our sense of self when stocks are going up.

In the context of a strained sense of self, normal market anxiety predisposes investors toward herd mentality. As I pointed out in chapter two, one of the characteristic side effects of anxiety is jigsaw-puzzle thinking. Under the pressures of anxiety, our capacity for abstract thinking with the big picture in mind tends to break down into concrete thinking, and we can perceive only the individual parts of a whole picture. We then tend to make decisions based on one or two components of a whole picture. This is all the more likely when there's a glut of complex and often-contradictory information at hand. Under these circumstances, the most recent and vociferously presented information—typically isolated facts thrown at us by the herd—assumes undue importance in our investment decisions.

For example, Louis, an investor who was following Cytyc Corporation, a company with a new pap smear test that was becoming widely used, heard from a broker friend that another company, Tripath Imaging, had developed a similar test and that Tripath's test had been well received by the medical community. He called, anxiously wanting to know what I thought of the company. Although I had never heard of it, a quick glance at their filings and press releases revealed no information that was useful in comparing their product to Cytyc's.

In his anxiety to find out information that would confirm his hunch, Louis focused on the difference between Cytyc's $2.8 billion market cap and Tripath's relatively paltry $270 million market cap. "One has room to grow, and the other doesn't," he concluded. "I know I'm on to something here! I think I should buy it in the morning." What went unnoticed in Louis's anxious enthusiasm for his new idea, based on market cap comparison, was the fact that Cytyc was trading at 10 times revenue, and Tripath was trading at 240 times revenue. Also unnoticed was the fact that we literally had no information about Tripath on which to base any rational decision. But because the herd (the brokerage firm pushing the stock) was telling Louis that this stock could be a big winner, his enthusiasm caused him to ignore the whole picture and trust the brokerage recommendation, without regard to its underlying motivation.

Under conditions of risk, when our sense of self is under pressure, the strain assaults our confidence and forces us to question our judgment. We have a tendency to tune into and fit into the opinions and beliefs of others. Within this collusive bond, we tend to subordinate our own judgments and convictions to the accepted wisdom of the herd. From an evolutionary perspective, this emphasis on respecting authority over our own researched content and belief had adaptive value for the survival of the group. In fact within the investment community there are often high rewards for actions based on imitation rather than independent thinking. But for individual investors, this kind of compliance generally leads to conformity and average performance, if not underperformance. To understand how compliance can foster a blind and self-destructive faith in others' opinions, we need only recall the number of investors who blindly followed leading Internet analysts to buy their recommendations at the height of the Internet bubble, only to watch their stocks fall 80 percent to 90 percent.

A stressed sense of self is usually accompanied by a lack of assertiveness. We feel inhibited and constricted because we fear a true exhibition of "I am!" will bring a negative reaction from the surrounding community. This lack of assertiveness generally leaves investors looking to *react* to their surrounding environment rather than to take advantage of it. Within the investment community, those who lack the capacity for self-organization and self-direction find themselves continually on the defensive, reacting to market events rather than anticipating and forecasting them. Once again, given the dearth of worldly information available in evolutionary time, the capacity of herds to react successfully to sudden events was more important than anticipation and planning. But in the modern investment arena, reactivity to a deluge of information fosters an aura of constant danger. We sit in front of the computer waiting for any negative news requiring a reaction. And instead of anticipating trends we should be able to discern from all the available information, we turn to the herd for reactive guidance.

The pressures that weaken our sense of self foster a strong identification with the herd. Perhaps because we perceive herd mentality as an evolutionary necessity, we tend to experience our reactions to pressure in our investment activities not as troublesome but as adaptive and natural. The paradoxical fact is that successful investing requires us to stand firm against the herd despite the weight of evolutionary drives. Although bucking the evolutionary tide is still maladaptive in most ordinary circumstances, it can be a road to success in today's market.

WHY HERD MENTALITY
CONTINUES TO PREVAIL

Although it is understandable that investors who experience a shaky sense of self when playing in the market will be more inclined toward herd mentality, there are many investors who experience themselves as strongly independent when making investment decisions. While I was at CNN to tape a segment on the psychology of investing, one of the network correspondents asked me a thought-provoking question that addressed this issue: "We know all about herd mentality, and you give a lot of reasons for its existence, but why does it continue to work, and how does it work so consistently when we are all aware of it?" What indeed is it about our psyches that prevents us from changing?

SELF-SUSTAINING EXPERIENCES

There is a concept in psychology that helps us to answer the CNN correspondent's query. Just as we need oxygen to ensure physical survival, we also need to feel surrounded by empathic emotional responsiveness to ensure psychological survival.[18] Contrary to the prevailing assumption that independence is the end point of human maturation, several decades of research have suggested the need to be surrounded by this perceived emotional responsiveness from birth to death.

The mode of this responsiveness varies and changes with the individual's development. At first a child needs the physical responsiveness and holding of others. Later, while the need for self-sustaining experiences has not diminished, a wide variety of other experiences can partially substitute for the concrete presence of loved ones. In other words, in adulthood our needs can sometimes be met in a more abstract way by a connection with symbolic cultural representations such as art, music, literature, and nature, as well as social roles such as going to work and caring for families, enjoying hobbies, or investing.

Thus the adult may at times not need the intensity of the physical connections required by a child but may secure self-sustaining experiences by listening to a favorite composition, riding a horse, or walking in the woods, or through group, religious, familial, occupational, recreational, or intellectual experiences. The experiences evoked by the relationship with either people or their symbolic cultural representatives help us to feel good about ourselves and maintain a sense of well-being.

If human development always requires embeddedness in a sea of self-sustaining experiences to maintain a sense of well-being and self-esteem, it follows that one important attribute of our psyche is the capacity to organize our experiences to create a self-sustaining tapestry of experiences. It is the ongoing and normal process of creating this very tapestry that biases human beings toward herd mentality. Within the investing world, we create this tapestry in several ways.

THE SOCIAL ROLE OF INVESTING

Active investors in individual stocks or mutual funds often identify themselves as "investors." This is a social role that in the new economic era performs a self-sustaining function. It often affords these investors a mirroring validation for their success in the market. They pursue the advice of purported authorities in the field, either directly or indirectly through books, seminars, and meetings. They may join an organization such as the American Association of Individual Investors (AAII), which evokes a sense of pride in belongingness. These and many other ways of creating a social identity of ourselves as investors act as a self-sustaining experience that unconsciously supports our well-being without regard to success or failure in the market. As one investor, Henry, said to me, "You know, sometimes I think it doesn't matter if I succeed or fail in the market; being an investor lets me into a world of other people that I enjoy, and I can turn to them when I need advice."

At the same time, however, the belongingness inherent in the social identity of "investor" biases even the most psychologically healthy investors toward herd mentality. Remaining part of the larger group assumes a greater importance than successful investing. Even within the professional community, we see analysts who refuse to "go it alone," hesitating to recommend stocks that fellow analysts refuse to follow.[19]

REMINISCENCE

Reminiscing is another way to create a tapestry of self-sustaining experiences. Investors in particular love to reminisce. Adventures, colorful personalities, battles with the shorts or longs, Mergers & Acquisitions adventures, major losses or wins, and the reification of statistics all play an important part in the narratives told in investing circles. In fact I've never met an investor who didn't have an interesting story to tell about personal experiences in the stock market. After a point these stories become as irritating as the elderly individual who continually unearths images and recollections of the past in front of a younger generation trying to live in the present or prepare for the future. This parenthetically is also why some older folks who appear to be isolated rely on an active capacity for vivid recall to feel much less lonely than their offspring believe. For investors these reminiscences weave a net of self-sustaining experiences that enhance their psychological well-being.

Before the 2000 bear market, many older investors argued that the new breed of portfolio managers who had never lived through a prolonged bear market were ignoring the past at their own peril. Some cited their experiences in 1973, evoking memories to organize and invigorate their present state and enhance their self-esteem. While self-sustaining experiences that support our well-being often emanate from reminiscing, they can also lend false confidence to the recollector's future predictions. The very memories that are essential to maintain self-esteem encourage in oneself and others an absolute reliance on history to predict the future. As Barbara Tuchman once commented, "History has a way of escaping attempts to imprison it in patterns . . . [because] . . . data which are shut up in prearranged boxes are helpless. Their nuances have no voice."[20]

Such temporal organization of experience is often incorrect, as we witnessed with those who relied on traditional valuation measures to forecast the market during the emergence of the Internet phenomenon. Reminiscence makes it harder to believe that conflicting views of the world can be valid. In this sense it can have a tendency to pull many investors into a herd-mentality mode while also helping them feel better about themselves.

IDEALIZATIONS

Idealized figures play an important role in the self-sustaining experiences of every individual, and they play a particularly active role in the dynamics of the investment community. Much of the investment business is learned by apprenticeship. Self-appointed investment gurus are continually prognosticating on television, the Internet, and in the print media. Investors often feel better if they experience themselves as connected to a charismatic authority. Indulging in a little name dropping like "I had a chance to talk with Peter Lynch yesterday after his speech" does wonders for some folks' self-esteem.

When I first appeared on CNBC's then-popular program *Buy, Sell, or Hold*, a call-in show in which investors ask the guest expert his opinion of a specific stock, I was clearly nervous. My publicist had arranged the appearance, and I had no idea how the process worked until being ushered into a studio room fifteen minutes before we went live. The producer explained that she would begin taking calls and then ask me if I was familiar with the caller's stock. If I said yes, she would place the caller on hold until the show began, then the caller would pose his or her question live and I would respond on camera. If I said no, she would quickly move on to the next call. The first ten queries involved stocks I was not familiar with, and the producer's worried expression only heightened my anxiety. Finally a caller asked about a small company I had just finished researching. The enormous relief was palpable, and my producer even smiled for the first time. Fortunately we came up with the requisite five or six companies just before airtime. In response to the live question about the small company that had done so much to relieve my anxiety, I smiled and enthusiastically gave an explanation for a buy recommendation. The following day the stock climbed nearly 50 percent on three times its normal volume. To my utter surprise, I received numerous phone calls during the week from people saying they could tell from my "enthusiastic smile" that TGI Widget Company was my favorite, so they bought the stock. They were totally unaware that my "enthusiasm" was no greater for TGI Widget than for the other companies I recommended on that first appearance. What they perceived as my enthusiasm was actually my relief at finally getting a question on a company I knew well.

This human tendency to use a connection with admired others to sustain our own well-being promotes herd mentality in three ways. First, it exerts pressure to conform. To remain connected to the admired other, investors feel a pull to agree with the "expert's" views and resist the implementation of their own ideas.

Second, the more intense an investor's commitment to the ideals and beliefs of people they look up to, the less creative he will be in formalizing his own investment style and ideas. The best investors tend to have original thoughts that transcend prevailing theories and philosophies. But even the best investors, when committed to admired others, tend to produce or adopt more tradition-bound thinking.

Warren Buffett idealized Ben Graham, but only to a point. Because his idealization was limited, Buffett was able to go beyond his mentor and develop his own investing theories and style.

Third, for many investors, new ideas are threatening to their status quo mentality. Unfortunately, because they tend to experience themselves as connected to an idealized other who supports their belief system, new ideas can be dismissed with the thought that everything important is already known by the idealized other to whom they are connected. Perhaps Alan Greenspan provides a good example with his comments on the stock market. The Dow tends to plunge or rise several hundred points following his remarks. While the Fed's actions clearly influence market trends, offhand positive or negative remarks by the Fed chief can create this level of market volatility only if investors' admiration for Greenspan (or his power) traps them in their compliant connection to a perceived omnipotent figure. The protection of our self-esteem through such a strong fantasized bond is a major contributor to herd mentality.

VALIDATION AND AFFIRMATION

Another important platform for securing psychological security is the sense of having our exhibited or expressed self validated and admired by others. Most individuals seek out affirmation of their beliefs and actions. One way to achieve this "mirroring" is to tune in to or fit in with others' theories and opinions in return for their validation of our intelligence, sensitivity, and judgment. For example, a broker calls a client and suggests that he sell his shares of XYZ because they have appreciated 100 percent: "Our analysts believe the stock is overvalued and you've made a good profit." To experience the affirmation of the broker and his firm, the client sells without regard for the fundamentals of XYZ or the reasons he bought the stock in the first place. Subordinating our sense of self to another's mirroring responses, while making us feel good, is also a common contributor to crowd behavior.

HERD MENTALITY:
A PSYCHOLOGICAL SYMPTOM

Perhaps the most important psychological element underlying herd mentality that has emerged from my conversations with investors involves a breakdown in our sense of "self-agency."[21] This is a term coined by Dorothy Levinson and George Atwood to mean feeling like the authentic author of our actions. Daniel Stern, the well-known researcher on infant development, addressed the same phenomenon when he said, "The sense of volition (or agency) makes our actions seem to belong to us and to be self acts. Without it (we) would feel what a puppet would feel like, as the non author of its immediate behavior."[22]

Most of the time we feel as though we are "independent centers of initiative,"[23] capable of formulating our own thoughts, opinions, and beliefs, and making our own decisions regardless of what we read in the newspaper, view on television, or see on our computer screens. Under conditions of risk, however, this feeling of authentic action rooted in our own beliefs and judgments can break down and become an unauthentic accommodation to ostensibly knowledgeable others.

As an example, let's say that one of your favorite stocks climbs by 50 percent from $20 to $30. But then the unexpected happens. Seemingly out of the blue, a government regulatory agency files a complaint alleging that one of the company's recently acquired major divisions violated the law. The company is surprised by the action. Trading in the stock halts while the CEO holds a conference call to discuss the event and management's response. Despite reassurances, the stock suddenly plummets five points after the call, opening at $25. The concerns raised by investors are all similar. The company has broken through its technical resistance level and therefore will plunge further in a matter of days. Rumors were rampant that the commission of the agency was shutting down the company's operations, that management was dishonest, that customers would abandon the company. The feeling "sell first and ask questions later" pushes the stock down another 20 percent and preempts more rational thinking and investigation. When clearer heads prevail, however, buyers of the stock in the $20 range see their shares appreciate quickly back to $25 per share in a matter of a week. Exploration after the fact indicates that the government's action was based on a miniscule number of complaints made over a period of several years before the acquisition of the offending division. Since acquiring the division, the parent company had instituted policies to ensure compliance with all government regulations.

When investors look further into the situation, what they find is no immediate evidence of anything fundamentally askew with the company, its current operations, or prospects for executing its business plan. Management confirms that there are no changes in the publicly announced fiscal revenue projections or projected earnings per share and they publicly reassure investors that the management team is comfortable with its business practices. So what is it that causes us to compromise our sense of agency and volition at these times in accommodation to the herd or, in Stern's metaphor, to become puppets whose strings are being pulled by some invisible controllers of rumor?

Understanding the reasons for our inability to exert our initiative in the face of pressure from the herd requires that we understand the double-edged nature of any symptom. To begin with the simplest analogy, think about physical symptoms. If you have cardiac problems and are jogging three miles, you may feel pain in your chest. This pain is a symptom of some underlying disease process. But equally important, it represents a warning not to run the next three miles. In other words, the pain represents both the expression of disease and the tendency toward health. Or take another example. You have a minor skin infection. A wall of white blood cells forms around the infection, causing symptoms of pain and swelling. On the one hand, while these symptoms represent the disease process, an infection, the wall of white blood cells represents the body's healthy defensive response for preventing the infection from spreading. Once again we can easily understand how the symptom represents both pathology and the mechanism for dealing with it to sustain our health.

If we view herd mentality as a symptom, we can understand more readily why, despite our awareness and insight into crowd behavior, it's so difficult for investors to maintain their independent thinking. When we are making decisions under conditions of risk and uncertainty, there is always a compromise to our sense of agency. The more we have at risk, the more frightened we are of the consequences of loss and the higher our anxiety level. As anxiety increases, we slowly lose the capacity for independent judgment and self-reflective awareness. The inability to be self-aware makes it impossible to carry out the usual dialogue with the market. In other words, as I suggested in chapter one, we all have predetermined conceptions or emotional convictions that interact with market data when we make buy–sell decisions. For example, if I am a large shareholder of ABC Company and see the stock plummeting, the organizing lenses that determine how I see the world will interact with the data I'm observing on my computer screen. If one of my unconscious emotional convictions is "I'm an unlucky person, since every time I buy a stock it goes down," then the stress I feel when I see ABC's stock plummet will likely confirm my emotional conviction and cause me to sell with the herd. The only way to counter this tendency and its pitfalls is to step back and use self-reflective awareness: "Oh, yes, this is one of those times I can't let my paranoia of being unlucky undermine my positive assessment of the company." Unfortunately since self-reflective awareness is all but impossible when I become anxious, I'm much more likely to sell prematurely. Like any symptom, however, the selling represents not just my disturbed equilibrium (my anxiety), but also my attempt to overcome my anxiety by extricating myself from the situation in hopes of regaining my normal balance (independent thinking). Thus there are both healthy and unhealthy psychological motivations for selling the stock.

Second, when we are involved in investment decision-making under conditions of risk, we are confronted with a host of opinions about our stocks. These opinions, often expressed vociferously, and the events on which they are based remain outside our control and volition. Under these conditions, our sense of agency is typically threatened. We experience agonizing doubt whether our beliefs and judgments are sound: "Am I sure I'm right about this stock? What am I missing in this picture? Maybe my judgment is wrong about management, or maybe the guy who told me to buy this stock has bad judgment or some unknown agenda. Whose perspective is the clearest?"

This sort of paralyzing doubt leads to heightened obsessing about the buy–sell decision: "If I buy more as the stock is tanking, I'll look like a hero when it recovers. But what if it goes lower and I lose even more?" These are the ceaseless dilemmas that can lead to unrelenting worry and depression. In the absence of clear information on which to base a balanced decision, there is a natural human tendency to express what's left of our receding sense of agency in self-defeating ways. For investors, this usually takes the form of high-risk trading. It might include buying too much of a tumbling stock on the way down or selling all of your position prematurely and immediately buying another high-risk investment without doing careful research in the belief that you will have control over this new investment. This behavior again reflects both sides of the coin—a destructive action resulting from loss of a sense of agency, coupled with a healthy action aimed at restoring that sense of agency, although both lead to hasty decisions.

Third, because investing is a lonely endeavor, with each of us solely responsible for our gains and losses at the end of the day, all investors tend to experience a feeling of being alone in a crowd. This nullifies our sense of personal agency and leads to experiences of estrangement and discomfort even in familiar surroundings. These experiences are concretized in the form of symbols representing disaster—fantasies of a bear market, the loss of all assets, another 1929 crash. In other words, when familiar orientations are lost, the resulting threat to our sense of self is expressed in our imagery as concrete disasters. This is particularly common when a company we believe we know well announces a negative surprise or when a market that has been predictable suddenly becomes volatile.

For example, in September 2001, following the World Trade Center disaster, all of my indicators turned very bullish, and, while nervous, I felt some confidence that the market had suffered through its correction and was ready to turn around. The next two weeks were miserable, suggesting that my models must be totally wrong. I felt lost in a sea of surrounding familiarity. Indicators I'd relied on for years seemed suddenly inaccurate. Have they lost their predictive power? Are they no longer relevant in this economic environment? Am I reading them incorrectly? The answer was probably no; sometimes the general direction of a plane is correct despite unexpected crosswinds requiring a compensatory but temporary heading adjustment. As our control, volition, and sense of agency become threatened, however, we are more likely to deny that we are wrong. We cut ourselves off from the information that would not only confirm the soundness of our overall model, but also guide us in making the necessary adjustments. We treat the crosswinds as the major reality and lose sight of the correct course. This restores our sense of agency. We now feel competent in handling the crosswinds, but we undermine ourselves by treating them as the primary reality.

These examples clarify that our difficulty in resisting herd mentality stems from its daunting mix of both destructive and constructive forces. While siding with the herd often represents a relinquishment of volition, it also tends to enhance our self-esteem and build connections with others. Like combating an infection with an antibiotic that gets the job done despite some temporary stomach upset, resisting the siren song of herd mentality demands independent initiative that may initially leave us feeling alone and adrift. The good news is that our awareness of this herd behavioral paradox should help us navigate around the crowd. When confronting the pressures of the crowd, keep these guidelines in mind:

• Recognize the paradox that, as a result of the Internet, herd influence will become more intense while becoming less important to your investing behavior.

• Replace traditional contrarian thinking with "price-conscious" and "personal niche market" thinking. In the new economy, what the herd is doing will matter less than finding a market niche that fits your personality. The closer your holdings match your personality, the easier it will be to resist joining the herd.

• Because electronic communication creates more volatility in the market and speeds up the frequency of corrections while shortening their time-spans, you will need to focus more on entry points for your stocks than the usual buy and hold strategists recommend. You must have the psychological patience to wait for prices to come to you rather than buying when the momentum investors are driving the herd.

• The most important consequence of the market's heightened volatility is the need to keep a much higher level of available cash to take advantage of the more frequent buying opportunities that intensified herd behavior will create. As radical as it may seem, a 20 percent cash level will in the long run enable you to achieve higher returns than being fully invested.

• Heightened herd behavior means that fundamental research has been replaced by momentum- and trading-based behavior. The investor who learns to do solid fundamental research will in the long run outperform peers without having to pay much attention to the herd.

FIVE

On Not Being Able to Wait

In *Othello*, Shakespeare's character Iago makes an eloquent observation about one of the key ingredients of successful investing:

> *How poor are they that have not patience!*
> *What wound did ever heal but by degrees?*
> *Thou know'st we work by wit, and not by witchcraft;*
> *And wit depends on dilatory time.*

Although Shakespeare was probably not an investor, he understood the importance of using our intellectual and perceptive powers ("wit") to patiently gather and interpret relevant data before making decisions. He also understood the importance of developing the patience to know when to act and when to wait.

Few would disagree that patience is an essential element of investing, but no one has really defined what it means to be a patient investor, or clarified how we should use patience to our benefit in the market, or prescribed an antidote for impatience. We know that patience has its roots in our subjective experience of time and our ability or inability to wait. We also know that we can shoot ourselves in the foot (or worse) by waiting too long to buy, not waiting long enough to buy, waiting too long to sell, or not waiting long enough to sell. All investors must learn to deal with the many variations of waiting, but for most of us the topic evokes a latent animosity. We tolerate the role of waiting in the investing process (and in life) but rarely seek to profit from understanding its dynamics. If we could gain that understanding, we could have a competitive edge because our capacity to take an initial position in an investment, to tolerate volatility, and to decide when to accumulate and when to sell stock is all affected by this delicate skill.

WAITING (AND NOT WAITING) TO TAKE AN INITIAL POSITION

Consider a few examples that illustrate possible consequences of too much or too little patience. I once suggested to an investor, Ginny, that she buy Aura Systems when it was at $0.37. The stock more than doubled before falling back to its original recommendation price (and subsequently crashing) on concerns that the company would not meet its revenue projections. After the stock retreated, Ginny called to tell me that she had not bought AURA when it was at $0.37 the first time: "I thought if I waited a few days the price might come down. But it just went up. I thought it might pull back again if I waited, but no such luck. Next thing I knew, it was $0.70. So I took the plunge. As soon as I bought it, of course, it fell back to $0.37. Do you think I should double up?"

Like so many of us, this investor had trouble deciding when to take an initial position. She explained that investing at $0.37 seemed like going to a doctor's appointment early. She felt out of control when the doctor kept her waiting. If she arrived late and kept him waiting, she felt much more in control. It was the same with stocks: "If I buy a stock and it does nothing for months, I can't tolerate it. I'd rather buy it on the way up when I know it's moving." It appeared that her need for having a sense of control over her stocks, even though it was admittedly a need that she knew was impossible to fulfill, caused her to continually postpone her actions and wait for time to come to her rescue. It reminded me of Sleeping Beauty waiting for Prince Charming to awaken her.

I know another investor who is a study in contrast to Sleeping Beauty. Sam typically buys stocks as soon as he reads a recommendation he likes. He bought American Healthways at $36 after seeing a positive write-up on the company. He did no research, nor did he watch the stock to see how it traded. Within a week the stock retreated to $24. As Sam explained, "I was afraid if I didn't buy it as soon as I saw the recommendation, everyone else would, and the price would run away from me. I can't stand watching a stock move up when I know I should have bought it at a lower price." He then compounded his error by selling at $25 because "I couldn't stand seeing the stock crash, and I knew everyone else would be getting out." Shortly thereafter the stock moved up to $43. His inability to wait had its roots in his fear that waiting will lead to loss, his concern in this case that the stock price would run away from him. Sam had suffered several emotional losses and was always on guard and hypervigilant, afraid that if he ever let down his guard, he would suffer another loss.

IMPATIENCE: WHEN THE STOCK DOESN'T MOVE

Another investor I know, Todd, bought Facelifters (FACE) in November 1993 at $5.13. The stock moved very little for a few months and then went to the $7 range, where, with the exception of a few temporary upward and downward moves, it remained for nearly one and a half years. Todd became bored and disinterested in the stock, despite the company's steady increase in revenues and earnings. In September 1995 he finally sold his shares in FACE at just under $7. During October the stock price quickly increased to $10.25, which would have given Todd a 100 percent gain in two years. If he had waited a little longer, he could have watched the stock go into the mid-$20s before the company was bought out.

Todd had a rational-sounding explanation for his decision to sell: "I was getting impatient waiting. There were too many other good opportunities out there that could give me a quick 25 percent gain. I know I should have held on, but I felt like I was in that Beckett play *Waiting for Godot*. Nothing was happening." For him, waiting for FACE to move became impossible. Time began to move very slowly. Passively sitting with the stock seemed much less productive than pursuing other opportunities, even though FACE was reporting very positive developments. For some reason, though, the news wasn't integrated into his decision to sell FACE. There was too much perceived uncertainty for him to feel comfortable waiting. Sitting with a stock that is stuck in a trading range is always a challenge for those with an emotional conviction that activity leads to profits while passivity amounts to helplessness.

HOLDING ON TOO LONG

In June 1993 I bought Air Methods at $4.63. Although I knew that many people were hyping the stock, I had confidence in the long-term outlook of the company. In short order the stock rocketed to $14. I felt brilliant about my choice. The excitement of watching my money triple so quickly turned waiting into a pleasurable phenomenon. I was eager to wait for more good news, and just as intent on denying that the upturn could be quickly wiped out if my concerns about some of the company's recent decisions were on target. As it turned out, I overstayed my position.

Susanne Langer once said that waiting is an act of suspension:

> The principle of waiting is clearly exemplified in the conjoint actions of multi-enzyme systems, in which not the fastest but the slowest catalyst involved in a transformation is the "pace-maker," since chemical reactions are not driven by successive impulses, but require their own exact times, so that complex cycles are possible only if the faster reactions can be suspended until the slowest is completed.[1]

Langer is describing what in biology is known as the "rate-limiting step." In simpler terms, waiting occurs because a whole process can move only as quickly as the slowest element. In the case of Air Methods, the fastest step was the movement of the stock price, and the slowest rate-limiting step was the poor decisions being made by management. It would be necessary for the stock price to suspend its forward movement until the poor decision-making was fixed. This indeed happened when new management was brought into the company, and the stock subsequently returned to the $11 range. Holding on too long almost always involves impatiently paying attention to the fastest element while closing our eyes and denying the rate-limiting step.

DEVELOPING PATIENCE

Bull and bear markets evoke impatience. In a bull market we are all impatient for quick gains. Stock prices are going up, and all our friends are ostensibly making big money. Trading schemes promising huge gains flood our computer screens, and no matter how skeptical we are, there is always that flicker of hope that maybe, just maybe, some new system hot tip will help us beat the market.

The Internet bubble was particularly hard on our patience because it coincided with the rise of instantaneous electronic communication. Everything happened rapidly. Time passed quickly; we had instant access to information; e-mail replaced snail mail; we could communicate with virtually anyone in the world from anywhere at any time; instant dot-com millionaires appeared on magazine covers each week. Instant gratification was at a premium. It played havoc with our ability to be patient. Long-term thinking was out, and short-term thinking was in. As a group, we investors were terribly impatient.

In the bear market that followed the collapse of the Internet bubble, a different kind of impatience emerged. It is perhaps best expressed by Coleridge's Ancient Mariner, who, after sailing with fair breezes into the Pacific Ocean, was suddenly becalmed:

> *Day after day, day after day,*
> *We stuck, nor breath nor motion;*
> *As idle as a painted ship*
> *Upon a painted ocean.*
>
> *Water, water, everywhere,*
> *And all the boards did shrink;*
> *Water, water, everywhere,*
> *Not any drop to drink. . . .*
>
> *And every tongue, through utter drought,*
> *Was withered at the root;*
> *We could not speak, no more than if*
> *We had been choked with soot.*[2]

Not only did investors regret their failure to exit the market in March 2000, but impatience with the market permeated their thought processes. As one investor said to me, "I have no patience for waiting this out. I should have sold everything like they said on TV. I don't even want to look at the market anymore. I feel like a kid who wants to pick up her toys and just go home. I've lost so much money that maybe the market isn't worth playing anymore." Short-term thinking was now out, but long-term thinking was difficult to maintain. Investors didn't know how long they would have to wait. Indefiniteness breeds impatience.

THE PSYCHOLOGICAL FOUNDATIONS OF PATIENCE

The September 30, 1994, issue of the *Roxbury Quarterly* stated, "We were surprised to hear Peter Lynch, the brilliant former portfolio manager of the Magellan Fund, say recently that he believes over half of the people who invested in his fund lost money." According to Lynch, if you had invested $1,000 in Magellan in May 1977 when Lynch began managing the fund and then liquidated in May 1990 when he retired, you would have left with $28,000.[3] That's a compounded annual return of 29.2 percent.[4] So how is it possible that so many investors lost money? Although Fidelity denied this fact and Lynch later recanted, additional research[5] has confirmed that Peter Lynch's assessment, as most of his wise comments, applies to mutual-fund investors in general. The reason has much to do with the psychology underlying impatience.

The prototype for developing patience is the infant who cries when hungry and cannot tolerate any delay in the feeding process. What makes it possible for the infant to eventually wait to be fed? Many psychologists believe that responding to the infant's or child's needs reasonably quickly offers them an illusion of omnipotence, since the repeated sequence of "I am hungry, I cry, and someone feeds me" gives them the feeling that the feeding process is under their control. Seeing the parent preparing the food augments this process by visually reinforcing the feeling of omnipotence and control. A similar process, repeated thousands of times for each variety of needs, eventually lends a feeling of magical control over our surroundings. As infants mature, however, they gain a growing intellectual understanding of delay (for example, it takes time to prepare food), and the feeling that they are magically in control of their environment begins to wane. Over time that feeling becomes internalized as a realistic capacity to wait. It is only when children's needs are not met within a reasonable time, or at least empathically acknowledged by attuned adults, that they lose or fail to develop a capacity to wait and instead reinstitute attempts to force the environment to magically meet their needs immediately. That spells trouble. They become impatient and feel entitled.

Applying this psychological concept to the investment world, we know that investors who feel a strong sense of self—wholeness, aliveness, vitality, and an inner core of solidity—tend to be more patient than those whose sense of self is easily disrupted by the normally dysfunctional market. The investor in my Sleeping Beauty example, Ginny, who was unable to pull the trigger on an initial investment in Aura Systems, operated with a sense of self that felt continually vulnerable to disappointment. Her procrastination was a defensive strategy that protected her from further disappointment. My example of the investor who jumped into American Healthway after reading a positive write-up on the company was at the other end of the spectrum. His sense of self felt disrupted when confronted with wild volatility in American Healthway's stock price. His precipitous selling, while costing him significant capital appreciation, restored his sense of continuity, which at the time was more important to him than his investment decision. Only after his sense of self was restored was he able to think more clearly and recognize his mistake. For the investor in my third example, Todd, who got bored waiting for Facelifters to fly, the feeling of not knowing how long he needed to wait for the stock to move up left him feeling out of control. He lost his healthy sense of confidence about his investment decision, and the resulting anxiety was handled by selling the stock prematurely. Investors with a shaky feeling of continuity and control tend to be much more frightened of sitting long term with a stock that is not moving.

Unfortunately even a healthy sense of continuity and control is no assurance of success in the market. Investors in this category are vulnerable to impatience through their excessive feelings of grandiosity. Where our confidence is not contained within reasonable bounds, as with my decision to sit with Air Methods, we can miss important signals and find ourselves replicating the plight of Icarus and his contemporary counterparts discussed in chapter two.

PATIENCE AND THE PSYCHOLOGY OF TIME

Time is the investor's best friend and worst enemy. It is the most important variable in executing and understanding any investment program. The length of time an investment is held influences not only risk level and rate of return. It is also the most significant factor in determining asset allocation, individual stock choice, and the manner of utilizing different investments.

Time is both an objective and subjective phenomenon. Objectively we can define time as the duration of seconds, minutes, hours, days, months, and years. We can clock it and measure it according to any agreed-upon standards. We all agree that a week has seven days. But if you tell your two-year-old that you'll be gone for a week, he will have no conception of the length of your absence. Once you leave, your child may experience the week as forever. Time can be an equally subjective phenomenon for us grown-ups. We all experience time differently, depending on our developmental stage and emotional state. Vacations pass quickly; the workday drags interminably; time occasionally stands still; time passes more slowly for children than for adults. The relationship between everyday clock time (objective) and time as an agent of our psychological life (subjective time) dramatically influences investor behavior. Surprisingly, like many other aspects of psychological influences on investing, it is a subject left virtually untouched by both investors and psychologists.

INVESTMENTS AND OBJECTIVE TIME

To give you a feel for the importance of objective time in the investing process, consider the effect that compounding has on money growth over a horizon of five to thirty years:

COMPOUND RATE OF RETURN ON $1,000	INVESTMENT PERIOD (IN YEARS)			
	5	10	20	30
4%	$1,216	$1,480	$2,191	$ 3,243
6	1,338	1,790	3,207	5,743
8	1,469	2,159	4,661	10,062
10	1,610	2,593	6,728	17,449
12	1,762	3,106	9,646	29,960
14	1,925	3,707	13,744	50,950
16	2,100	4,411	19,460	85,850
18	2,289	5,234	27,393	143,371
20	2,488	6,192	38,338	237,376

To think that $1,000 invested in a retirement account at a compounded annual rate of 14 percent when you are forty years old would yield nearly $51,000 at age seventy is simply astounding. If you had invested $10,000, you would have more than half a million dollars. It is no wonder Albert Einstein mused that the greatest human invention was compound interest.

Of course, like many things, compounding can be a double-edged sword. Consider its effects on eroding our purchasing power through inflation:

RATE OF INFLATION	TIME TO CUT YOUR MONEY IN HALF
2%	36 years
3	24 years
4	18 years
5	14 years
6	12 years
7	11 years

When thought of in inflationary terms, time has a truly daunting power. A modest 4 percent inflation rate can reduce a $1,000 investment to only $500 worth of purchasing power by the time a newborn is ready for college. If you are forty years old and saving for retirement in a bank account or through CDs paying 2.5 to 3 percent interest, that 4 percent annual hit is patently destructive to any long-term plan for accumulating wealth. Even before taxes on interest income, your $1,000 invested at 3 percent for thirty years will leave you with $2,427. Subtract more than 50 percent purchasing power from that, and you have about what you started with, with taxes adding insult to your injury.

Since most investors are well aware of this basic reality, why is it that sophisticated individuals don't take better advantage of compounding to increase their returns over time by long-term investing in equities? The answer seems relatively simple. Despite all our cultural, intellectual, and technological advances over the last few centuries, human emotional development has remained essentially static. And the power of human psychology can undermine even the savviest investors who are not cognizant of their psychology of time.

INVESTMENTS AND SUBJECTIVE TIME

Subjective time can be defined as the distortions of clock time inherent in our idiosyncratic psychic lives. A familiar scenario may help with the distinction. Let's say that eighteen months ago your favorite analyst recommended Express Scripts (ESRX), but you passed on it, and its share price has now tripled. So of course you're kicking yourself: "Why didn't I buy ESRX at 13? How often will I get a chance to triple my money in so short a time?" On the other hand, the same analyst now recommends Air Methods based on an evaluation suggesting that the stock could double or triple in eighteen months. You think, *That's a long time to tie up my money if nothing happens down the road.* Why do we experience eighteen months as unbearably long when we are about to commit money to an investment while the same period seems incredibly short when we could have successfully committed money in the past?

T. S. Eliot illuminated this phenomenon with characteristic deftness in "Burnt Norton":

> *Time present and time past*
> *Are both perhaps present in time future,*
> *And time future contained in time past.*
> *If all time is eternally present*
> *All time is unredeemable.*[6]

Indeed our feelings from the past as well as our hopes and fears about the future are continuously active and alive in the present. This seems especially apt for investors. When we wear our investor hat, we seem to function emotionally almost exclusively in the present without realizing how past and future fears and hopes unwittingly influence our time perspective. In this way our human emotions frequently move contrary to our economic interests by interfering with long-term investing. Consider the following obstacles to patient, long-term investing.

The Accumulation of Past Fears and Losses. Committing our hard-earned savings to the prospect of future returns is always influenced by past losses and fears. Our capacity for long-term investing can be impaired not only from past losses in the market, but also from any significant personal losses, which can act unconsciously on our long-term resolve. In fact my interviews with investors indicate that the greater their history of losses or fear of loss, the more likely they will focus on short-term trading rather than long-term investing. The former offers the sense of more control over our investments, however illusory. Long-term investing appears more risky because of the length of time we experience being parted from our money and therefore the diminished control we experience over the results. To some degree this is absolutely true, which is why we demand a higher return for longer payoff or illiquid stocks. But it is important to remember that the feeling of control over an investment and the actual risk it presents are not necessarily interrelated.

The Need for Immediate Feedback. Most people appreciate immediate feedback on their actions. In fact most of us search continually (often unconsciously) for immediate gratification in the form of confirmation, validation, and appreciation of our thoughts, values, beliefs, and actions. When this mirroring is not forthcoming, we frequently become more tentative and unsure in our decision-making. To invest a significant amount of money in a stock that languishes for a year or more (or worse yet goes down) before beginning its ascent frustrates our need for immediate feedback. During the long wait, we have a natural tendency to doubt ourselves and discount the positive fundamentals that motivated us to buy the stock in the first place. Too often it is only after we act on our emotions (in the absence of validation of our stock picking) and sell that the stock begins to appreciate in value.

The Fear of Missing Out. Do you remember as a child not wanting to commit yourself to accepting an invitation to a party two weeks in advance because something more interesting could come up in the interim? The same phenomenon occurs in investor psychology. We hesitate to commit funds long term to equities or a specific company because a more lucrative investment may be waiting just around the corner. Or we hesitate to use any of our cash reserve because the next round of economic statistics to be released tomorrow may affect the market, not to mention the PPI (Producer Price Index) and CPI (Consumer Price Index) to be announced soon. We always have a rational reason to procrastinate for fear of missing out on something important. But unless we are able to make investing decisions in the here and now, with all its uncertainty, we not only *feel* continually held back, we *are* held back.

The Need for Efficacy. We all need to experience the feeling that we have an impact on others in our surroundings, that we are effective at our work, for example, or that our favorite activity provides a sense of mastery. For investors this need translates into the capacity to demonstrate that we can, via the knowledge and skill inherent in wise investment choices, accumulate wealth or beat the market or choose a stock that goes up immediately. But for investing to have a serious impact on our financial security, years of patient discipline are usually required. Many people cannot tolerate that long a delay in gratification. Some eschew long-term investing for the dramatic feeling of mastery that day traders occasionally achieve.

The Need for Essential Alikeness. All human beings feel a sense of well-being in the presence of like others. As noted earlier, this phenomenon is one of the reasons that crowd psychology is so powerful. With the advent of instant communications and instantaneous, computerized capacity for statistical measurement of performance, most public discussions of investment success emphasize quarter-by-quarter results posted by well-known money managers. Investors gain a sense of belonging and alikeness when they experience themselves in the company of these experts. To eschew quarterly measurements and focus on performance over a three-to-five- or ten-year horizon generally produces the best results but takes a mix of courage, independence, and, of course, patience that many investors lack.

WHAT MAKES PATIENCE POSSIBLE

Whenever I talk about patience, investors always say, "Sure, we know patience is important, but what makes it possible? And what if my personality makes it seem impossible?" These are important questions. At least part of the answers turn on several underlying psychological characteristics that contribute to our capacity to be patient. With an understanding of those variables, we can see which investing styles mesh with different psychological capacities for patience.

The Capacity for Personal Reality. Hope is the single most important factor that drives our investment activities. Whether it is a hopeful expectation that we will become wealthy, make optimal decisions, achieve independence, learn enough about the process to help others, or enhance our self-esteem, it comes down in each case to hope. Whatever the idiosyncratic hopes of any investor, we could not buy a stock (or short a stock) without the expectation that we will be successful. And no matter what form of hope drives us, we still need to base investment decisions on our evaluation of what we believe is reality—assessments of the fundamentals, technicals, products, services, and management that we routinely perform during the research process. In fact some economists suggest (incorrectly, I strongly believe) that all decisions are made in a rational manner based solely on the real utility or value of a potential investment.

In between our hopes and realities, we have an accumulation of experience I call *personal reality*. Children understand this experience best because their normal play activities encourage them to adapt other children's reality to their own fantasy life. As investors, our capacity for personal reality is based on our adeptness at adapting external reality, as objectively perceived, to our subjective understanding, which is always infused with emotional convictions and fantasies. For the personal reality about an investment decision to be balanced, its external reality (all the ostensible realities represented by earnings, revenues, cash flows, and so on) must be infused with our hopes and expectations in appropriate proportions. Too much subjectivity and we end up with delusion; too much reality and we end up succumbing to generally accepted external beliefs (the herd). Both of these states interfere with our capacity to be patient. Just the right combination, however delicate, contributes to enormous capacity for patience.

To illustrate, as detailed in chapter one, I recommended Zi-Corp at the end of 1996 at $3.13, and then again in the fall of 1998 at $2.19. It took some time for Zi's innovations to catch on, but by March 2000 the stock ran to $40. While I had recommended a stop loss of $25 as a sell point in the event of a downturn, I also kept the stock in my model portfolio. What enabled me to be so patient over the years? It certainly had to be more than the external reality of the company's good product and potential for building a market in China. Nor was it only my subjective belief that management could turn an interesting technology into a major player in the interface solutions arena. What enabled me to hold on for four years, through many ups and downs, was the capacity for personal reality. I had managed to infuse what I believe was a reasonable assessment of external reality with my own internal, hopeful fantasies, the kind of feelings that may arise when listening to a pleasing concert or studying an intricate painting.

While describing these subjective feelings may be difficult, their importance is clear. Without them we simply cannot maintain enough internal belief in our companies and personal excitement about their prospects to weather their storms and sustain the prolonged patience required for many of them to achieve their potential. This doesn't mean allowing our own hopes and dreams to spill over into delusion. Keeping subjective belief from distorting our personal reality requires ongoing attention to our companies' progress and concrete prospects for executing their business plans successfully.

The Capacity for Inactivity ("Standing Still and Dancing"). Warren Buffett once said:

Inactivity strikes us an intelligent behavior. . . . When we own portions of outstanding businesses with outstanding managements, our favorite holding period is forever. We are just the opposite of those who hurry to sell and book profits when companies perform well but who tenaciously hang on to businesses that disappoint. Peter Lynch aptly likens such behavior to cutting the flowers and watering the weeds.[7]

What Buffett does not say here is psychologically just as important as what he does say. Inactivity for Buffett refers to an optimal hesitation to doing something—buying and selling or trading. What Buffett is really talking about, however, is the capacity for *being*. My guess is there is a lot of activity going on, but it's in his head rather than in the market. What allows for patience is the capacity to be cognitively and emotionally active—to study the market, to create a host of scenarios and play them out in your head, to review a myriad of potential investments while acting only on the few that require action.

In an interesting series of papers, Vadim Rotenberg and his associates described four possible responses to situations with indefinite outcomes: rigid stereotypic responses from the past that are used without thought; disorganized panic behavior; withdrawal and refusal to participate; and search activity involving our attempt to actively change a situation or our attitude toward it while simultaneously monitoring the effects of our behavior.[8] Rotenberg also observed that the benefits of search activity for our mental and physical health are primarily from the search itself rather than the outcome: "What is important for the subject is to perceive himself as a problem solver, a conqueror."

My clinical-research findings support an extension of Rotenberg's premise to the phenomenon of patience. People seem to develop and sustain patience by engaging in mental search activity—using our minds actively to find creative solutions to the uncertainty around us. A simple example in a bear market would be making mental notes for what stocks we would buy right now if we had the money. Search activity in a bull market might take the form of imagining all the things that could go wrong with our portfolio. To use singer–songwriter David Buskin's metaphor, we are actively "standing still and dancing" with little regard for the actual outcome. Impatience, by its nature, pulls us away from ourselves and toward external solutions. The search for external solutions results from a subtle feeling of emptiness or disorganization that underlies the impatience, as if some important organizing principle or belief system has been invalidated. Seeking an external solution is a way of filling in that emptiness with other people's feelings, judgments, and perceptions.

In search activity, however, these abortive solutions are avoided, and our creative imaginings serve two important functions. First, the fantasies we develop in actively searching (imagining what stocks we would buy when the market bottoms or what indicators might suggest a market bottom) provide us with a sense of validity and competence that would otherwise be absent. Second, the mental process involved in search activity puts us in a useful state of suspended animation (patience) in which we are able to wait, as Langer suggested, until the actual "means of continuance arrives."[9] The active search restores some sense of control over our environment and helps increase our capacity for patience.

There are several cognitive activities that contribute to this process and promote patience. Reading our companies' recent 10-Ks and 10-Qs, listening to their conference calls, and talking with their management are among the most obvious. Making lists of stocks you want to buy or sell and determining the price at which you would purchase or sell them, making lists of stocks you would buy if you were to sell one of your holdings, searching for a niche in the market that corresponds to your personality, developing your own way of valuing companies, and talking about stocks with a small group of trusted others all help you to be patient. As Bernard Baruch once allegedly suggested, at the beginning of each new year, performing an exercise in which you ask yourself which stocks you would buy if you were starting from a 100 percent cash position often leads to revealing insights.

Cognitive activity always bolsters our capacity for patience. At the risk of oversimplification, let's go back to my illustration of the hungry infant who gets cranky when his demands for food are not immediately satisfied. As the child develops, he can imagine his mother or father in the kitchen preparing food, and through this cognitive imagining he builds a capacity for delay. Maturation eventually leads to patience. Those who were fortunate to have their needs met in a timely manner while growing up develop patience almost automatically; those who were unduly frustrated often feel more need for immediate gratification, fearing that an opportunity not seized immediately will be lost forever. People in that category may need to work harder at patience, but that doesn't mean it cannot be developed through search activities and similar cognitive functions that substitute being for doing.

The Capacity for Using Emotion. Every psychological study of affects (emotions) concludes that they are central to the development of our sense of self. According to Silvan Tomkins, one of the most prolific writers and researchers on the subject, affect "lends its power to memory, to perception, to thought, and to action. . . . Affect either makes good things better or bad things worse."[10] In the investment world, affect becomes important to the development of patience in two basic ways—as a signal that can guide our investment actions, and as an organizer of our experiences.

We all appreciate that patience tends to break down in the face of intense emotional states. Just remember the last time you saw one of your stocks dropping sharply and had no idea why it was falling or who was selling it. Without being able to modulate these powerful and intense reactions to the market, investors experience panic, tending to sell just after a stock has crashed and then buy when it recovers (often at the top) for fear of missing further upside. Patience requires the active containment and modulation of these strong emotions. And this kind of patience is achieved only if your affects act as signals alerting you to a change in your psychological state rather than as indicators of something traumatic in the market.

Let me give you an example of how knowing your own affect can dramatically improve your decision-making. After I recommended American Healthways at around $30, the stock quickly fell to $24. My first reaction was to send out an urgent alert to sell the stock. But I knew from experience that this urge was based on my own internal panic rather than some fundamental flaw in my analysis of the company. On the other hand, I was also aware that when a stock dropped precipitously and I stayed very calm, it often meant there really was something going awry at the company. If we pay attention, we can learn to identify our idiosyncratic internal signals and use them as clues to the appropriate action. In the case of American Healthways, I interpreted the sense of panic as a signal to do nothing, and the stock shortly recovered, ultimately breaking $40 before splitting three for two. The more understanding we have of our emotional reactions to different market scenarios, and the more trusting we become of their signaling properties, the more patient we can become in the face of turmoil.

Patience also suffers when we experience contradictory feelings about an investment. There is a tendency in the investment world to see things as all black or all white. Similar mind-sets in the broadcast and print media reinforce this tendency. In reality most investments are a "mixed bag"; most companies and their management have many strengths and admirable qualities as well as vulnerabilities and deficits. In fact, becoming too knowledgeable about a company probably creates more contradictory feelings than remaining a bit more detached, since too much familiarity tends to imbue all the superficial warts with more importance than they deserve.

Not long ago I received a call from an investor, Jeremy, who was extremely critical of my sticking with a buy–hold recommendation on a particular company. He said his meticulous research showed that management had "made a decision that favored the large shareholders over the smaller retail shareholders." He urged me to sell the stock immediately. I reminded him that the last time he called me he was equally adamant that management could do no wrong. At this point Jeremy acknowledged that he felt both ways, but "the negative feelings had taken over this week."

Patience requires the integration of conflicting feelings about a company. Only if we can hold both the positive and negative feelings at the same time can we see the subtle shades of gray that exist for all investments. Patiently examining both sides of the picture leads to much more productive buy-and-sell decisions than experiencing only an isolated side of the picture.

Optimism and Self-Trust. An old Zen poet once wrote:

> *My house burned down.*
> *At last, a clear view*
> *Of the Moon.*

Admittedly the poet could become either a gifted investor or a disastrously delusional one. While the non-Zen saying that investing requires an optimistic outlook may be a cliché, it is also true. Not only do we need optimism about the future, we must be optimistic about a management team's ability to execute, a product's or service's appeal to the public, a company's ability to integrate acquisitions, its ability to meet its projected numbers, and our own ability to make judgments about these factors.

AND IF I AM IMPATIENT?
(A DIFFERENT KIND OF TRADING)

What if you have examined your sense of self carefully and decided that it would take too many years of psychotherapy to become a patient long-term investor? Or perhaps you're perfectly comfortable with your imperfect self and your distaste for psychotherapy. Don't worry. Remember that one of the keys to successful investing is to match your personality to your investing style. And in my experience, the particular investing style is less important than understanding your personality. There are plenty of successful investors with different investing strategies; the key is knowing which one fits your personality.

I frequently receive calls asking if I believe in trading and, if so, whether I know of good trading systems that can be used for people who either want to add trading to their longer-term investment strategies or are just not patient enough to be only long-term investors. My answer is a simple yes and no. My experience is that most individual traders lose money, and even those who make money spend an inordinate amount of time in front of their computer screens, often not justifying the returns they achieve. I also believe that the largest returns are by definition achieved on long-term investments in small companies at an early stage in the development cycle when there is a significant discrepancy between their intrinsic value and their stock price.

With that said, it is also true that trading is fun, stimulating, and at times rewarding. Many long-term investors and money managers supplement their long-term strategies by occasionally trading when they find a suitable opportunity for short-term gains. So for those who enjoy the process and want to spend the time and energy understanding both themselves and the market, setting aside a limited amount of funds to trade is a reasonable option.

TRADING SYSTEMS
FOR THE QUASI-PATIENT

Most trading systems and their accompanying educational materials are expensive. Online systems typically require monthly fees and offer a continual flow of ideas. Some large companies offer workshops and seminars to teach trading. Many investors learn by trial and error. Professional traders will tell you that it takes many years of patience, practice, and psychological insight to become a good trader. But if you want to try your hand at trading, I have developed a system that you can adapt to your own needs and patience level.

From my perspective any trading system must fit with your lifestyle and investing style. I'm not interested in sitting in front of a computer screen all day when I could be more profitably researching companies for long-term investments. I also cannot tolerate investing in a vacuum, so pure technical analysis makes me uncomfortable unless it is used just to complement my fundamental understanding. In addition, I think shorting stocks as a trading methodology is too risky for the average investor except in unusual circumstances. With these admitted biases, I recommend that any trading system

- Must be based on fundamentals.
- Should not require you to be in front of your computer all day.
- Must not rely on complex technical analysis.
- Should not depend on shorting stocks for success.
- Should be based on a four-week time frame.
- Should not be overly dependent on your ability to predict short-term market movements.

Incorporating these characteristics into a trading system should allow you to be flexible and thoughtful without feeling like a slave to the stock market's every twist and turn. Within this system, however, there are certain guidelines that I recommend to limit risk and enhance performance.

Limit Your Funds. Learning to trade or invest requires actual participation in the market. If you try out trading systems on paper, you will always be a winner because playing on paper eliminates 90 percent of the emotions that contribute to investment errors. That's why trading-system advertising always invites you to try out a program for sixty days on paper. They know you will win and want to buy their service. But in practice you must accept that you will make mistakes and could lose real money. If you can force yourself to study those mistakes, you can improve your odds. If not, my old tennis coach's saying will likely apply to your trading as it applied when I wouldn't change from a Western grip to an Eastern grip: "Practice doesn't make perfect, it just makes permanent." So be careful not to entrap yourself in a cycle of repetitive errors. And be sure to remember my two primary rules of trading. First, since some losses are bound to occur in any trading system, do not use more than 10 percent of your investing funds to start trading. The second rule is just as simple. Under no circumstances violate the first rule.

Fundamentals, Fundamentals. Once you've decided on your pool of money, select a group of fifteen stocks whose fundamentals you either know well or want to learn about. Some may be stocks that you already own for the long run. Many traders use only the exchange-traded funds that represent an index (for example, the QQQ or "cubes"—the Nasdaq 100 index tracking stock) for trading, but you'll have two strikes against you in that arena. You will be competing with some of the best professional traders on Wall Street, and your results will depend solely on your market direction calls. So I prefer trading within a portfolio of stocks you own or know well. The more comprehensive your understanding of your companies' fundamentals, the greater your chances of deciphering spreads between intrinsic value and fluctuating market prices.

For example, let's say Titan (TTN) reached an intraday high of $29 on day one. On day two, Merrill Lynch downgraded the stock, and AG Edwards jumped on the bandwagon with a downgrade on day nine. By day twelve, the stock price had retreated to $21.86 but appeared to be turning around. In the meantime, Titan had been selected by the U.S. Postal Service to use its SureBeam technology for eradicating anthrax, and the company was awarded part of a $400 million contract from the Department of Defense. If you believed in Titan's fundamentals, which were certainly reinforced by those announcements, you probably would perceive a darn good risk–reward ratio at $22. Subsequently the stock began its climb back toward $28. So you could have made six or seven points on the trade over a few weeks. But you would have needed enough familiarity with the fundamentals to know that the Street's downgrades were an opportunity rather than a warning.

Trade in Small Amounts and Set Limits. When you begin trading, it's best to trade in small lots. This will protect you from substantial losses as well as ameliorating the emotional baggage that often accompanies losing trades. I have found that most investors are comfortable with trading one hundred to five hundred shares of a stock depending on the price of the stock and their tolerance and capacity for loss. It is also important to trade on the basis of limit orders for both the buy and sell side, since a greedy market maker can substantially affect your results if left to its own devices by filling your buy orders at a high price and your sell orders at the low end of the range.

Become Familiar with Your Stock's Personality. Just as each individual has unique personality characteristics, every stock has unique trading patterns. Some stocks trade up in the morning and down in the afternoon. Others do just the opposite. Some stocks continually reach their highs or lows for the day at midmorning or midafternoon. Select a few of your portfolio stocks and study how they trade for several sessions. You will notice clear patterns emerging over several days. You can observe trading behavior without paying for streaming quotes or Nasdaq level-two market-maker information. While this information is useful as you become more experienced, you should begin with an online trading firm that provides you with free real-time quotes.

You may be surprised by the predictability of particular patterns. Stocks that are traded mostly by retail investors often move the most in the first hour of the day; stocks traded by professionals often move toward the end of the day, although there are many exceptions. Some stocks trade actively for the first few hours of the day, followed by an observable lull, with another wave of strong volume before the close. Whatever the pattern, you do not need sophisticated technical analysis to understand it. As Yogi Berra once said, "You can observe a lot by watching." What you are searching for is a reliable pattern of trading that will give you a feel for the stock's rhythms during the trading session and repeated opportunities to capitalize on predictable movements. For example, if your stock has repeatedly traded down in the morning and up at the end of the day, you could take advantage of the spread between the price near the opening and the price advance before the close.

Set Mental Stop-Loss Limits. Whenever you trade, you should set a mental stop-loss limit for each stock. This is the price below which you won't allow it to go without selling. Many traders have found that a 7 percent to 8 percent stop loss works well. Once you establish your limit, never violate it, no matter how much your psyche tries to convince you that the stock will come back in a few days. Because this trading system assumes that you may have a substantial long position in the stocks you trade, be sure to distinguish between your long-term investing and your short-term trading. For example, you may be selling a stock in your trading account when it drops below the 8 percent limit, but you may also be buying the same stock in your long-term account after it has lost 15 percent. One of the difficulties traders experience in their novice stage is confusing their long- and short-term investing goals. Remember that short-term trading requires a constant flow of cash to remain liquid, so despite the excellent long-term prospects of a company, your short-term philosophy must hold sway in trading accounts.

Take Advantage of Volatility. Most long-term investors feel anxious during volatile stock markets, even though they offer an ideal opportunity to accumulate larger positions at lower prices. But there is no ambivalence for traders. Volatility is always their good friend. To make the most of it, you should search for stocks within your portfolio that have the potential to move one to three points in a short time on large volume. Reviewing the trading pattern of your stocks by looking at a chart (try Barchart.com) will give you a good feel for volume and volatility. If you had followed Manugistics in the late fall of 2000 into the winter of 2001, for example, you would have seen that it climbed from $6.41 at the end of October to about $20 in January. In between, however, it offered you many opportunities to jump on board. Once it reached the $14 level, it pulled back to $11 and then immediately jumped three points to $14 again on large volume. Most beginning traders find it extremely difficult to buy stocks when they are going down, which is exactly why I recommend that you know the fundamentals of your companies. It gives you the confidence to take advantage of traders who use nothing but technical analysis to buy and sell stocks. These traders will sell when their charts tell them to, driving the price arbitrarily down to levels that you can exploit because of your confidence in the fundamentals.

Take Advantage of Arbitrage Opportunities. Arbitrage used to be defined as the simultaneous purchase and sale of stocks on two different exchanges to take advantage of price differences in different markets. But I am using the term as it applies to exploiting opportunities that follow public announcements of extraordinary transactions such as buyouts, mergers, acquisitions, and restructurings, which involve risks of not being completed as planned. For example, on November 21, 2000, when its price was at $35.20, DRS Technologies announced that it filed for a secondary offering of three million shares. Six days later the price was $ 30.75, presumably reflecting concerns about dilution. If you were confident about DRS's fundamentals and knew that in general whenever a company announces a secondary offering, the price tends to fall, you would have jumped at the chance to buy DRS at the depressed price. Your major risk would have been an unusually quick deterioration of the fundamentals or a major delay in the secondary.

Above All, Be Patient. Most investors assume that trading involves frenetic activity. But the type of trading I recommend for those with the yen for quick results still requires enormous patience and thought.

You trade selectively and only when the difference between value and price becomes clear. Warren Buffett has quoted Ted Williams, one of baseball's all-time greatest hitters, on this matter. Williams said, "My argument is, to be a good hitter, you've got to get a good ball to hit. It's the first rule in the book. If I have to bite at stuff that is out of my happy zone, I'm not a .344 hitter. I might only be a .250 hitter."[11] To be a good trader in this system, you must stay patiently within your "happy zone," trading stocks only when you can exploit your knowledge of their fundamentals and trading patterns.

Now that I have delineated a few characteristics that underlie your capacity for patience and offered you an alternative to solely long-term investing, your job is to decide where you fit on the continuum of long-term investor to trader. Each requires a different type of patience and skill, and a deeper understanding of yourself is the best way to decide how much patience you can live with comfortably.

SIX

Letting Go

How much money you make or lose in the stock market depends ultimately on when you sell your holdings. Because of the enormous importance of selling decisions, you would expect to see considerable study and theory on all aspects of the phenomenon. Curiously enough, however, there is a dearth of literature on the subject compared to the many books, articles, and commentary on buying stocks.[1] Part of the explanation may lie in the complexity of the subject, for selling at the right time is an art that depends on an elusive combination of skill, knowledge, judgment, luck, and psychology that can never be reduced to a coherent or comprehensive formula. The rest of the explanation may be that every investor faced with a selling decision brings unique psychological variables into the formula. No matter how much we know about a company or fund, no matter what guidelines we follow or systems we use, and no matter how superior our judgment may be, our sell decisions are strongly impacted by our own particular organizing lenses, especially those emotional convictions involving the psychological association between selling and loss.

As I've indicated in a variety of ways in the preceding chapters, all market decisions involve the interweaving of external information into the texture of our imagination. We dream of enormous profits; we fear substantial losses; we commit ourselves to philosophical causes (for example, environmentalism); we become fascinated with technological development (for example, telecommunications). Subtly but surely, all these personal visions influence our buying and selling in ways that are barely conscious. Consider the following scenarios:

• You've just bought a stock after doing a week of careful research. The company is a high-tech business operating in a complex area of the insurance industry. Although you don't know very much about this type of insurance, you're intrigued, and you read up on the company, download articles on the industry and the company's products, and become convinced this stock has significant growth potential. The following week the company announces unexpected downside earnings due to the one technological glitch you failed to consider. But psychologically it's hard to acknowledge that you made a mistake and that the punishment has been so swift. While the realization of an error is sinking in, you watch the value of your stock plummet for another week.

• You're a strong supporter of the environment, and you're a member of local community groups that promote clean air. You recently invested in a company that is a leading proponent of the cause. The company is a manufacturer, but all of their products and factories are built with the environment in mind. They use only recyclable packaging, and they attempt to minimize their energy consumption. Unfortunately, despite all the positives, the stock slowly but surely tanks. You don't want to sell because it feels like giving in to your broker, who has lectured for years not to pick companies to invest in based on their environmental policies.

• Your favorite stock drops precipitously on high volume. The company then reports a slowdown in sales for the quarter. You panic at the thought of your favorite company having a poor quarter and sell after the stock drops. Maybe things are turning down for the company, and maybe it will never recover. You begin to wonder if the CEO recruited within the last year is up to the job, and you start to think that the growth spurt for this company is over. It feels like a relief to sell. But three weeks later you learn that the slowdown was a temporary glitch from unexpected delays in shipping, and you watch as the stock rebounds.

Similar and equally distressing scenarios are infinite. I could probably write several books just recounting all the mistakes that occur during the selling process. But the psychological underpinning of virtually all selling-error scenarios would be surprisingly consistent. We imaginatively perceive the external realities and incorporate them into our latest hopes and fears in ways that can feel truly congruent with our organizing lenses while being starkly discordant with market realities.

DIFFERENCES BETWEEN BUYING AND SELLING

Ideally when we buy a stock on the basis of a company's fundamentals, there is a period of intense research and due diligence that precedes the purchase. During this process, evidence accumulates that supports our high hopes for the future success of the company and our confidence in that evaluation. A brief period of anxiety often surrounds the actual buy order, but it usually dissipates shortly after the order is executed. The psychologists call this "cognitive dissonance," the process of accumulating evidence that supports a decision once it is made, while ignoring evidence that would contradict our actions. When cognitive dissonance is resolved, the resolution helps us feel proud, intelligent, and positive about our choice. Self-esteem and judgment are both validated, especially if the next move in the stock is up. Even when the stock drops immediately after the purchase, we often look for explanations to support the ultimate wisdom of our buy decision. We then tend to move on to intensive research on other stocks while paying less attention to the recently purchased ones. Hope and confidence are the primary emotions that accompany a well-researched buy decision.

While the hope, optimism, and self-confidence that follow well-researched buying decisions are fairly straightforward emotional experiences, selling evokes a myriad of more complex emotions. The contrast can be traced in part to the difference in variables. The buy decision is made on all available information at a given point in time. But once an investor owns the stock, the choice between sell or hold is subject to a mercurial set of subjectivities. As Stephen Jay Gould, a keen observer of the natural world, once said in another context:

The divine tape player holds a million scenarios, each perfectly sensible. Little quirks at the outset, occurring for no particular reason, unleash cascades of consequences that make a particular future seem inevitable in retrospect. But the slightest nudge contacts a different groove, and history veers into another plausible channel, diverging continually from its original pathway. The end results are so different, the initial perturbations so apparently trivial.[2]

The unforeseen little hiccups in the companies we buy, and the natural, human quirks of their management, presage scenarios impossible to discern when we initially purchase our stocks. The countless permutations of changing circumstances and paucity of time to monitor stocks already in our portfolio contribute to a more complex set of emotions than those feelings that follow an initial purchase: anxiety from the uncertainty; threats to self-esteem from having made a potential mistake; mental depletion from following too many stocks; anger from uncontrollable and unforeseen events or management errors. The list could go on infinitely, but what seems important is that the buy decision tends to evoke more hopeful emotions, while the sell decision evokes a wide range of more complex emotions including guilt, anxiety, anger, loss, shame, gratitude, greed, and relief. It is natural to experience these emotions as you sell. The only mistake is to let them get into the driver's seat and steer your investment decisions.

THE EMOTIONS OF LOSS AND SELLING

Behavioral problems with selling can often be traced to difficulties, conscious or unconscious, in handling the emotions of loss. Loss is associated with selling a stock in a variety of ways, not all of them purely financial. If a stock retreats below its buy price, investors become concerned not only with taking a loss, but also with how much of a loss is reasonable to bear and when to bail out and accept the loss. To one degree or another, the loss at issue involves more than money. At least as important are loss of time, loss of self-esteem, and loss of validation by others. Similar emotions of loss can also play a role when a stock has appreciated, since letting go evokes fears of foregoing future upside potential in the stock being sold, as well as lost opportunities elsewhere in the market if the stock isn't sold. More subtly, and sometimes unconsciously, investors become concerned with loss of their connection to a company they know well. This can also involve fear of losing a close working relationship with admired members of the company's management. Sometimes we also have difficulty letting go of a stock that we experience as an important possession. Stock ownership can provide a valuable attachment, and such a sense of belonging can be difficult to relinquish.

Many investors will deny that the idea of emotional loss enters into their investment decisions. As one investor commented, "I don't have to deal with emotions because I use a computer system that tells me when to sell." In other words, a system obviates the need for emotional involvement. As pointed out in Chapter Two, however, my qualitative research into investment errors in both amateur and professional investors suggests otherwise. In fact the strength of these denials seems generally proportional to an investor's resistance to introspection. It betrays the fear that a glance inward at our psychological reactions will destroy our capacity to concentrate on the external reality of everyday buy and sell decisions.[3] While all systems are designed to eliminate emotions from buy and sell decisions, if strong enough, those emotions can overrule any system at just the wrong moment.

LOSS SYNDROMES THAT INTERFERE WITH SELLING DECISIONS

The specific ways our feelings about loss impact investment decision-making, particularly selling, have not been well studied. We do know, however, that all adults were once children and that we cannot grow up without experiencing either emotional or real losses on many levels. In general the fewer losses we experience, and the more help we get in dealing with those that do occur, the stronger our sense of self in adulthood. Feelings of loss, when unrecognized, have the potential to seriously interfere with the selling process, as the following examples illustrate.

Separation Anxiety. One very intelligent investor who consulted me about his difficulty selling stocks realized he frequently lost profits because, as he stated, "I know intellectually when to sell, but I just can't seem to let go of the stocks when I should." Carl provided numerous examples dating back several years of how he failed to sell his holdings in a timely fashion, each time ending his example with "I just could not seem to let go." I finally told him that I was struck by his repetitive use of those words—*could not seem to let go*—and wondered if they had some unusual importance in his life. He smiled and told me he hadn't remembered this in a long time, but when he was young he had difficulty leaving his mother when going to school. Other kids used to tease him about "not being able to let go of her." And "teachers used to tell me that I had to let go of her. I always thought something terrible would happen if we were apart." Carl's "separation anxiety," to use the psychological jargon, hadn't been particularly severe and hadn't lasted very long. But as Carl realized that day, his feeling that something terrible would happen if he "let go" was influencing his behavior in the stock market.

The obvious question from this example is whether Carl's insight into his "separation anxiety" would cure his inability to sell when he knew the time was right. While intellectual insight rarely cures all ills, the investor in this case was able to make more timely sell decisions. His recognition of an important organizing lens—letting go leads to disaster—didn't remove it. He still felt anxious when he sold stock. Yet at least he could say to himself, "I know I'm feeling anxious, but that anxiety belongs to a time in my childhood that is unrelated to current market realities. Letting go here actually leads to protecting myself." This was a happy ending, since it involved an expansion of his organizing lenses or emotional convictions, and it turned out to be one of the keys to his future investing success.

Unresolved Losses. Investors who have grown up experiencing unresolved losses often have specific difficulties in selling their stocks. Where feelings of loss are still raw and exposed, the idea of losing money in the stock market can be intolerable. Any potential loss in the market telescopes all former nonmonetary losses into the present. As a result, these investors are likely to sell too early. Their decisions are not based on the fundamentals of their investment but on the need to avoid rekindling the emotion of loss. As one investor said, "I just can't tolerate the feeling of loss. It has nothing to do with my stock; I just sell before a price drop gets too big so I don't have to confront the feeling." Arbitrary rules to sell when your stock retreats 7 percent or 8 percent below your buy price may prove to be the right choice in some cases or exactly the wrong choice in others. Either way it often reflects a technical rationalization of an emotional need to avoid feelings of loss and disappointment at any cost.

On the other hand, emotional conflicts from unresolved losses can also steer investors in the opposite direction. Where the conflict is from the denial of painful losses, an investor is more likely to hold on to a losing position well beyond the time indicated by the fundamentals. These are the investors who are likely to say, "It isn't a loss until I've actually sold my position, so I think I'll just hold on for a while longer." In other words, as long as we can deny that our loss is real until we sell, we tend to hold on to our losers while selling our winners, just the wrong strategy for success in the market. Selling the winners too early convinces us that we are not playing a loser's game, while reinforcing our denial that keeping our losers avoids a real loss.

The effects of this type of unresolved loss on investing decisions are most dramatic on the anniversaries of the emotional losses, even if they occurred many years earlier. These anniversaries can be represented symbolically when they become associated with particular seasons, holidays, or months. Many investors do best not making important investment decisions during those anniversary periods.

SUDDEN LOSSES IN THE MARKET

Sudden and unexpected losses have become commonplace in today's volatile markets. Even after performing thorough research, it is the rare investor who doesn't confront negative and sometimes dramatic surprises. When these disruptions occur, the suddenness of the loss can short-circuit the processes that normally work on autopilot to organize our experiences into meaningful percepts.

I first became aware of this phenomenon in my psychotherapy practice. Patients who had established a stable and positive relationship with me would emerge from an isolated session feeling I was unattuned to them, and then they would return to the next session dressed in clothes that were obviously and uncharacteristically mismatched, like striped pants and a plaid shirt or two different-colored socks. When I observed similar phenomena in the investment world, the analogy was clear, except that the sudden loss or disruption for investors interfered with their capacity to make sound decisions with their investments rather than their clothes.

For those investors, the loss interfered with their capacity to understand and act on the usual market signals. Their self-organizing capacity, while usually automatic, was temporarily disrupted. As one investor commented after he lost a significant amount of money at the beginning of the 2000 crash, "Right after I was blindsided by the technology collapse, I found myself doing things, making decisions I never would have made under ordinary circumstances. I bought the next stock without even thinking about it. No due diligence, no research. It wasn't me." With his emotional equilibrium suddenly disrupted, he clearly had lost touch with the inner experiences that typically guided him intuitively to make sound buy and sell decisions.

COGNITIVE DISTORTIONS

Loss, or anxiety about loss, can affect our capacity to use our self as an observing instrument. The ability to observe data through our preconceived, unique, and familiar lenses provides the means for profitable investment decision-making. It determines which data we think important and how we choose to explain the selected data. When fear of loss disrupts this intuitive cognitive style, it leaves us without a framework to structure observations, resulting in severe doubt about our subjectively perceived truths. It is similar to the disorientation we may experience when alone on a deserted road at night with no sense of connection to our milieu and the people within it. Otherwise manageable fears can expand out of all proportion. This is why it becomes important for investors, in the face of loss, to have others with whom they can discuss their market decisions. The connectedness with like others restores our disrupted sense of self so that perceived data can be metabolized in a more normal way.

SELLING, ASSERTION, AND LOSS

Selling requires an assertive decisiveness cultivated by most successful investors. There are many people, however, who have grown up in an atmosphere where assertiveness was off-putting to their parents. Instead of welcoming assertiveness, their parents withdrew slightly or reacted negatively. Children raised in that type of environment are left feeling that assertiveness, including attempts to express independent ideas, carries a destructive potential for loss and disconnectedness from needed others. Transposed into the investment business, this common syndrome creates continual internal conflict over selling because the investor experiences a sense of danger and potential loss each time a sell decision (assertiveness) is imminent. It also encourages investors to place undue emphasis on compliance with others' needs. The combination of these factors fosters both herd mentality and emotional turmoil whenever they sell a stock. Most investors do not consciously experience this sequence; rather they feel anxious and attempt to find ways to eliminate it. But an understanding of the connection between assertiveness and fear of loss often helps to circumvent the behavioral problems associated with selling.

Consider Jamie, a generally successful investor who became puzzled about her inability, at certain times, to sell stock when her investment-club friends advised her against selling her holdings. In Jamie's words, "I usually don't have trouble selling, but I began to realize it's a problem when I'm the only one who thinks I should sell. Then I feel like if I go against the group consensus I'll somehow alienate people in the club. I know I'm right, but I just can't bring myself to click the mouse. And invariably it turns out my instincts are proven accurate."

Jamie grew up in a family that prized consensus. And although her parents paid lip service to the importance of Jamie's developing her own opinions, she sensed they pulled back and distanced themselves whenever she expressed a strong independent opinion. Through the years, Jamie learned on an unconscious level that it was emotionally dangerous to assert herself. Without realizing it, this emotional conviction permeated her investment decisions whenever she tried to assume a contrarian stance. After becoming familiar with this pattern, however, Jamie became progressively able to monitor her responses to her investment partners. She learned to recognize the extraneous source of her conflict with consensus sell decisions. Realizing it had no bearing on her analytic capacities, she became more comfortable acting on her beliefs.

SELLING LOSERS AND
ANALYZING WHAT HAPPENED

There are times when no matter what you do, at least one of your stocks will be a big loser. What matters most at this juncture is that you maintain your emotional equilibrium. In a well-diversified portfolio, a few losses are to be expected, and they will not undermine the increasing value of your overall holdings. The greatest value that comes from losses is the chance to review exactly what you did and what went wrong. Was it predictable? Was it inevitable, or did you overlook something? Do you have other holdings where the same situation might develop? Was the mistake a psychological one or a flaw in financial analysis? Asking these types of questions is the best protection against future losses. Too many investors fail to analyze what happened and merely want to forget the situation and move on. Continual postmortems and self-analysis following any selling in the investing process is as important as it is in examining the dissolution of interpersonal relationships.

There also are many psychological reasons, both positive and negative, for selling stocks that transcend the idiosyncratic problems connected with loss. When you write about the market, everybody asks you about when to buy and sell stocks: "What do you think of EMC down here? Will it go any lower? Should I sell it?" "How about Oracle? Now that it's been downgraded and lost a few points, is it time to get out?" "Will IBM be a good turnaround play like it was the last time it tanked, or should I cut my losses?" "Could you check out Bitstream for me and get back to me in an hour or so? I heard from a reliable source that they have some good sales coming this year, but I've held it so long, I just want to get rid of it." "I noticed that Trico Bancshares has gone from $14.50 to $23. It's up almost 60 percent. Time to sell?"

There are several interesting assumptions in these questions. The first one is that I, or any investor, has a good grasp of nine thousand stocks and can offer an informed opinion on any one of them at any time. Patently false. Most investors follow relatively few stocks closely enough to have any strong or informed opinions. EMC's a great company with superior management. It's got some problems and some potentially difficult competition in the storage market. That's about as far as my knowledge of EMC goes. I haven't read their SEC filings or analyst-research reports on the company. Oracle? Another interesting company that a lot of folks think is undervalued. Probably the best of the database management and business-systems companies. Do I have a detailed understanding of their business model or their financials? No way.

Could I check out Bitstream for you? Sure, but not in the next hour. It's difficult to read and digest a company's full annual report and most recent quarterly reports, check out some research reports, talk to the company's management (or, more likely for a large-cap company, their investor-relations staff), and watch how their stock trades all in a week, to say nothing of an hour. A number of years ago, when I consulted at one mutual fund, their buy-side analysts used to take a couple of months to develop their five-year models on the new companies they followed. So I can't tell you whether to sell Bitstream. As for Trico Bancshares? A friend recommended it to me at $15. I wish I had researched it and bought it because it's nearly doubled since then. But I didn't, and I don't have a clue if you should be selling or buying.

If you asked me about some companies I follow, like Aura Systems, Zi-Corp, SFBC International, SureBeam, The Titan Corporation, Tag-It Pacific, Air Methods, Cubic, Gaiam, DRS Technologies, Educational Lending Group, Openwave, or Express Scripts, I could give you the nitty-gritty, probably more than you'd have time to listen to if you're in a hurry to buy or sell them. But that's because I've spent months studying them. So the first important rule when it comes to selling is almost a cliché, and it has more to do with common sense than psychology. You have to know something about your stocks; everybody who's an investor is more than willing to offer you their "sage" advice on when to sell your stocks, but their opinions are generally based on what they've read in the press and heard on television or from a friend who knows a friend who knows someone who works at the company. Invariably these sources will all lead to poor selling decisions.

The Real Basis for Selling Stocks. The mountain of requests I receive for stock information stimulated my curiosity about how investors actually decide to buy and sell stocks for their portfolios. So I began asking folks for the major criteria they used to make their sell decisions. This was not quantitative research using traditional methodologies; it was clinical research based on interviews with many investors from 1999 through 2001. Very few investors, in fact fewer than 5 percent of those I talked to, used fundamental research as a preferred tool. When asked why, nearly all of them said it took too much time and energy. Although they had access to the information, most readily admitted they didn't know how to judge that information, so they relied on other means for their decisions. And they were stock-pickers, not index-fund investors.

Recognition. An important variable in stock selection for nearly all the investors I interviewed was recognition of company names. A familiar name translated to a safe company with a history: "I know I can't go wrong with one of the solid, well-known companies. Bristol-Myers isn't going out of business anytime soon. Neither is IBM." Unfortunately Enron and K-Mart were also recognized names in this "can't go wrong with" category. The same phenomenon also occurred quite often to rationalize not selling: "IBM is a great company, and I know that buy and hold has worked for a lot of years, so why should I sell IBM just because of an earnings warning? It'll come back just like it always did. It's a great name." And so it is. But not always a great stock. As Don Cassidy pointed out in his excellent article on selling, "If you had bought the seven largest [well-recognized] U.S. computer companies in 1984 and not sold them for ten years, you would have lost money in all of them—in the leading industry and during a great bull market."[4]

In recently reported research, Gigerenzer postulated a recognition heuristic: "If one of two objects is recognized and the other is not, then infer that the recognized object has the higher value."[5] So for most investors, if I mentioned two hypothetical portfolio stocks, America Online and Rita Medical Systems, and asked which they would sell if they had to choose, they would pick RITA rather than AOL. When asked why, the answer was always some variation of "because I know it's a good company. I've never heard of RITA." At the time Rita Medical was significantly undervalued while AOL was grossly over-valued. But psychologically, a familiar name, in addition to providing a feeling of safety, also offers a mirroring confirmation that the investor knows something about the stock market. Because RITA had no recognition and therefore no meaning, investors were even re-luctant to ask for details. As one investor said, "I don't like to keep stocks that people haven't heard of. You're only supposed to invest in things know about." The problem, of course, was that beyond recog-nition, most of these investors knew nothing about *either* company.

Affect. A second variable important to stock selection and selling is the investor's emotional associations to a specific company, which can often be strongly negative or positive. When I asked investors to choose between Philip Morris and Yahoo! to sell from a hypothetical portfolio, invariably they chose Philip Morris. Tobacco companies often evoked strong negative affect: "I would never even buy Philip Morris. I have such bad feelings about their hiding all that medical evi-dence." Technology companies often evoked very positive affect: "Yahoo! is such a great company. It just came from nowhere and cap-tured the market. It's the only place I check stock prices. That's why I bought the stock, and that's why I wouldn't sell it."

In an interesting study conducted by Donald MacGregor and col-leagues in which investors responded to industry groups with images, associations, and affects, MacGregor concluded that "affect and imagery appear to have a strong influence on judgments of the quality of financial stimuli, particularly under conditions where specific, indi-viduating information about a particular company or firm is absent."[6] What I am finding from my own research is that even where informa-tion on a particular company is readily available, affect and imagery play an important role in buy and sell decisions. For retail investors, warm, fuzzy feelings about a company or management often play a more important role in holding on to stocks than time-consuming research into fundamentals. This applies even though these same investors will admit, at least privately, that they know they should "not be selling stocks on the basis of feelings about the company." Although a premise of this book is that emotions can play a very constructive role in successful stock picking and selling, the converse applies in the absence of sophisticated self-knowledge.

Noise. Perhaps not surprisingly, investors frequently sell stocks on the basis of noise, a term coined by Fischer Black to describe information that was useless static rather than information relevant to the fundamentals of a company.[7] Classic examples of noise trading are decisions based on television, Internet, or print media sell recommendations: "I sold Worldcom because I heard some guy on CNBC saying it was a sell. They wouldn't have had him on if he wasn't a reputable analyst." Or how about an investor who confided that he sold his stock based on a brief streaming video of a financial reporter on the Internet. As Jeremy said, "After I saw that, I thought I better get rid of the stock." I then asked him what the commentator had said. Here's an excerpt:

> We're forty-eight hours into the brand-new world of incomplete 10-Qs that nobody cares about. What's the point of filing a 10-Q if half the pages are missing from it? No one seems to care. We're speaking of course of . . . There's been a lot of controversy about that stock; a fair amount of it was stirred up by us in a column we wrote saying just to read the plain meaning of the public record, and it looks like these people were selling their products to their own vice-president of marketing and never declaring the related party transactions in their financial filing. . . . Well, anyway, they've now filed their 10-Q, and it's missing . . . the four key pages. I didn't see anything this morning indicating they filed an amended one; maybe they have, or maybe I just haven't caught up with it yet. But something's going on because as we talk the stock is off $0.80. That's down nearly 15 percent. . . .

The question isn't whether the Internet report was accurate. As it turned out, there was a technology glitch on Edgar, the electronic database for all SEC filings, rather than a failure to file the proper disclosure. But even if the Internet report had been accurate, why was it being used as a basis for an investment decision without further research? My sense from interviewing the investor and many more like him is that our new age of instantaneous electronic communication has made noise the medium that carries the messages to the herd. And because noise is more accessible than direct company information—and far louder—investors tend to pay more attention to it. Adding injury to insult, the noise is also mutually reinforced by the groupthink that mobilizes so quickly in electronic spaces.

Analyst Recommendations. Investors report strong biases toward blindly acting on analysts' recommendations. During the Internet bubble, Mary Meeker and Henry Blodget became folk heroes, with investors hanging on their every word: "I bought all those technology stocks because those guys said to; I thought they had figured out a new way to value technology companies, and I never questioned it. They never told me to sell, so I just thought the stocks would keep going up." The Street would have us believe their estimates are high or low by no more than 5 percent. This, of course, is a near impossibility in real life. The realities of analysts' estimates are undoubtedly much closer to the nightmare uncovered by David Dreman's research, which has painstakingly pointed out how analysts' estimates have historically been way off the mark.[8] In fact his research shows that in the final eight years of a study encompassing some 500,000 estimates by professional analysts, the average error was *50 percent.*

So why does everyone expect analysts or other market forecasters to be accurate? In part because the need to look up to expert others as a source of power, knowledge, competence, and organization is built into the human condition. The need for heroes remains a part of our psyche until we begin to assume more personal responsibility for our actions, including our investment decisions. Until then these heroes will shine as beacons of investment insight despite our understanding, at least intellectually, that it is impossible for them to be precisely correct in their earnings forecasts, and, until the investment industry changes the underlying foundations of their business, it is unrealistic to expect them to sacrifice investment-banking priorities and biases in favor of individual investors' best interests.

Intuition. Many of the investors I interviewed relied on their intuition to sell stocks: "I just got a gut feeling this company wasn't going to succeed after all. I can't tell you exactly why, but I'm usually right when I follow my hunches." Depending on the constituents of our intuition, some of us can be very right for periods of time using nothing but our unconscious intellectual attributes (intuition). Most of the time, however, pure intuition will carry us only so far. Intuition is too often based on idiosyncratic organizing lenses that we use to filter information emanating from the market. When we are not aware of the biases shaping these lenses, rosy colors or dark colors can distort our decisions while making them feel absolutely sound. This problem is compounded by the tendency we all share to some degree to feel overconfident in our instincts, which adds a definitiveness to gut feelings at just the times we should impose a healthy skepticism on our intuitive judgments.

Result. If more than 50 percent of households own stock and most investors are making important sell decisions based on a combination of recognition, affect, noise, hero-worship, and intuition, we are likely to see increasing amounts of volatility in the markets. This can become a vicious cycle, since the strongest external factor that motivates misguided selling is high market volatility. This syndrome is fueled by the phenomenon that selling based on emotions requires continual changes in investment decisions. The only silver lining is a built-in circuit breaker in this phenomenon: As market volatility and emotion-driven selling increases, so does the likelihood of greater discrepancies between intrinsic value and stock prices. Ultimately this will lead to demand for undervalued stocks. It will also give investors who take the time to perform fundamental analysis a strong competitive advantage in the market.

CASE EXAMPLE

Before concluding with some guidelines for selling, let's consider a case example. While selling under stress is a complex subject that defies simple answers, this case may help illustrate how to deal with some of the difficulties created by psychological factors in making sell decisions.

The Fundamentals. I once recommended Infrasonics (IFRA), a company that manufactures and markets respirators. My research indicated that it was a technological leader in respiratory care, a $3-billion industry that was continuing to grow. Its competitors were still selling ventilators with outdated technology, and most of the ventilators in the field were well past their normal life expectancy. IFRA was spending significantly more money on research and development than its competitors, so it could be expected to maintain its technological lead. It was working on a ventilator that could revolutionize the industry by automatically adjusting itself to patients' real-time blood gas levels. Financially it had $5 million in the bank, $18 million in working capital, and $26 million in stockholders' equity. It also had solid management. CEO Jim Hitchen, who had a background in physics, brought the company from nowhere to $0.19 per share and had steered new products through the Food and Drug Administration at a fast and steady pace, nearly one every fourteen months throughout his tenure.

After a difficult couple of years when the stock went from $12 to the $2 level, the company was projecting significant profitability during fiscal 1995 and approximately $0.02 for the quarter ended December 31, 1994. Two weeks after my final contact with management, the company reported its quarterly results, with an unexpected net loss of $0.10 per share due to decreased margins on essentially flat sales.

How could this happen to a company with superb management and an innovative product line? How could management not have predicted a loss for the quarter, and why couldn't I see it coming? I spoke with Hitchen following this unexpected reversal of fortune. He was quite candid about the situation. In November 1994 the company trained all of their European staff; in December they trained their U.S. staff and participated in a trade show. All expenses for these events were straight-line budgeted and spread over twelve months. When the auditors came in during January, however, they took the position that all these expenses should be booked in the fourth quarter, resulting in a large SG&A (selling, general, and administrative) spike for the quarter.

The CEO also cited another unanticipated development adding to the poor quarter. In fall 1994 Infrasonics received two large orders worth approximately $663,000 from the Mexican government for the company's adult ventilator. In December the Mexicans requested that the company speed up their order and deliver it ahead of schedule. Infrasonics decided that using their higher priced inventory and reconfiguring all the machines to function in Mexico would be worth the extra cost by forging a more secure relationship with Mexico. The decision was clearly harmful in the near term, since the extra costs killed their gross margin. It also made the company look inept because costs don't get rolled up until the end of each month. When the figures started coming in during the first and second week in January for the month of December, the costs were a shocker. As Hitchen said, "I just wasn't aware of the rework expenses." Obviously I had to wonder where the CFO was during December.

My follow-up had made it clear that the combination of surprising high costs of sales on the Mexican order and the unforeseen need to record all the training expenses in the quarter had led to the unexpected loss. In the meantime, a preliminary press release had already been prepared announcing the profit that would have been realized for the quarter in the absence of these developments. Management was now in possession of inside information that they did not feel comfortable sharing with investors until the actual results were publicly released.

The Issues. When company expectations unravel quickly, we're left in a vacuum without a map or compass to guide our investment decision. The situation reminds me of Warren Buffett's story of "the fellow who applied for a job and stated he had twenty years of experience—which was corrected by the former employer to read 'one year's experience—twenty times'"[9] The humorous comment is important because it suggests the complexity investors confront when trying to decide whether to remain with a company experiencing difficulties. There are a number of guidelines I use for making these decisions, and while it would be next to impossible to prioritize them, as a whole they do provide a working map of the selling terrain.

• When trouble occurs, is management willing to discuss openly and candidly what happened? Many CEOs enjoy talking to shareholders and the investment community when things are going well but seem to disappear into the woodwork when the inevitable failures and disappointments occur. How management reacts to unexpected adversities or poor judgments can be an important signal to the investor. A small-cap CEO and senior executive of a large company should be willing to accept calls from brokers or shareholders, explain what happened, assume responsibility for mistakes, and have a reasonable plan to correct or at least address the situation. Any company whose management attempts to dissemble bad news and avoid personal responsibility should be immediately sold. Infrasonics received high grades in this area. Management was honest and open with me and the public while acknowledging its responsibility. Because the SEC's Fair Disclosure rules, which took effect in October 2000, prevent management from selectively disclosing material nonpublic information, most companies now provide a forum for discussing quarterly results through phone-conferencing facilities. Any investor can listen in and participate in the Q&A segment.

• Is the company's product or service continuing to fill a niche in the market? A poor quarter is usually overdetermined; it has multiple causes. A slowing economy, accounting adjustments, accruals or non-recurring write-offs, acquisitions, and share dilution all can affect the bottom line. Even long-term investors are sensitive to quarterly results that can signal trends. To remain invested in the company, we need some indication that an unexpected shortfall or adverse event is not presaging a decline in demand for the company's services or products or other threat to the company's prospects. For Infrasonics to reverse the impact of their significant quarterly loss, their sales would have to grow at a rapid enough rate to reflect healthy market demand on a consistent basis. Whether a slowing economy would prevent hospitals from purchasing new ventilators at all or merely delay their purchases for one more year remained an open question.

• Will the company's profit margins rebound from their temporary difficulties? Even if strong demand for a product or service continues, voluminous sales will mean nothing if profits do not increase commensurately. Infrasonic's margins decreased due to the high cost of sales involved with the Mexican order and the recognition of training costs during one quarter rather than twelve months. These had all the makings of nonrecurring events. If so, profit margins during the next six months could be expected to normalize.

• Has the company adequately explained the reversal of fortune and taken appropriate steps to address it? How long will this take to accomplish? Infrasonics had been attempting to grow sales quickly, emphasizing the top line while assuming the bottom line would take care of itself. In other words, management assumed that emphasizing research and development, sales, and market expansion would eventually lead to an increase in the bottom line. After a disappointing quarterly loss, management was reconsidering this philosophy. Instead of quadrupling the sales force, they were considering just tripling it; they were reconsidering spending 10 percent of the budget on R&D. Their reevaluation seemed to reflect an appreciation for the practical requirements of producing profits consistently. Rather than looking at costs monthly, all orders and gross margins were being monitored daily.

While I was encouraged that changes were being made, I still had concerns about the timing, which I could clarify only after hearing management's outlook for the coming quarters. Like many things in life, timing is important. It's important in evaluating stock sales because investors tend to overreact to bad news. In some situations, that may require selling at the first signs of trouble and, ideally, jumping back in before a rebound to take advantage of this pricing inefficiency.

• Is management taking steps to show its confidence in the value of the company? The investment community definitely gets that message from reported events such as adoption of a stock repurchase program (for the right reasons), exercise of outstanding stock options by management, and absence of significant insider selling. Any of these positive indications should generally contribute to a decision not to sell. At the time that Infrasonics announced its quarterly loss, I had no answers on these questions from the company.

• Will the company need additional financing to execute its business plan? Obviously we would prefer no need for additional financing to resume growth, particularly debt financing, which can strap earnings mercilessly if a company becomes overleveraged. And while equity financing is neutral for overall earnings, it can be dilutive to earnings per share, particularly if new shares are issued privately at a discount to an already-depressed market price. A quarter of poor earnings followed by stock dilution only pushes the resumption of a positive bottom line further into the future. To my knowledge, Infrasonics was not planning an equity infusion at the time, nor was it expecting to take on significant debt to fund its expansion initiatives.

• Are the short-sellers out of the stock? My experience, which is contrary to popular belief, suggests that stock prices of companies in difficulty generally do not begin to turn around until the short-sellers begin covering their positions. But maybe I'm missing something, since most of the financial commentators argue that companies with a large short position are good buys because the shorts must eventually cover. "Eventually" can take a very long time, but it was academic with Infrasonics, which had no significant short position.

• Are the reasons you bought the stock in the first place still sound? Remember that list I recommended you make whenever you buy a stock, summarizing all your reasons for the investment? Before selling the stock, take a good look at that list. If nothing fundamental has changed and the listed points still apply, it may be time to test the courage of your initial convictions. If the list is out of date, the updating process may clarify your selling decision.

Although not all-inclusive, these questions offer you a beginning outline for assessing a sell decision in the wake of bad news. My decision on Infrasonics at the time, after analyzing the financials and thinking these questions through, was to sell the stock. It was a difficult decision. The deciding factor was my assessment of the timing issue rather than any questions about the quality of management or the company's product. It appeared that it would take longer than others were suggesting for the company to get back on track. Infrasonics was bought out shortly thereafter, but at a price significantly below my original recommendation.

GUIDELINES FOR SELLING

You can avoid some of the difficulty in making selling decisions by remembering that, for most investors most of the time, the right answer to the question "When should I sell?" is ideally "As rarely as possible." Why? Because every sales triggers brokerage fees and potential tax consequences (outside of IRAs and similar tax-deferral vehicles) as well as reinvestment costs and risks. Transaction costs and any resulting taxes will lower your portfolio profits, and the investment of sale proceeds will tax at least your time and possibly your overall returns. This sentiment is common among long-term investors, but its impact has real meaning only if we look at the underlying assumptions. If you invest $10,000 in a stock for twenty-five years and it appreciates at 15 percent per year, at the end of twenty-five years you will have a stock worth $329,190, without regard to any dividends. You will then have to pay taxes, let's assume 20 percent on the long-term gain, which will leave you with $263,352, or 13.98 percent per-year growth. Now let's assume that you invested the same $10,000 but sold your holding each year, reinvesting in stocks that also appreciated at 15 percent per year. You now owe 35 percent of the $1,500 you made in the first year, which leaves you with a $975.00 gain. You're now averaging 9.75 percent per year for twenty-five years, which leaves you with $102,356 at the end of twenty-five years. The difference is astounding.

When Express Scripts fell from $30 to $20 on rumors about the impact of Clinton's health-care package on the pharmaceutical industry and a rumored sale of a large block of shares by one insider who needed the money, investors could have sold out with more than a 50 percent gain. They would have missed a 200 percent gain from the stock's rebound. They would also have avoided the taxes and commissions from the ill-advised sale or the additional brokerage fees to buy back in at a higher price.

In a perfect world, if you have been careful in your selection of companies to invest in and are investing for the long term, the turnover in your portfolio should remain low. More profits are lost by not allowing your companies to grow over a period of at least several years than are won by impulsive selling whenever the crowd overreacts to company news. It is also true, however, that we don't live in a perfect world. Companies make mistakes, we sometimes need extra cash, and exciting new investments continually entice us with promises of wealth. So we need some guidelines to complement our psychological understanding of our selling impulses.

• First, you should always have *a basic understanding of why you bought the company*. And I say *company* rather than *stock* because too often investors forget that in purchasing shares they own part of the company. As a long-term investor, "making money" is not a good enough reason to buy; if you would not want to be an owner of Xco, there is very little rationale for purchasing the stock. Similarly when the reason you bought the stock (good management, proprietary technology, little competition, safe product, earnings momentum) changes, you should consider selling. Unlike many advisers, I do not believe that you should have a selling plan ahead of time. For example, to say I'll sell when the stock appreciates 20 percent typically deprives you of a careful analysis of the company after it has grown 20 percent. By the same token, to sell a fundamentally sound company arbitarily because it drops 7 percent below your buy price often leads to taking many unnecessary losses. Systems are for professional traders. Instead of relying on computer-generated buy and sell signals, you should take advantage of a unique asset—your own careful analysis.

• If you are buying growth stocks for capital appreciation, particularly small-growth stocks, *it is a good idea to sell if institutions (banks, insurance companies, pension plans) acquire more than 50 percent of the shares*. At this point they are in control of trading large blocks of stock, and the individual investor loses an edge in the competition. If you own large stocks such as Pepsi or AT&T, you don't need to worry about institutional ownership unless it disappears.

• Consider selling when *the financial health of the company deteriorates for two quarters in a row*. Sales, earnings, and profit margins are what drive stock prices up. If you see these figures trending downward over several periods, consider selling unless management provides a convincing explanation why the downturn is aberrational. One period of poor earnings in an upward trend is typically not reason enough to sell. In addition a poor earnings report in a volatile market environment will generally send the stock spiraling downward before you can get out. Don't panic. You don't want to be selling just when the crowd is overreacting. And while it is true that one surprise often is not the last, prices usually bounce back a bit after a sell-off, so you still have time to investigate before making a decision. While you should always sell in the face of unexpected disaster (failed technology or regulatory problems), one poor quarter is not necessarily a disaster, and it often provides a good buying opportunity.

• Earnings and sales figures can often be manipulated by creative accounting procedures. What can't be manipulated as easily is the amount of cash the company maintains and generates. Although dishonest management can manipulate this indicator before year-end audits, and there is always the possibility of an Enron-style meltdown, distortion of a company's cash position and cash flows is generally a remote risk, particularly for investors holding a well-diversified portfolio. You can assess this indicator in two different ways. If your company pays a dividend regularly, any decrease in the dividend should be a warning signal that the company is encountering difficulty. Reported earnings may be increasing, but the failure to generate enough cash to maintain historic dividends should make you worry. If you own a small company that does not pay dividends (and most small companies either cannot or do not because they have no earnings or reinvest them to fund their growth initiatives), looking at how much cash it maintains and how much cash flow is being generated by current operations will tell you if it has the resources and capacity to overcome any temporary setback. If the internally generated cash flow is trending downward, you should think about selling.

• You should always investigate the reasons behind *a large buildup of inventory* with an eye toward selling. Unusual accumulation of products is often the first warning sign of a company's ensuing sales and earning problems. Comparing inventories on the balance sheet in your company's quarterly reports is a quick way to sense the trend. You may find that temporary inventory gluts have explainable reasons. If not, head for the exits.

• While you are looking at figures, *be sure to check the long-term debt to equity ratio* of your company. It should not be carrying more than 25 percent of debt relative to the stockholders' equity (total assets minus total liabilities), except in unusual cases such as industries that require high debt levels to operate effectively. In addition the company's current assets should remain approximately 1.5 to 2 times current liabilities to ensure enough working capital. Beware, however, of companies with too much working capital that is not being used efficiently.

• Consider selling *if your company begins to diversify into business sectors where it has no experience*. Peter Lynch calls this "diworsification." Most companies know most about their core business, and attempts to grow by acquiring other unrelated businesses typically fail unless accompanied by an experienced management team that can coexist with existing management.

• If you discover that management is selling significant numbers of shares *(insider sales)*, you should take this as a warning signal warranting further investigation. Insiders are among the most knowledgeable investors within a company. Sales can occur for many reasons, such as college tuition or unexpected cash needs, and they are usually not nearly as important as insider buying. But if the president, CEO, or other senior executives of your company sell more than 100,000 shares or 10 percent of their holdings, you can almost always assume that something is up, and it is usually not good. The smaller the company you own, the more important you should view any insider sales.

• A *significant change in management*, a new CEO or president, or a change in focus of the company from its purpose when you first bought it are reasons to consider selling. You can gather this information easily by reading the annual and quarterly reports. These are generally sent to you automatically if you own the stock. While the glossy pages are often fluff, the CEO's letter is important in giving you a sense of whether the company's mission remains the same from year to year. And the MD&A (management's discussion and analysis) section, while often tedious, can be portentous.

• Finally you should review the qualitative changes within your companies' industries. These include the consumer appeal of new products, competition, and service and technology trends within the culture.

SEVEN

Talking with Management

Informed investing requires careful study of a company's financial data, an understanding of products and services, industry trends, and market psychology, a little luck, enormous patience, independent thinking, and helpful contacts. While most of us would agree with this formula, few of us have the background or contacts to compete with the professional analysts who cover a particular industry or sector. When other constraints of time and energy are added to the mix, it should not surprise us if the meticulous personal research required to practice what the formula preaches takes a back seat to newspaper or magazine articles, television talking heads, analysts' reports, hot tips, and recommendations from friends. As a result, despite the opportunity to spend weeks accumulating data from the Internet about our companies, most investors are much more likely to invest $5,000 on a "can't lose" speculation overheard by a "helpful contact" at a cocktail party or to bail out when the pundits panic.

To avoid the pitfalls from this path of least resistance, let's go back to the formula. Years of experimentation with its components have led me to conclude that contacts are key, and the most useful, knowledgeable contacts are typically senior management of the companies we're evaluating. These insiders have more information about their companies than any outside analyst or annual report can possibly convey. But they are also among the sources most underutilized by individual investors. To make the most of this resource, I have developed a model for gaining a competitive edge through the management interview process. It's based on tools to increase our understanding of the psychological processes involved in interviewing management. This is particularly important if David Dreman is correct in suggesting that analysts' earnings forecasts, typically based on interpretation of hard data rather than application of basic human psychology, are highly inaccurate. While analysts have more information available than ever before, what they seem to lack is any psychological system for assessing management and discerning the messages underlying management's statements about their companies. If they were able to glean more from their interviews with management, I suspect their forecasting errors might be reduced.

Now that the SEC has passed Fair Disclosure rules known as Regulation FD, designed to equalize access to corporate information, more individual investors are participating in analyst conference calls. These are quarterly presentations by management, followed by Q&As, on the current state and prospects of their companies. Regulation FD prohibits selective disclosure of material nonpublic information, so we cannot expect to get any earth-shattering information from these calls or from separate interviews with management. But that doesn't matter. They both provide opportunities to read between the lines and assess management's ability to do their job. Some of the following psychological tools may be useful in doing your job to stay informed about your investments and maximize your return.

If you're not a professional analyst, you're probably wondering why I would try to arm my readers with interviewing tools and encourage investor interaction with self-important CEO millionaires who are unlikely to return calls from investors they don't know from Adam. Contrary to popular belief, while you may have trouble contacting the CEO at AT&T, you can speak with investor relations personnel, and you might be surprised at the access afforded these days by executives at small-cap companies. They tend to be highly sensitive to the importance of good grades for investor relations and may be quite willing to talk with you. It may even be possible to develop a personal relationship with management over time. But that will depend on you and your interactive skills.

In every interaction with management, we bring an idiosyncratic history (personal and sometimes professional) that influences how we elicit and interpret both hard and soft corporate information. Of course, management also comes to the interaction with their own unique ways of viewing their company's numbers and prospects, as well as members of the investment community. This means that a single model that applies to how all of us should go about the interview process is probably not realistic. It doesn't mean we can't develop a model for thinking about the psychological phenomena that occur during the process, adapt that model to our interviewing style, and use it to gain insights we might otherwise miss.

MANAGEMENT IS HUMAN

Let's begin with the concession that senior corporate executives are human, even though we're likely to lose sight of this when our stock in their companies takes a nose dive. But that's the first mistake, because management shares the same needs as you and I. Just like us, a CEO needs to develop, organize, and maintain his or her sense of self. Job and investor pressures may heighten that central, motivating need. Despite all the abstractions and ambiguities in the concept of self, when our sense of self is functioning well, as I pointed out in Chapter Two, we know it with certainty and clarity. We experience a sense of wholeness, togetherness, vitality, and inner solidity. Our self-esteem remains consistent in the face of the bumps and bruises of everyday life. When our sense of self is strong, we experience ourselves as independent, worthwhile, and capable of enthusiastically pursuing our ambitions and ideals. When our self-esteem slips, however, we often feel slightly anxious, depleted, and unenthusiastic and are more prone to feeling injured by others. We feel unsure of ourselves and are generally less capable of carrying out our ambitions and ideals. Our self-esteem acts as a barometer that gauges the integrity and vitality of our sense of self, and there is usually a place on the gauge that feels like home.

The most important thing to understand about a company's CEO or spokesman is that he feels the same emotions we do, and his self-esteem is affected by the same phenomena that affect ours. Just as our self-esteem as investors rises and falls with fickle moves of Mr. Market, CEOs judge their self-worth by how well their companies perform.

When a CEO makes a presentation, he is holding up his judgment, vision, ideals, and business acumen for validating or mirroring confirmation from the investment community. And protestations notwithstanding, the reaction to that presentation does affect a CEO's sense of self. The CEO is putting his life and career on the line at a certain level. He yearns for affirmation that his ideas are worth listening to. More important, the response to his presentation does affect what he consciously or unwittingly communicates to us.

The psychological phenomenon of *idealizing* also plays a role in the lives of CEOs. Idealizing refers to the experience of security evoked when we are allowed to share in the knowledge, power, calmness, organization, and ideals of others. This process plays out on both sides of the analyst–management dialogue. In searching out companies, we tend to idealize (or devalue) particular management and technologies. Management idealizes their company's services, products, and prospects, clandestinely longing to be worthy of those investors (professional and amateur) they respect.

Partnering also plays a role. This refers to experiencing the sustaining effect of human sameness—a sense of we-ness that fosters a feeling of belonging to an important group that shares the use of similar tools, skills, or beliefs. Management has a strong need for their audience to think like they do, and they often feel confused, angry, and hurt on a personal level when the investment community's perceptions of the company differ from theirs.

Efficacy is a person's need to experience himself as having an impact on someone or something. In trying to convince an analyst or investor that his company presents a superior investment opportunity, executives derive a heightened sense of self-esteem from the experience of efficacy. In fact whenever we have succeeded in some difficult bodily or mental task, such as exercising our analytic skills, we derive a sense of efficacy. The CFO who finds a way to save his company money or the CEO who formulates a particularly innovative vision derives a sense of efficacy from being perceived as having an impact on the company's future.

WHY IS THE PSYCHOLOGY
OF MANAGEMENT IMPORTANT?

This overview of the CEO's psychological needs is important because

1. Knowledge of these needs can help us structure initial relationships with management.
2. These psychological forces form the basis for long-term relationships between management and investors.
3. Understanding these needs will help us deal with management's resistance or stonewalling.
4. Once these needs are recognized and addressed, you're more likely than the competition to elicit useful information.

This last point is the key. Once you have unlocked the way managers feel and think when they discuss their companies with investors, you will know how to assess what they say. You will also have a better chance of discerning the underlying meaning of their rhetoric. One thing you won't be able to do, given the new Fair Disclosure regulations, is persuade managers to reveal material nonpublic information or "news" on the company in private conversations. You shouldn't even try. But you may be able to discover emotional messages that give you a critical edge over your fellow investors and the analysts who follow the company.

COLLECTING SUBJECTIVE DATA

How do we figure out a manager's psychological needs? When we accumulate data about the financial aspects of a company, we immerse ourselves in 10-Ks and 10-Qs; when we accumulate subjective data, we immerse ourselves in the emotional nuances of management's communications. This enables us to collect a unique kind of data to supplement the more quantitative facts in our research endeavors.

It is important to remember that part of management's job is to let you read them. When we become skilled in collecting this more subjective data, we often know what management is going to do before management does—a kind of legal inside information.

Empathy is the tool used to collect this data. Empathy has a triple function. It's not only a methodology for collecting data, but also a sustaining activity that shores up the self-esteem of the data provider as well as a means of creating a powerful bond between manager and interviewer.

As a tool for collecting data, empathy refers to the "capacity to feel or think our way into another's inner life and view the world from that person's subjective vantage point."[1] In this sense empathy does not mean sympathy, support, or kindness. In fact empathy can be used for inimical purposes. (A used-car salesman can tune into customers' needs and wishes and develop the ability to sell on the basis of making the customer feel those needs and desires are understood regardless of whether the product is needed.) Nor does it mean trying to figure out how *you* would feel if *you* were that CEO. Empathy means "becoming the subject rather than the object" of management's feelings or intent.[2] In other words, you try to feel what management might feel at any given moment. Using empathy you can put yourself in the manager's place and decipher what *he or she* will feel and do when confronted with new events.

For example, CEO Jones is telling the public that his company's normalized growth rate is 10 percent per year. My model says it's 8 percent per year. Instead of putting him on the defensive to explain this discrepancy (which may be a perfectly reasonable action), an empathic approach would be to first ask myself, *What is it like for Jones to be telling me something that he knows is contradicting my figures?* Is he afraid of our questions? Does he want to show us up? Is he testing us, or is he telling us we're missing something?

Feeling my way into Jones's world, I get a sense of his self-confidence; he's clearly proud of his statement. I continue to wonder how he can expect to grow at 10 percent when his software division can bring in only X dollars. But what I would say empathically addresses the state of Jones's self, his pride and confidence. Addressing that state, I said, "I feel as though I should be congratulating you. You're obviously pulling something off that's going to surprise people." If my empathy is accurate, I will generally elicit more information than if I had originally challenged him by saying, "I don't see how you can grow at 10 percent when . . ." Jones smiled and confidently said, "Sorry, I can't talk about it." My attempt was not to elicit non-public information but rather to gauge his confidence. My antenna tells me that Jones believes his company will grow more rapidly than I expected.

The second function of empathy—to provide a self-sustaining experience for management—is a byproduct of trying to see the world through another person's eyes. If our attempts to feel and think our way into the subjective world of the CEO make him feel understood on some deeper level (as did CEO Jones), the cohesion of his self will be strengthened, self-esteem will increase, and he will experience an enhanced feeling of well-being. This should help to lower the usual defensive mechanisms. Through his relaxed attitude, he may give me clues that help me understand his company better.

Remember, empathy does not mean we are going to be sympathetic or kind; it won't keep us from asking the tough questions on a conference call. But it will allow us to do so in a way that elicits more candid and comprehensive answers. What we are really doing is trying to understand the emotions management is experiencing during our conversation. We are looking for the meaning that management's statement has for management rather than for us.

Because of this impact, empathy is the core of *meaningful engagement* in the world of investor detective work. This happens when an investor or financial analyst is able to perceive management's subjective experience and the executive perceives that someone understands him. When an interview becomes a meaningful engagement because an empathic connection is created, a number of interesting self-enhancing phenomena occur:

1. When management feels understood, it tends to feel invested in their story and motivated to tell you about it.
2. When management feels understood rather than criticized, it finds it much easier to verbalize embarrassing feelings, acknowledge mistakes, and expand on what was or will be done to correct them.
3. When management feels understood and appreciated, it's

encouraged to communicate more information with greater import.

RESISTANCE

When mirroring, idealizing, partnering, and efficacy needs are thwarted, usually because the interviewer failed to empathically address these needs, the failure will evoke resistance to the analyst or investor inquiries. When you encounter resistance or stonewalling, it doesn't necessarily mean you've zeroed in on a corporate soft spot. It's more likely that you've threatened injury to management's self-esteem.

I realize that a CEO's recalcitrance is instinctively assumed to mean he's covering a negative trend or hiding a looming problem. Forget that particular instinct. An empathic approach assumes that his resistance to talking with us is always motivated by fear of injury to his self-esteem. If the CEO on the other end of the telephone knows some damaging information, the reason for his stonewalling (in the absence of regulatory constraints) may not be only a reaction to questioning by a nonempathic investor; it may instead be the fear that his position and his self-esteem will be injured if the information gets out. But in either case, an empathic mode of observation and interviewing should elicit that possibility.[3]

Because resistance serves basic needs of the self, we expect that whenever managers anticipate criticism, they will become defensive. Some will go on the attack, others withdraw, and some will use denial. I remember talking with Alan, the CEO of a small company, two weeks before the end of a quarter. I wanted to see if he remained comfortable with the Street's earnings estimate of $0.04 per share for the quarter. He acknowledged that the estimates were still within his range of expectations. Several weeks later the company announced an unexpected $0.10 per share loss. Needless to say, I was upset and asked one of my colleagues, Sam, to call and find out what had happened. Sam returned telling me the CEO had gotten angry and essentially refused to talk with him. I queried him about the conversation, and Sam said he had confronted the CEO with the fact that he had told us he was comfortable with the Street's estimate and now there was a $.10 loss. Sam said it made us look foolish and demanded an explanation.

But the CEO only dug his heels in deeper. I decided to call the CEO and use a more empathic approach to collect my data. Here's how the first part of the conversation went:

DICK: Hi, Alan. It's Dick Geist.

ALAN: Hi, Dick. How are you?

DICK: Not real well given your earnings report, but I'm sure I feel better than you do.

Empathically recognize his state rather than challenge him.

ALAN: I think you probably do. I feel like people are throwing bricks at me—makes me feel like not talking to them at all.

I don't say, "So I noticed from the way you reacted to my colleague..."

DICK: People are pretty angry at the disappointing results?

ALAN: It's like I did this purposely to screw them. Hell, we didn't know 'til the last week. The four cents press release was already written when our auditors told us at the last minute we had to expense a bunch of things all in the same quarter.

Empathic response leads him to tell me more of what happened. I still felt there was more of a screwup than the unanticipated accounting treatment, but I decided to stay with his feelings.

DICK: So investors must have wondered how that could have happened without anyone knowing about it.

ALAN: I sure am wondering how it happened. I'm finding out,

I'm thinking, like where was your CFO

though, and you can be sure it will be fixed.

and where were you?

DICK: You mean, whose responsibility was it?

I wanted to know if he was willing to take responsibility.

ALAN: Yes, but ultimately it's mine.

Important information that he is willing to take the responsibility.

DICK: Sure, but I think people will stand behind you in the long run if you tell it like it is— even if they sell the stock now.

Idealizing.

ALAN: Well, that's what I'm hoping for. The other thing that's reflected in the loss is that our sales force just didn't do what I thought they could overseas. But I intend to fix that.

Here we see an important acknowledgment of his mistake in judgment, his willingness to accept responsibility for it, and his resolve to change it.

DICK: So, realistically, how long will it take to fix?

In this dialogue there is no resistance or stonewalling because Alan felt empathically understood. As a result I elicited the needed information, which was not so much factual as it was subjective. His willingness to take responsibility for the shortfall and acknowledge the company's mistakes while indicating a plan for fixing them provides a strong impetus to hold on to the stock for the long run. When interviewing management, he who initially asks pointed questions will get answers, but not much else. The most relevant information emerges when we create an atmosphere that helps the CEO to feel empathically understood.

The easiest way to gain a competitive edge over other investors in the market, particularly in the wake of reg FD, is by discovering this type of "soft" or subjective information about the companies you invest in. Chances are that few if any competitors made the right efforts to come up with it. To accomplish this you must have the courage of your convictions (or stupidity) and be willing to treat the interview as research in which, as Robert Noyce, Intel's founder, once said, "you may not always find what you were looking for, but you find something else equally important." This research process combines several elements, in addition to empathy, that we can separate only for the purposes of discussion.

ACTIVE OBSERVATION

Observation is a silent part of the interview process. I urge investors to pay attention to even small, seemingly unimportant details. Take in the tone, manner, and intonations of the managers. Pay attention to how they are dressed, what kind of environment they are creating, how their offices are set up—in other words, everything nonverbal about the interview. Watch body language, like rigid posture, clenched fists, laughing, blushing, restlessness, frequent glances at a watch or clock. Observe what subject matter is being discussed when this behavior occurs. Focus on whether management's manner is insular, charming, ingratiating, arrogant, or evasive. Try to envision thought processes—organized, scattered, clear, confused, words connected by emotion or logic. In isolation none of these observations necessarily provides anything tangible or definitive. But as the data begin to be integrated with other factors, these signals can generate hypotheses that can be tested and put to use later.

There's one other important prerequisite to honing your observation skills. Listen evocatively for answers to your questions. If ordinary listening is hearing concrete words, evocative listening is tuning in to the underlying meaning of what is said and organizing the meaning of the material around central themes. While listening evocatively, you avoid being a receptacle for numerous details that every other investor also possesses. Rather, based on your growing card catalog of experiences, try to capture the thread around which the interview is evolving. This type of listening may help you arrive at insights suddenly without being immediately aware of the thought processes that led to them. We don't know what sparks this intuitive insight, and we can't initiate the process deliberately. But it clearly is another overlooked avenue to knowledge, a creative sensing of relationships, meanings, and causal connections that should never be ignored or discounted.

In the mid-1990s I visited LifeUSA (Nasdaq: LUSA until it was bought by Allianz Insurance), a Minneapolis annuity company, and immediately noticed that CEO Bob MacDonald had no secretary. Although he shut the door when we were together, there were frequent knocks, and people seemed to float in and out freely, interrupting us and asking him questions and leaving. Obviously this could have meant the place was in chaos or it could have meant that the 147 employees had free access to the boss, which in turn could mean that he never got anything done or that he thrived on listening to new ideas. His office was full of plaques representing his hobbies, funny signs, pictures of family. I felt like I was in his home den. He maintained an imposing desk but preferred to sit and talk without any desk between us. As the hour proceeded, I found myself feeling more and more comfortable in this setting—relaxing, joking a bit, asking him more personal questions about his background and why the company was set up as it was. And I left feeling that this was the type of company that I would want to work for or do business with if I were searching for a job or insurance. Even though the numbers were poor that quarter, I came away with a belief that Bob could mobilize his forces to do exactly what he promised. I also sensed that I could call anytime and interrupt him with a question that would receive an honest response.

My first phone call to Bob following up on our meeting took me by surprise. The voice-mail greeting said, "Sorry, I can't take your call right now. I was called out unexpectedly to replace Jerry Garcia on a road trip. But leave a message, and as soon as I get off stage I'll return the call." Just the choice of Jerry Garcia confirmed my impression of a CEO who could comfortably buck the establishment and experiment with new ventures and novel ideas. In a dot-com company, I might have been suspicious, but in the insurance industry I thought this sort of offbeat creativity was unusual and innovative. Was this the kind of guy I wanted to trust with my money? The answer was a clear yes, even when every analyst covering LUSA lowered his ratings on the company.

As a private investor, you are entitled to talk with management and to observe them and their companies. It's worth it. These techniques may help you see beyond the current operating results and other hard data to discover what really makes the company work or struggle. They are the same techniques used consciously or intuitively by most good financial analysts. Using them in your own investing may help you distinguish opportunity from calamity.

EMPATHY AND ACTIVE OBSERVATION IN PRACTICE

How these interviewing elements come together in practice is illustrated in the following brief conversation with Steve, CEO of a company whose earnings release didn't come out on time—often a harbinger of severe trouble for a company.

DICK: Hi, Steve, it's Dick Geist.

STEVE: Hi, Dick.

Said warmly, relationship in place. Don't have to go further. If the relationship were not in place, developing it would take precedence over gathering information.

DICK: How are you, Steve?

Not just being polite. Listening to see if emotional tone matches verbal response.

STEVE: Good, thanks.

Emotions and verbalization coincided.

DICK: I was just calling to check on your earnings release.

Release was late.

STEVE: Yeah, you and everyone else. It'll be out Tuesday. I know it's caused people all kinds of nervousness. We usually try to do it in the month following the quarter.

A bit of irritation in his voice. Was I going to be critical like everyone else? I'm looking for potential resistance.

DICK: Lots of calls, huh? We both know how the investment community responds to late earnings releases.

Partnering response— I'm part of his team, not the enemy. Notice that no questions are asked here, for example, When are earnings coming out? I am more interested in reflecting back to him an understanding of what he is expressing.

STEVE: Sure do. We're waiting for a calculation from an insurance broker on a workers' comp refund that we wanted to book into the third quarter. We though we'd have it by now and we just didn't. I keep beating up on the guy, so I'm hoping for tomorrow. And John's out of town today, and I'm trying to get my own finance committee to meet to approve the release and do fourth-quarter projections. That's like herding calves because they're all over the world. I've given up on that so I'm going to deal with each individually. I hope to have numbers finalized tomorrow.

Feels we're together and explains the delay, and then conveys hectic nature of atmosphere and gives clue on how he deals with it.

Deals with chaos calmly, which is important in my evaluation of a CEO.

I really hope we can have it then because as you know we don't want to release things on a Friday We are telling everyone we're on course, though, although I don't know what the exact numbers are yet.

Sense of partnership here allows him to share information freely.

DICK: But we're not looking for any negative surprises?

First real question follows only after feeling that we have established a partnering connection.

STEVE: No, I would have let the investment community know ahead of time. You've been good to us. I wouldn't surprise you.

Confirmation of the relationship, as well as the regulatory landscape.

DICK: Thanks, I think everyone appreciates your openly sharing information with us, Steve.

Value his efforts—and the association is to prospects of more information.

STEVE: We're also working on several news releases.

Information is forthcoming.

DICK: I was just going to ask whether business continues to go well. Congratulations.

Again, I appreciate his efforts, which leads to more information.

STEVE: You saw the announcement that a second order was delivered in Europe? I was just blown away by the potential down there.

Affect is enthusiastic. We can explore more here.

DICK: How so?

STEVE: They're just terrific people.   *Potential here looks large*
       Kind of a loose confederation.   *from his tone.*
       We're doing a great job on
       marketing. My concern is that
       if this thing takes off they won't
       be able to handle the demand.

DICK: Do they know how to run   *Can this really work?*
       the software yet?

STEVE: Yes [*laughing*]. They've learned.   *The important message here*
       But I don't want to get ahead   *is the concern with promising*
       of ourselves. There's nothing   *something and not*
       worse than promising   *delivering. This gives me*
       something and not delivering   *insight into the quality of*
       on it.   *management not only on this*
                                            project, but going forward.

DICK: That's encouraging. What else?   *He's talking about what he's*
                                            encouraged about—wants to
                                            tell his story, and this is
                                            where we can pick up
                                            emotional nuances that
                                            others may miss.

STEVE: We're starting to get a lot of   *Implicit that costs are going*
       attention worldwide, so I'm   *up, but more interested in*
       really encouraged there, too.   *fact that they need to hire*
       And we're hiring more people   *because they think they will*
       in anticipation of the business   *have so much work. To begin*
       growing.   *asking about costs here would*
                                            be like a kid coming home
                                            with three A's and a C and a
                                            parent asking, "What
                                            happened with the C?"

DICK: Next year could be a very good year.

If encouraged, what's his forecast?

STEVE: Here's hoping. I'm always going to be nervous on the domestic side because it's my background and because of changes taking place in the industry. How do you make money on that side?

Here's where the problems could arise.

DICK: Not like XXY [*a competitor that went out of business*].

How will he avoid XXY's fate?

STEVE: That's right. I don't want to do what XXY did and try to buy market share with essentially no-margin contracts. When the board comes out next week, we'll work on that. We're continuing to do traditional contracts where it works, but I really want to push different models for the future.

Here he's telling me he can work with his board.

DICK: Good that you work well with the board.

Appreciate his creative ideas. Encourage him to talk about it.

STEVE: They're always supportive. I've got some new ideas for directions to present to them.

Tone is a little nervous. Always pick up on the affect when its strong, not the content.

DICK: You sound a little nervous about them.

How does he respond to risk?

STEVE: My board will be nervous. While it's a little riskier, we can combine a group of things to save money. I really think we'd be taking a bigger risk not to do it, though.

He can tolerate some risk and has a vision for the company.

Talks about board several times. Sounds like he has issues but can work with them.

STEVE: It's exciting. Our plate is really full. I had a long talk with an investor the other day who had a whole bunch of ideas for expansion. But we are also considering what would make financial sense and are not going off the deep end and taking on more than we can handle.

Excited, but will control risk.

DICK: What did you think of his ideas?

Is he responsive to ideas from outside?

STEVE: Some of his ideas weren't very good, but he had a point with others. It may be time to reorganize our business a little. If we can price contracts correctly, the business could really move. That's what we're betting on. As you've seen, we've also retained an IR [*investor relations*] firm to try to improve whole areas of communications without hyping the stock. I don't want the stock to get ahead of itself.

Realistic about stock price reflecting business.

DICK: I think that with three profitable quarters under your belt in this turnaround, you can afford to let the investment community know about your accomplishments.

Unsolicited advice, but given in clear support of the company.

STEVE: I think so, too, but the board wants to stay conservative.

DICK: Tell the board the investors are on their side now, so any news will be well received.

STEVE: I'll convey the message.

DICK: I've taken enough of your time. This has been real helpful, Steve.

STEVE: Thanks for your support, Dick. I'll talk with you after earnings are released.

The goal of the dialogue is to listen from management's perspective, putting yourself in their shoes, without judging the material (until we get back to the office or off the phone). We want to grasp management's subjective experience and offer our tentative understanding as a form of open-ended statement. In essence we convey the notion, "Tell me if I'm hearing you right, you're saying that . . ." In other words, there is an attempt to join with management to grasp the essence of what they are expressing. When management feels understood, their self-esteem and confidence increase and they feel more comfortable to engage in a genuine exploration of their thoughts. And in doing so they can reveal many important facets of their management style.

In this interview we avoid material nonpublic information, but we gain some very important insights. The CEO functions well in the midst of chaos; he is forthright in conveying what information he feels allowed to share; he works well with his board; he is willing to take calculated risks as long as they can be managed; he wants the stock to fairly reflect the value of the business; he feels realistically confident about the future; and he's thinking creatively about new ideas.

PERSONAL REACTIONS TO MANAGEMENT

In doing investigative work, we are more than collectors and interpreters of data. We are active participants in the dialogue with management. Our own thoughts, feelings, and reactions have an influence on how management responds and how those responses are interpreted.

Because there is always an interpersonal dynamic, our internal reactions can become a help or a hindrance to our research work. Remember that we share the same needs that I attributed to management. We all have lifelong needs for a modicum of self-affirmation, being worthy of some idealized other, or of being like an acceptable other (and therefore being acceptable oneself), and we all have needs for the strengthening of the self that come from the exercising of a bodily or mental activity. For analysts and investors, it's that feeling of fulfillment from looking at a stock chart and knowing you bought in just before the chart headed up.

In other words, just as management brings their subjective views of the company to us, we bring our subjective feelings about the company, its products, services, and financial projections to management. No matter how objective we are in analyzing the numbers, no investor or financial analyst can be totally neutral and free of bias about management. It is just as important to keep track of these personal reactions as our catalog of observed and empathically perceived ones. Here are some examples of the role personal reactions can play during conversations with management:

When feelings from your personal life influence your decisions. There may be times when life outside of work becomes so frustrating or upsetting that we may be temporarily unable to fulfill our usual analytic functions. If so we need to recognize our emotions and make a conscious effort to keep them from interfering with our professional activities and judgments.

For example, I once consulted with John, a brokerage analyst who had lowered his opinion from strong buy to hold on ABC when its quarterly earnings came in $0.03 under his estimate. John told me, "I put myself on the line recommending ABC to begin with, and management didn't have the decency to guide me to the right numbers. They made me look like a fool. I know I could go either way, but I'm going to put them on hold just to get back at them." The official explanation, of course, cited more rational reasons for the lowered rating and, indeed, there were more rational reasons for a lowered rating. In fact John later reversed his position on ABC and reiterated a strong buy recommendation. But for many institutional and individual investors, the damage had been done, as they probably sold out at very low prices. At the time, John was under pressure outside of work; he was feeling exposed and foolish for something that he had inadvertently done in his personal life. If he had recognized how what was occurring in his personal life resonated with how he felt when he missed his earnings estimate, he might have made a different call.

Using your emotional reactions to management as information. We may have a particularly strong reaction to management's refusing to give us information we consider nonmaterial, but necessary for developing our earnings estimates or financial models. Here again, it's important to recognize when and how our personal baggage may color our professional perceptions.

I remember an incident (prior to the adoption of Regulation FD) when a CFO cut off my request for his company's revenue and earnings projections by telling me rather curtly that the company didn't discuss earnings projections. I went on to ask my other questions but came away from the meeting feeling uncharacteristically angry. I didn't pay much attention to the feelings until the next day, when I still felt angry. I resisted the temptation to just blame management for not giving me the information I wanted, forcing myself instead to think about the anger and wondering what it reminded me of. To my surprise, I found myself thinking of a time in the distant past when I needed information to make an important decision, only to find out it was being purposefully withheld. I realized that it was not my style to get angry with a CFO for withholding information—so why now? I concluded that I must have been making a subconscious connection to the original situation. After making the connection, I went back to the company with a cooler head and asked questions that helped me to discover more sketchy evidence suggesting the CFO may in fact be trying to hide something. Two months later his company announced an unexpected 50 percent drop in earnings, and the stock plummeted.

Be suspect when you feel special. We must also pay careful notice to our reactions to a manager who implies he or she is giving us special information. This was a valuable rule of thumb before the adoption of Regulation FD, and it's even more axiomatic now.

For example, if we come away from an interview feeling special because we were offered what management implies is special information, we need to question the meaning and source of our reaction. The simple fact is that managers may not and don't give out material new information over the telephone or the lunch table; when they do, it is to promote their stock rather than to promote accuracy. Often management tries to make us feel special in order to seduce us to overlook a major negative. We should use the "self-reaction" information to guide our evaluation of the company and be wary of rather than seduced by its supposedly special nature.

PRACTICAL LESSONS IN INTERVIEWING

Now that you understand the importance of an emotional connection to management, here are some practical recommendations that can also help you be a better interviewer. For starters, keep in mind that part of management's job involves talking with investors. But with plates at least as full as yours and mine, most top executives are likely to have developed various survival tactics to manage their IR time allocation. Their receptivity to your calls is likely to depend on several basic factors.

First, they want to feel that you've done your homework and that you know something about their company and its products or services.

That means that you've read the latest 10-K or "glossy" annual report and proxy statement, the most current 10-Q quarterly report, and their latest press releases.

Second, they appreciate hearing that you have specific questions generated by your interest in the company (for example, "I noticed in your last quarterly report that inventories are significantly higher than last year, and I couldn't figure out why; could you help me out with that?"). Initially specific questions help management feel more comfortable talking with you than do vague inquiries such as "Where do you think the stock price is headed?" or "How are things going this year?" Once the specifics are answered and management has a sense of your bona fides, it's much easier for them to add some general positives or negatives about the company.

Third, management is much more receptive if they believe you are truly interested in their company rather than just calling to challenge every statement in their latest annual report. An adversarial stance will usually inhibit discussion.

Your general approach to contact with management should be one of an inquisitive investor who is interested in maintaining and perhaps increasing your stake in the business they are running. Try to experience the conversation from the vantage point of management. With all the crazy litigiousness that has become endemic to our landscape, management will be hesitant to say anything or make specific predictions that could lead to a class-action lawsuit that would disrupt the functioning of the company. Expect some hesitation at first, but don't be put off by it.

With large hierarchical companies, a good place to start is with the IR representative. He or she will be glad to field your queries and provide additional (albeit canned) information. If the IR department cannot answer a specific question, it should tell you so and offer to call you back with the information, if available. Any representative who is unwilling to respond to legitimate questions not involving selective disclosure of material nonpublic information should raise an immediate warning flag. If the front line perceives shareholders as a threat, you can be sure it reflects top management's views. I once was very interested in buying the stock of a small-cap company and telephoned the company with my questions. When IR refused to answer my questions, I asked to be put through to the CFO, who promptly told me that he did not make a habit of discussing his company's prospects with shareholders. Needless to say, I did not buy the stock, which in the next two months dropped 90 percent. Refusal of any public company to talk (or at least hold hands) with its shareholders is always an ominous sign.

WHERE TO BEGIN

Whenever you're considering investing in a company, remember that patience is always worth more than money. If XYZ Corporation is a good long-term investment this week, it will be equally suitable next week. Before committing any money, call the company and ask for investor relations. Ask them to send you a complete package of their recent periodic reports and press releases and to add your name to their mailing and e-mail lists. This request assures that you will receive all current quarterly and annual reports and press releases, hopefully in a timely fashion.

Your call to IR initiates the first part of your assessment of the company. How do they respond to your call? Do they send you the material in a timely fashion (within two weeks)? If not, be wary and ask for an explanation. Although a courteous and prompt response does not ensure anything, a company that does not execute a simple request for information may well have difficulty executing its basic business plan, let alone any major plans for expansion.

After you have read the financial packet, you may want to do some research into trends for the industry in which the company operates. It is also helpful to become familiar with its major customers and competitors. Following your review of the financial packet, you should be able to formulate a few specific questions for management.

QUESTIONS FOR MANAGEMENT

You are now in a position to call the company. With large companies, ask for investor relations; with small companies, ask to speak with the CFO or CEO. Tell them that you are a prospective investor who is very interested in the company, have read their disclosure package, and have some questions you would like help in answering. In terms of your assessment, you are listening here not only for their answers, but, more important, for the quality of their response to your interest—whether they seem to welcome curiosity about their products and ways of doing business and how willing they are to share their thoughts with you.

It's important that your initial questions be researched and specific. Here are just a few examples of questions you can ask:

• Ask them about their biggest customers, subscribers, or clients. They may have changed since their last 10-K report. Are these relationships good, and do they expect future sales to these organizations? Ask in an empathic way: "It's great you do so much business with Sears. Is this going to continue to be a major sales site for your products?"

• Look to see if they have booked any unusual investment- or training-related costs. These will often tell you about their plans to make the company better in the future. For example, "I notice that the company has invested in a procedure/training program or a new IT system. Looks like you're improving the company's productivity. Can you tell me how this is going and if you have other plans to make the company more efficient?"

• If there is some recently announced development you are concerned about, ask them how they will respond to it, again in an empathic way: "I noticed you've cut down SG&A. What happens next year when you need to hire more people and costs begin to go up again?"

Remember, you're not looking for a specific answer—or at least that's not the main goal of the questioning. Rather you are looking to see what emotional reaction you elicit. Is the CEO or IR officer confident? Do they have answers in response to questions about the company's plans? Are they open about some areas of questioning and defensive about others?

After your specific questions are answered (why the slowdown in sales, or the increase in operating expenses, or the rise in inventories), it is helpful to ask a series of more general questions. In the glossy annual report (but not the Form 10-K filed with the SEC), there is always a letter to shareholders that typically addresses future directions of the company. While most investors consider this nothing more than fluff, it allows you to question management about their public pronouncements on future directions. Have they completed whatever projects they outlined for the following year? If not, why not? You are listening here for whether management can follow through on their promises to shareholders. Can they follow through with promised goals to enhance growth?

I also like to ask my company contact to tell me briefly about top management. Here I'm not so interested in their credentials (you can find this in the proxy statement); rather I'm interested in any recent changes in management (and the reasons for them) and the quality of the description—the feeling that management is working as a team, that this is "our" company, not "my" company, and that each member of the team brings a particular strength.

Every executive should be optimistic about his or her company's prospects. In fact in answer to my questions, I expect to hear a slight overvaluation of what can be accomplished in the next few years. In the same way that a psychologically healthy parent tends to slightly overvalue his or her children's strengths, management will overemphasize the company's strengths, but without "puffing" or being grandiose about the possibilities. This overvaluation should be tempered by the capacity for a realistic assessment of what might prevent the company from achieving its goals. These should appear as "risk factors" or "special considerations" in a prospectus or transactional proxy statement and as part of management's discussion and analysis of financial conditions and results of operations (or MD&A) in the annual report.

I'm always interested in knowing how much of the company is owned by management. While this information is also in the proxy statement, I usually ask for it anyway because the inquiry leads easily to follow-up questions such as whether there has been recent insider buying or selling and, if so, the reasons for each.

Because of the rules against selective disclosure of material nonpublic information that now apply to all publicly held companies under Regulation FD, many companies have begun to disclose their revenues and earnings projections in press releases or current reports on Form 8-K. If these have been issued by analysts but not released by the company itself, management won't discuss their earnings projections; but they will usually tell you if they agree with the Street estimate. You should know any Street estimates before you call and can obtain them from Zack's or I.B.E.S, or your broker can locate the figures quickly for you. I am less interested in the quantitative answer to the earnings question than in listening for some indication that management is truly committed to increasing shareholder value. A comment such as "We don't comment on earnings projections, but I think our shareholders will be pleased" conveys that management has the owners on their mind.

Management should be able to discuss both the specific competitors of their company and the competitive position of their products or services. The discussion should leave you with a sense of confidence and assurance that any competitive disadvantages are acknowledged and are being addressed. If they are hostile to this question, you may have hit on a key insecurity. They may be seriously worried about one of their competitors, and it may be time for you to switch your stockholding to a more efficient company in the same business.

Toward the end of the conversation (try to keep it under fifteen minutes), I usually suggest that I've been asking a lot of questions and wonder if there is anything I should have asked that I didn't as a potential investor. I invite management to comment on any positives or negatives that I might not have asked about. I encourage my contact to tell me where he or she sees the company in five years. What I look for here is not so much the content as the emotional tone for the company's prospects. "Business looks promising" can convey very different meanings depending on whether it's accompanied by an upbeat or a somewhat depressed tone.

DEVELOPING YOUR OWN "GOOD ENOUGH" PSYCHOLOGICAL ACUITY

As you talk with management, I think you'll develop your own set of questions and clues to help you read between the lines, but these suggestions should help you to get started. Try to remember that most questions about the financial results and prospects of the company can be answered by reading the financial statements and MD&A. What you are really interested in is evaluating the psychology of management and the psychological nuances beneath the surface of their responses.

Like most skills, this is developed with practice and patience over time, not inherited or mastered overnight. It also requires continuity. Don't take too much time off from calling management or you'll lose your psychological acuity. Do it regularly and you will build up an astonishing array of psychological skills and the ability to add immeasurably to the knowledge you've gained from looking at financial statements and MD&A. And remember, you'll never be perfect; you will never be able to act like a telepath or fortune-teller. You may sometimes be fooled, but that shouldn't stop you from being good enough at these interview skills to keep your portfolio going in the right direction.

I want to close this chapter with some of my questions, in no particular order, that have evoked the most useful responses from CEOs and CFOs after an empathic connection has been established.[4]

- What makes you different from the competition?
- What keeps you up at night?
- What positive and negative surprises are we most likely to encounter?
- Who follows you best from the sell side? Why do you think so?
- What is your plan for increasing shareholder value?
- What do you spend the most time doing?
- If something were to go wrong, how might it happen?
- How will the company be different in five years if everything goes as planned?
- What are some of your biggest mistakes? What have you done about them?

- What's the hardest question you get on a road show?
- What do most people not understand about the company?
- How quickly should we expect things to change?
- Can you tell me why I should invest in your company?
- What should I have asked that I didn't?

EIGHT

Thinking Small

John Cole, one of our most prolific observers of the natural world, once described the flight of the rarely seen frigate bird in a way that reminds me of many of us who invest primarily in small- and micro-cap stocks:

> [T]hese birds are designed for flight, not perching; for gliding, not walking, running or scratching in the ground like wild turkeys. The air's upper reaches are where the frigate bird lives most of its life, soaring, riding the thermals like a skier on invisible, airy slopes, finding hills in the sky, dipping along the rim of a great cumulus, then soaring suddenly higher on a windward thrust those of us watching from below will never feel, see or comprehend. We know it exists because it has been defined by the flight of a magnificent frigate bird.[1]

Like the frigate bird, small- and micro-cap investors are not made for perching or walking or even gliding. We are searching for those potential once-in-a-lifetime opportunities—the ten-baggers, as Peter Lynch coined them—that will make life a bit easier if we are right about their prospects for soaring suddenly higher on a windward thrust of the thermals. We know the well-established companies, however successful, will trade below those windward thrusts, their market values likely to continue appreciating year after year at a slow but healthy enough rate to assure comfortable wealth by the time we retire. Yet for entrepreneurial investors, there is something missing in this traditional path.

According to Gerald Holton, Einstein once commented that "he was brought to the formulation of relativity theory in good part because he kept asking himself questions concerning space and time that only children wonder about."[2] Einstein added, "From a psychological point of view, play seems to be the essential feature in productive thought—before there is any connection with logical construction in words or other kinds of signs which can be communicated to others."[3]

Perhaps it is this kind of playfulness in the small- and micro-cap world that appeals to entrepreneurial investors. But it is not for everyone. It means taking losses in speculative stocks of small companies that never make it, while maintaining the courage of our convictions that creative research and intuition will pay off with enough large winners to far outweigh the losers. It requires the discipline to do more research than most are willing to perform, the capacity for assuming higher risk than most are willing to take, the balance to experience grandiosity yet keep it well controlled, the patience to endure the long time frame often required for innovative products and services to catch on, the confidence to eschew the investment community's fixation on short-term results and quarterly statistics, and the knack for viewing the world in a way that is both highly focused and expansive.

The goal of micro-cap investing is no different from that of traditional investing. We all want to increase our personal net worth. The main difference is in the process. For me the emotional rewards of the process give micro-cap investing its personal value. There is a difference, psychologically, between the motivation for investing in general and the motivation for buying and selling micro-cap stocks. What generally makes people invest is intimately related to money and its many connotations (power, control, intelligence, judgment, creativity, self-esteem, ambition, and competition). What makes individuals buy and sell micro-cap stocks often involves more than just monetary wealth. Part of the allure involves the process of discovering and participating in exciting business opportunities, a process that can stimulate our imagination and augment the psychological cement that holds our sense of self together.

My interviews with small- and micro-cap investors suggest that their investing decisions are activated by healthy emotional motives that transcend purely monetary gains. These investors are looking to get much more involved in their companies than large- and mid-cap investors do in GE, Coca-Cola, and Citigroup. They are seeking opportunities not just to make money, but also to enhance self-esteem by getting involved in business successes, being rewarded when their insight and advice pays off, strengthening their confidence and security through savvy judgment calls, and ultimately increasing their feeling of well-being.

For entrepreneurial investors, participating in the micro-cap market provides opportunities to enhance their understanding of the business world and to profit from their participation in it, both financially and psychologically. Their participation evokes unknown aspects of their self, and self-discovery can be part of the rewards. Of course, compared to investing in large, established companies, this road less traveled is far more demanding and perilous.

EVALUATING MICRO-CAP OPPORTUNITIES

The organizing lenses suited to the air's upper reaches are very different from lenses meant for ground level. Micro-cap investing requires different tools and a different psychology to achieve success. Most analysts who attempt to understand a company's intrinsic value use similar tools and models. Their forecasts rely on normalized earnings, return on invested capital, financial leverage (debt), appraisal of management's past performance, development of discounted cash flow models, industry conditions, and numerous other financial analyses suited to blue-chip and middle-market stock. The relationship between the market price for these stocks and the results of that fundamental analysis determines whether they are overvalued or undervalued.

Determining intrinsic value becomes much more difficult when dealing with development-stage companies with no historic patterns on which to base forecasts of future performance. When comparing valuation approaches for large- and small-cap companies, Ben Graham once wrote:

> [U]nseasoned companies in new fields of activity, in striking contrast, provide no sound basis for the determination of an

intrinsic value. The risks inherent in the business, an untested management, and uncertain access to additional capital combine to make an analytical determination of value unlikely if not impossible. Analysts serve their discipline best by identifying such companies as highly speculative and by not attempting to value them even though we recognize that there will be pressure to make valuations . . . [4]

Some would argue that the Internet analysts of the late twentieth century should have heeded Graham's advice. But despite the vagaries of evaluating development-stage companies and the high risks of investments in their stocks, the few that occasionally succeed can provide great rewards. The obvious question is, how do we evaluate and invest in these companies while minimizing the very substantial risks of losing our principal? In discussing the intuitive leaps that often contribute to scientific discovery, Peter Medawar has stated that "it is of no use looking to scientific papers, for they not merely conceal but actively misrepresent the reasoning that goes into the work they describe. . . . Only unstudied evidence will do—and that means listening at the keyhole."[5]

LISTENING AT THE KEYHOLE

Medawar's metaphor has enormous power, for it points to the connection between discovery and the detective's tools of observation: careful listening, curiosity, imagination, and experiential "feel" for collecting hidden data. Given the inherently speculative nature of development-stage companies, we need guidelines to help us navigate our way through the investigative process, both economically and psychologically. I like to use a series of lenses to filter the ideas and address the questions raised in the process of examining early-stage investing opportunities.

Visionary Product or Service? The best micro-cap companies have visionary products or services that could change forever the way large groups of people, or whole cultures, carry on their lives. These usually involve a breakthrough technology to provide new solutions to old problems. The advent of the personal computer, the discovery of anti-biotics, the airplane, and possibly the information highway are all examples of innovations that altered society's infrastructure. Follow-ing the terrorist attacks of September 11, 2001, new technologies in the security industry and new developments in biotechnology will also alter how we live and heal.

Of course, most novel products either never reach the market or fail to catch on when they do, and many companies trying to launch inno-vative products or services have ended in bankruptcy. The successful groundbreakers are few and far between, and you can count the ones that have transformed society on your fingers. Because of all the hur-dles and uncertainties, selecting development-stage companies that ultimately succeed is in part an art, and certainly not a science. Given the odds, you should never put all your money in only one of these visionary but high-risk baskets.

While writing this book, I evaluated and invested in many small visionary companies with innovative products or services. They appealed to me because their visions were exciting and their innova-tions, if successful, could have major cultural and industry implica-tions. Here are some examples:

• Aura Systems (OTCBB: AURA) spent ten years developing a patented mobile power device that fits under the hood of a car and turns a vehicle into a mobile generator. My research indicated that Aura's technology had the potential to alter the capabilities of several industries, including utilities, rescue and emergency vehicles, and mil-itary capabilities. If this potential could be reached, the technology could have a profound impact on how we generate clean electricity, potentially addressing a variety of needs as we face a severe power cri-sis, as well as the mobile power needs of both the military and the RV and motor-home industries.

• SureBeam (Nasdaq: SURE) developed an electron-beam tech-nology that destroys harmful food-borne bacteria such as E coli, sal-monella, and listeria much like thermal pasteurization does to milk. Unlike older irradiation technologies, the SureBeam process does not use radioactive isotopes for irradiation. Instead the system uses ordinary electricity and operates in an efficient and environmentally responsible manner. I was intrigued by the potential of this technology to establish a new standard for food safety, an exciting prospect in an age when consumers are becoming increasingly concerned with food-related illnesses.

• Education Lending Group (OTCBB: EDLG) is a technology-based financial services company that markets financial aid products, services, and solutions to the Federal Guaranteed Student Loan Industry. The company originates federally guaranteed educational loans to students, parents, and schools. In addition it provides other financial aid products such as student financial aid counseling, debt counseling, debt management, loan service management, and secondary market loan acquisition services. I was intrigued by their solid management and by the fact that within the graduate school lending market, EDLG offered the only current nationally marketed program that pays schools a premium on the school-generated loans.

• Zi-Corp (Nasdaq: ZICA) developed a technology for connecting people to short messaging, e-mail, e-commerce, web browsing, and similar applications in almost any written language. It was the first technology that allowed Asian-speaking populations to use a keyboard without having to learn English first.

Will These Products or Services Appeal to a Niche Market? After searching for visionary products and services, I ask whether they have the benefits, allure, mythology, or charisma to fulfill the needs or fantasies of powerful niche groups that are underserved by the existing products or services and are willing to think in contrarian ways about new methodologies and tools. I was not looking for products or services that would be embraced by the general public, which historically is slow to accept innovation at the visionary level. Even major corporations can miss the boat on visionary approaches, as when IBM discounted the possibility of personal and minicomputers replacing most of the mainframes. What I was looking for was some evidence in the literature or due diligence reports that these products would be embraced by their targeted niche-market players.

My due diligence provided some positive indications. Aura Systems' product was being used by General Motors for some of their vehicles and by the military after extended testing. SureBeam's electron-beam technology was embraced by not only large retailers such as Hannaford's, but also by the Department of Agriculture and the FDA. Zi-Corp's input technology was endorsed by Ericsson, one of the world's largest telecommunications companies. Education Lending was being embraced by graduate and professional schools, where 82 percent of students received financial aid. The key I was seeking was the prospect for acceptance of the technology or service by a niche market, not the general public. If these companies were to succeed, they needed to get their foot in the door with a strong niche group of customers.

In fact, once novel ideas become accepted in the general marketplace, the margin of safety for investments in new but unknown products is lost. That margin of safety is your low entry price for the stock of an undiscovered innovator. In deciding to buy Aura Systems at $0.37, Zi-Corp at $2.00, Education Lending Group at $3.85, and SureBeam at $1.93, I was fairly confident about my margin of safety against the volatility inherent in small- and micro-cap stocks. Even with this perceived protection, however, I could not be sure all these companies would necessarily thrive or even survive.

Can Management Drive the Company to Success? In a development-stage company, no matter how good the product, a poor management team will inevitably lead to failure. I look for a team of people who can work well together, from the CEO and CFO to the scientists and COO. At small- and micro-cap companies, investors generally have much more access to senior management than at large companies like Exxon or J.P. Morgan Chase. To make the most of this, the psychological skills discussed in chapter seven can be useful. Here are some illustrations of how they can be put to good use to assess the attitude and skills of a prospect company's management.

First, be on the lookout for a CEO who tries to run the company alone without listening to his team. In my experience this is the main culprit in a high percentage of failures. Recently I sat in on a meeting with management of a high-tech company whose CEO talked a lot about the importance of teamwork but immediately cut off other team members the moment they began to offer spontaneous thoughts. This alone was enough to turn my attention to other prospect companies.

I also look for a management team with the confidence to rely on their own business experience and vision rather than conventional wisdom. This may create havoc with investors or analysts who try to tell management how to run their company, but it's a positive sign for me, since I want to have confidence in their decision-making. I want them to speak honestly with investors in good times and bad. I want to be convinced they have the capacity for change and flexibility, which are especially important in small companies that often have to shift their business plans quickly to survive. I want them to overvalue their company in the same way that parents overvalue their children. I want them to take on risk judiciously rather than protect against it.

I call them and meet with them if possible, and I make a psychological assessment, using the empathic techniques discussed in chapter seven, to make sure they know I am on their side. I look for any hint of defensiveness, dishonesty, or anxiety. I find the entrepreneurs who run these companies generally more real and down to earth than the investor-relations pros at the large-cap companies. Use this to your advantage—it makes psychological assessment easier.

Is This the Right Time to Buy? Timing your purchases of development-stage and other micro-cap companies, while nearly impossible to perform with any certainty, is still a job that needs to be done as well as possible. Ideally you want to buy at a point when nothing appears to be happening at the company but your scuttlebutt research has uncovered indications of positive developments—an unknown interest in the company's product, talks with potential strategic partners, the prospect of adding a highly regarded director to the board, or even the potential for a buyout. If these prospects are too uncertain to be publicly reported, the appearance of status quo will usually be reflected in a low market price for the company's stock. Even if the anticipated developments never materialize or take longer than expected, your low entry price provides a margin of safety, although you may have to tolerate a drop in price as investors begin to give up on the company.

Like all timing decisions, it's important to understand our own idiosyncratic psychological considerations. I have a friend who thinks that a stock should move within two weeks of buying it. If it fails to react within that time frame, he complains that he shouldn't have made the purchase. He obviously does not have the personality for investing in emerging but speculative growth companies, since suffering losses or at best waiting several years for significant rewards are the rule rather than the exception. Make sure you understand the emotional factors that influence your timing decisions before you make the intellectual decision to purchase these stocks.

Does This Company Have the Potential for Market Leadership? The best small- and micro-cap prospects have opportunities to create a niche market for their innovations if they succeed with their business plans. Ideally they can even achieve that leadership before the competition can catch up. When Zi-Corp began selling its eZiText input system in China, it was not displacing anyone. The company was creating a new market, not entering an established one. Market share and competition would come later, but at the outset we want the development-stage company to be creating new and hopefully long-term customers, with enough market leadership to defer the zero-sum game of market competition for several years down the road.

Can the Company Develop Valuable Strategic Partnerships? One of the best ways for development-stage companies to penetrate niche markets quickly is through cooperative arrangements with well-known strategic partners or investors. These connections not only provide valuable introductions, they also reflect a vote of confidence from a respected company that has done its due diligence and taken a chance on the fledgling upstart. This was a comforting factor for my prospects. For example, Ericsson's relationship with Zi-Corp facilitated its entry into the cellular marketplace. Aura System's shares were quietly being accumulated by some of the best money managers in the country, and its products were being quietly purchased by the military for use in Afghanistan. SureBeam had been developed, nurtured, and spun off by the Titan Corporation.

Does the Company Have a "Whole Product"? When all is said and done, the survival and ultimate success of any development-stage company comes down to what the technology industry calls a "whole product." It's great to have visionary ideas that are exciting and appealing in concept. But the concept must eventually be developed into a product or service that players in the company's niche market will buy. The fact that this bottom line is obvious doesn't always protect investors from losing sight of its importance.

For a development-stage company to have a whole product, its prospects for *immediate* appeal to the consumer market are secondary at most. That can come later. What matters at the development stage is the prospect of developing an innovative product or service that can *completely* supply the exacting needs of a niche market that demands a *particular* solution to a problem.[6] If participants in the targeted niche market have the financial leverage to ultimately create a customer base, so much the better. All of the companies in my illustrations had whole products that scored high marks on this front. The retail-food distributors targeted by SureBeam clearly had the resources and the motivation to support its product to address consumer concerns at a time when attitudes toward irradiated food were undergoing significant change in the face of growing risks of food contamination. The military certainly had the financial clout to put Aura Systems on the map. The telecom industry could be expected to support the eZiText input sytem. And colleges and graduate schools would likely embrace superior student-loan services for their students.

Does the Company Have Effective Financial and Public-Relations Support? The most common pitfall for small companies is undercapitalization. The search for micro-cap prospects should therefore include an evaluation of both their existing financial position and their financial backers. It is extremely important that financial backers be long-term players willing to support the company's development. All small companies need money as they grow. If they cannot count on their investors for continued support, their chances for survival diminish exponentially over time.

Small- and micro-cap companies also need a very specific kind of public-relations effort. They need a discreet, targeted approach that large PR firms usually cannot supply unless they have special insight into the issues and problems small companies face. I like to see a management team that understands the need for a PR firm with strong connections to both retail micro-cap investors and to brokers who are market makers in micro-cap stocks. In addition the PR firm must be able to introduce management to niche markets, help small companies with acquisition ideas, forge investment-banking relationships, and help management improve their skills and sensitivities in communicating with the investment community. Relationships with larger PR firms that excel at arranging TV interviews and magazine articles can come later.

As we access the opportunities in emerging growth stocks that cross our desks, it is important to understand the lenses we use to filter the many variables: the nature of the innovative and sometimes visionary products or services; the chances for acceptance of the technology by a niche market as opposed to the general public; the skills and temperament of managment; the likely time frame for transition from a development-stage company to a sales and marketing company; the prospects for creating markets through internal growth; the potential for developing relationships with strategic partners; the distance between the business concept and the realization of a whole product envisioned by that concept; and the availability of financial support. In addition to getting a handle on all these variables, it is equally important to understand whether your own psychology gives you an advantage or a handicap when investing in the micro-cap market. Success in this type of speculative investing depends not only on understanding and evaluating products, services, and management, but on your personality and emotional responses to the fragile and unpredictable phases of growth and setbacks experienced by all development-stage companies.

VISIONARIES:
THE RIGHT SIDE OF THE BRAIN

Almost all successful startups begin their development stage with a visionary concept for a product or service that has the potential to change the way large groups of people carry on their lives. To foresee the potential of their forward-looking ideas, managers and investors must have a particular cognitive capacity. I view that gift, whether innate or learned, as the ability to engage the right side of the brain.

We know that the left and right sides of the brain function somewhat differently. The left side helps us with linguistic, sequential, rational, intellectual, deductive, disciplined, analytic reasoning. The right side directs spatial, holistic, artistic, symbolic, emotional, intuitive, inductive, imaginative, and contemplative thinking. Cerebral hemispheres are not fully functional at birth. They continue to mature and evolve into complex systems that can generate new information in processes we describe in terms of discovery, creativity, and originality. The bundle of two hundred million neurons called the corpus callosum that connects the two halves of the brain is not operative until about two years of age and not fully functional until age ten. This has implications we usually take for granted. For many years, adults must help infants and children to join emotion and cognition appropriately. In this sense we act the part of the corpus callosum for our children until that structure can take over. In the course of this development, one side of the brain often receives more emphasis and attention than the other and, in conjunction with genetic predispositions, often develops to a higher level.

Most founders of visionary companies as well as their early-stage investors utilize right-brain cognition. Executives with this trait can appear to act irrationally or uncommunicatively and are prone to snap judgments that they do not explain clearly. These are examples of right-brain signals that are directly translated into decisions without being verbalized along the way. Traditionally trained financial analysts, especially large-cap analysts, often function more from the left side of the brain. While no one way is better or entirely exclusive of the other, the differences often create conflict between well-trained security analysts and entrepreneurial executives of young companies. This may be part of the reason why many of the large-cap company analysts are either negative or indifferent about small companies and their management.

This may also explain why investors in early-stage companies are likely to be more intuitive and inductive in their enthusiasm for new and revolutionary ideas. Their willingness to take risks appears unrelated to any traditional, analytic, and rational evaluation. It is more likely to be rooted in a kind of revolutionary thinking and basic trust in their intuitive judgments about both products and people. In some situations this cognitive style may contribute to naiveté, which can lead to major investment errors. It can also set the stage for intense conflicts with traditional investors (including many short-sellers) whose cognitive style evokes a much more skeptical approach to the world.

THE STRUGGLE: PARANOIA AND RAGE

The visionaries often spend years developing their product, ignored for decades or merely dismissed by the rest of the world as mad scientists. Several of my visionary-company illustrations are good examples. Aura Systems spent ten years developing its technology before launching a whole product. Zi-Corp spent ten years perfecting the mathematical logarithms for its input system. In each case a niche market in need of these innovations eventually discovered them, responding with great enthusiasm that was translated into initial product orders, paving the way for bringing these products to market. The stock prices of both companies suddenly moved significantly higher, fueled by hopes of conquering niche and ultimately consumer markets.

At this stage of the development cycle for most emerging growth companies, potential competitors enter the picture. They tend to become hypersensitive to the new kid on the block. The innovator suddenly poses a real threat to the market share and bottom line of the well-established companies in the sector. There may also be an unacknowledged blow to their self-esteem. The newcomer becomes a perceived attacker of the left-brained, rationally thinking competitor. A kind of paranoia sets in. With painstaking appeals to more rational customers and investors, the established companies and their supporters try to turn the rest of the world against the new kid on the block. After all, it has no earnings, no track record, no significant cash reserves, and no assurance of adequate financing. So they try to persuade the left-hemisphere-thinking masses that the new company cannot be a reliable supplier or a viable investment, even though all of the risk factors they harp on are part and parcel of every development-stage company. And indeed if we judged most emerging companies by traditional valuation methods or rational business-evaluative standards for established large-cap companies, no one would ever invest in them or take a chance on their products.

It is part of our culture, except perhaps in the art world, to measure intelligence and success by the criteria for left-brain functioning. As a result, the rational dissection of entrepreneurial, visionary companies can become a kind of sport for Wall Street, particularly the short-seller community. This can create intense public skepticism, which the shorts systematically reinforce when these companies face setbacks, however minor or transitory. When this happens, analysts get adversarial, and investors get nervous, questioning how the market valuations of these companies could have grown so high without any traditional evidence of sustained success. The high stock values are an open invitation for the short-sellers. No matter how much potential the company possesses, the shorts know that they can erode the confidence of anxious investors.

While short-sellers generally play an important and valuable role in the market, development-stage companies, particularly the innovators, tend to attract a well-established minority group of shorts who perceive them as lucrative targets of opportunity. Psychologically this group appears to have a chronic sense of mistrust and an inbred penchant for dissembling and vindictiveness, which they employ with little respite or integrity. These characteristics are also shared by a small minority of media personalities whose self-esteem appears to be enhanced only by their continual dedication to bursting the bubbles of embryonic innovators, often in the service of the shorts. In the absence of any regulatory restraints, this remains an unsavory and unfortunate aspect of micro-cap investing.

SHAME AND DESPAIR

For those investors who remain naive to the destructive, undercover machinations practiced by the predatory minority of short-sellers, the precipitous fall of their stocks after the shorts have done their damage can evoke a sense of shame and despair. These investors typically have neither the cash nor the confidence to buy more shares on significant pullbacks, and their original enthusiasm yields to a depressive sense of helplessness and fear. They are also likely to feel disappointed and let down by company management, who are often slow to think from a more rational, left-brain perspective, thus ignoring the realities of the struggle that is taking place until their companies are on the brink of extinction.

Investors can see their small- and micro-cap stocks lose 50 percent to 80 percent of their value quickly. Despair sets in, and they begin to question their original judgment. They experience a blow to their self-esteem, no longer feeling like someone to be admired for savvy invest-ment decisions. Brokers or analysts who originally recommended the stock often bear the brunt of these investors' anger. The despair and anger can last for months if the stock languishes at low levels. Feeling "once burned," these investors are not only "twice shy," but downright afraid to buy more shares, lest they end up compounding their per-ceived mistake. At the height of despair, when all but the most experi-enced and psychologically sophisticated investors have abandoned the company, an unanticipated catalyst stimulates a resurgence of interest. The short-sellers cover, and the stock price begins to climb back toward its old highs. At that point, institutions may suddenly become interested, and investors begin to rebuild their position, but now at much higher prices.

SUCCESSFUL DEVELOPMENT-STAGE INVESTING

To be successful in this type of investing, you need a rare combination of psychological characteristics. First, you must have the capacity for right-hemisphere thinking while still being guided by the more rational left side of the brain. One of the reasons development-stage investors are so passionate about their companies is that they use emo-tion, intuition, and creativity in their cognitive functioning. Without the guidance of a more analytical function, their passion easily leads to pipe dreams unfettered by realistic thinking about the hardships of transitioning from initial idea to marketable product. Bill Gates at Microsoft probably stands out as an example par excellence of suc-cessful two-hemispheric thinking.

Second, you must possess the psychological capacity to assume rather than manage risk. You must intuitively appreciate why I'm

repeating John Maynard Keynes's statement that "most of our decisions to do something positive can only be taken as a result of animal
spirits . . . and not as the outcome of a weighted average of quantitative benefits multiplied by qualitative probabilities."[7] If you are not
comfortable with that statement, you should not be investing in
development-stage companies.

Third, you have to possess an imperturbable optimism rather than
a more conservative affinity with tradition. It is this confidence in the
future that allows for failure, and you can count on having your fair
share in development-stage investing. And it is the same "spiritedness"
that will keep you in the hunt despite your failures, because that quality allows you to enjoy the process for its own sake.

Fourth, you must possess a healthy sense of self-esteem to protect
you from succumbing to the embittered gyrations of everyday life in
the emerging-growth market. The progressive paths of development-
stage companies are filled with enough potholes to derail all but the
most confidently centered investors. Those who use the stock price of
their companies as a mirror for their self-esteem are too nearsighted
and do not perform well in this speculative market.

Fifth, successful emerging-growth investors must have the capacity
to trust in their own research and judgments. You cannot depend on
media gurus for investment guidance, for you must frequently invest
against a very powerful herd whose pecuniary interest is tied to preventing the emergence of an embryonic product or service.

Sixth, development-stage investing requires enormous patience,
which must be enlisted to temper the sense of drivenness that often
accompanies investments in exciting new products. To remain with a
company while it makes the transitions of the development cycle usually strains the patience of the most dedicated investors. Companies
do not make this transition without major product glitches, changes of
management, lawsuits, and financial struggles. Investors do not succeed when they are consumed with the next press release or a 20 percent move in the stock price.

The process of growing from an embryonic company to an established innovator is both exiting and perilous. Your evaluation of these
companies and commitment of savings to their initially speculative
stock requires a willingness to develop and learn new ways of access-

ing them and understanding yourself as an investor. Just as important, it requires the realization that many of your investments will fail.

Despite the perils of micro-cap investing, individual investors have embraced this high-risk pursuit with a passion. Several factors account for the trend: the emergence of the Internet, with easy access to information and low online trading fees; $11.4 trillion in inheritance coming to baby-boomers over the next twenty years; an increasingly educated investor population; the fact that boomers need the thrill and challenge of the stock market; and the increasing responsibility that individuals must take for their financial futures. Many experts are wary of this new individual interest in small- and micro-cap investing. You don't have to look too far in the popular press to find naysayers and Cassandras who love cautioning us about all the terrible risks inherent in this type of investing. These expert opinions remind me of some eloquent lines from our former poet laureate, Richard Wilbur:

> Some would distinguish nothing here but oaks,
> Proud heads conversant with the power and glory
> Of heaven's rays or heaven's thunderstrokes,
> And adumbrators to the understory,
> Where, in their shade, small trees of modest leanings
> Contend for light and are content with gleanings.[8]

Small- and micro-cap investors are constantly in the shadow of large institutional groupthink. While claiming to be conversant with the power and glory of heavenly economic predictors, these people are secretly watching one another to ensure that none of their sentiments or recommendations strays too far from the group. On the Street it matters not if the whole crowd is wrong; it matters a lot if you stray from the herd and are wrong.

Micro-cap investors, those "small trees of modest leanings," are content to collect information and profits independently, bit by bit, and gradually. They know there are no investment gods on Wall Street, only statistical indicators waiting to be organized and interpreted. They also suspect the interpretation is an art, one that depends much more on psychology than mathematics or economics.

Statistics suggest that small companies outperform larger firms by significant percentages over the long term. Ibbotson Associates, a Chicago research bureau, has demonstrated that from 1926 to 2001 small-company stocks produced an annual compounded average return of approximately 12.5 percent versus 10.7 percent for large-cap stocks.[9] From 1971 to 2000 the small-cap averages were in excess of 15 percent per year. The reasons for their superior performance are important to understand, but equally relevant are the psychological underpinnings of small- and micro-cap investing. The investor who is not cognizant of his or her reactions to the specific psychological pressures of small-cap investing runs a high risk of failure. Here's my take on these points.

The Elimination of Groupthink. The first reason that small caps tend to outperform large caps is that developing enterprises need to be innovative, and that tends to free them from the constraints of group-think or herd mentality. Large institutions like pension funds shy away from smaller stocks because they literally have too much money to invest, and it is more efficient to spread their funds among fewer higher-priced issues than thousands of lower-priced ones. In addition, it is impossible for institutions to buy or sell large blocks of small-cap stocks without upsetting their market prices. Imagine trying to buy or sell 2 million shares of a company with only 3.5 million outstanding.

While the elimination of institutional participation levels the playing field for us individual investors and gives us a better opportunity for substantial profits, it also means we have to act independent of the conventional wisdom of the Street. As Bernard Baruch once said, most information reaches Wall Street through a "curtain of human emotions." With little institutional guidance, the small-cap investor is left alone to distinguish fact from fiction. Functioning in a virtual vacuum, our grandiose fantasies sometimes need only the slight stimulus of a friendly "can't lose" tip to play havoc with rational decision-making. Thus the small-cap investor must constantly guard against rumors, tips, and the fantasies stimulated by working in a more isolated environment.

Pricing Efficiencies. The second reason small stocks tend to outperform large-cap equities is the dearth of research coverage for emerging companies. Since institutions are generally disinclined to buy small-cap stocks, most institutional analysts don't conduct extensive research on their issuers. Instead of the usual ten to fifteen analysts' reports, we are lucky to find one or two, and these are usually from the company's investment bankers, who tend to be small outfits themselves and often have their own public-relations agenda. Without the typical consensus on earnings estimates, the potential for pricing inefficiencies (such as incorrect valuations) is greater, offering the individual investor a competitive edge.

Capitalizing on these pricing inefficiencies, however, exacts a psychological toll on the investor. Exceptional opportunities, by definition, are rare, and uncovering them requires thorough financial analysis and sound understanding of the company, the industry, the economic factors affecting the industry, and the company's products or services. Doing the job the right way demands enormous time and energy, commodities that are usually in short supply when we are preoccupied with family and a full-time job outside the investment field. So there is a tendency to create our own ostensibly rational assessment of a company based on fantasies woven from incomplete facts and inordinate expectations.

The lesson is obvious: Be careful. Don't go into this market sector unless you have time to evaluate all of the information you can find on target companies. If you are pressed for time temporarily, be careful making decisions, and ask yourself, "Is this based on the facts, or am I acting on my fantasies?" As a psychologically aware investor, you already know how fantasies of success or failure can drive your perceptions of the companies you invest in. Are those fantasies driving you now, or are you acting as a truly independent thinker?

Lower Liquidity, Higher Rewards. Small companies usually have fewer shares outstanding and fewer buyers and sellers for their stock. In other words, they are more thinly traded and not as liquid as large stocks. Because it can be harder to convert your holdings to cash at a moment's notice, investors demand a higher reward for the increased liquidity risk. Higher potential rewards, however, mean increased psychological pressure to tolerate uncertainty—the uncertainty of exiting stocks in the face of a sudden correction or bear market, the sense of doubt from realizing you cannot have all the information necessary for informed decisions, and the uncertainty that you have made a correct decision in purchasing a stock despite a temporary pullback in its trading price. The more prolonged an investor's uncertainty in the context of lone decision-making, the greater the likelihood of acting irrationally—selling at the bottom or chasing stocks and buying at the top.

Volatility. Small stocks possess more "company risk" than large caps. For example, they often don't have the financial strength to survive one poor year, whereas a Pepsico, IBM, or Microsoft merely restructures and continues its corporate life after adjusting to bad times. Volatility in this sense means that small companies have the capacity to disintegrate quickly. The small caps, of course, also have more volatility, and their stock can move precipitously and rapidly.

The psychological pressures inherent in the volatility of small caps can compel investors, mistakenly, to make snap decisions more akin to stock and commodity traders than to long-term investors. Quickly falling prices following a poor quarter or other disappointing developments elicit an urgency to sell at what may well turn out to be rock-bottom levels. Rapidly rising prices can elicit a craving for short-term profit taking, which calms the nerves but often at the expense of enormous upside potential. Because most brokers do not follow the small-cap arena carefully if they follow it at all, they frequently join in the panic, encouraging their clients to sell at just the wrong moment. Unanalyzed impatience is perhaps the most insidious psychological danger for the micro-cap investor. The small- and micro-cap markets are *not* for you if your self-esteem depends on Mr. Market's everyday approval. But if you can tolerate market pressures and risks on a long-term rather than a short-term basis, you will give yourself a fighting chance for meaningful rewards.

CREATING A PROTECTIVE PSYCHOLOGICAL SHIELD

The psychological effects of uncertainty, isolation, impatience, energy drain, and grandiose fantasy in small-cap investing, when combined with our tendency to use the stock market to confirm our self-esteem (intelligence, decision-making, efficacy, prediction, reasoning, etc.), places us all in an often unrecognized position of risk when managing our own or other people's money. There are several active steps you can take to minimize these psychological risks while maximizing your potential for financial gains.

Stick to a Long-Term Investment Horizon. Results in this arena take time. There are very few micro-cap traders who consistently make profits. The small-cap investor should not expect quick results, although this will often occur when we least expect it. A 400 percent gain in year four is obviously much more profitable than a 40 percent gain in year one. But few investors have the psychological capacity to tolerate several years of flat or underwater performance. Many small emerging growth stocks require this kind of patience, although a long-term horizon doesn't mean you should hold tenaciously when the fundamentals change. Whether your company information dictates patience or swift reaction, maintaining a long-term philosophy protects you from irrational impatience.

Uncertainty Is Best Tolerated by Working Through Different Scenarios Without Acting on Them. Ask yourself the following questions: What is the worst thing that can happen if I continue to hold this stock? What is the best possible result of not selling at these prices? Is there a company that I would rather buy than the one I currently am uncertain about? Do I trust management to bring the company back from a bad quarter or other adverse development?

By generating as many questions as you can or having an investor friend play devil's advocate, you can formulate a rational structure to handle the uncertainty and forestall premature actions.

Work on Your Investing Peer Group. The loneliness of the small-cap investor is best overcome by developing a network of investor friends and colleagues with whom to share and test ideas. As a psychologically aware investor, you can avoid the obvious danger of the group developing its own herd mentality and undermining your independent thinking, since you'll stay focused on the need for retaining individual responsibility for your decisions. At the end of the day, sharing ideas is almost always more positive than negative. As Barton Biggs reminded us in 1977, quoting Oliver Wendell Holmes, "Many ideas grow better when transplanted into another mind than in the one where they sprung up."[10]

NINE

Reacting to Loss in the Market

One of the toughest but most important skills we need to learn in becoming successful investors is dealing constructively with losses in the market. Unfortunately the path to mastering this art may bear a painful resemblance to Homer's epic story of Odysseus' wanderings in the west, as he struggled to find his way home after victory in Troy. With all its bewitching temptations, magical successes, and monstrous losses, *The Odyssey* captures metaphorically the travails of investors as they navigate the "twists and turns" of uncharted waters:

> *Many cities of men he saw and learned their minds,*
> *many pains he suffered, heartsick on the open sea,*
> *fighting to save his life and bring his comrades home.*
> *But he could not save them from disaster, hard as he strove—*
> *the recklessness of their own ways destroyed them all,*
> *the blind fools, they devoured the castle of the Sun*
> *and the Sungod blotted out the day of their return.*[1]

The Odyssey can teach us how fragments of our experience are woven together, either supporting our long-term goals and ambitions or unconsciously undermining our efforts and needlessly complicating our journeys. Even as a resourceful veteran of a ten-year war, Odysseus was "driven time and again off course, once he had plundered the hallowed heights of Troy." *The Odyssey* is such a useful allegory for investors because it so eloquently charts the losses Odysseus experienced and how he learned to overcome their potentially devastating impact on his road to ultimate success.

And no matter what anyone tells you, every investor in the stock market eventually incurs losses. In fact losing money is part of the investing experience, and dealing constructively with those losses is a key part of the maturation process from naive to experienced investor. When we focus only on our initial successes and fail to confront the plethora of emotions evoked by monetary loss, we become prone to a false confidence that all too easily can lead to complacency and grandiosity. This leaves us wide open to an unforeseen emotional defeat when eventually the winner's house of cards comes tumbling down.

Investment success is built upon a healthy respect for risk. Successful investors realize and account for the likelihood that five or even six out of ten investment choices will probably be faulty and that occasional corrections and bear markets can lead to devastating losses. Some investors cope well with losses and use them as a springboard for developing new and revised investment strategies. Others appear to be traumatized by loss. For a variety of reasons, they are far more devastated emotionally than financially, and they are unable to learn from their mistakes. For these investors in particular, it is important to understand how loss in the market represents an emotional shock and to find ways of recovering from that "trauma."

WE ALL LOSE MONEY SOMETIMES

Investors don't like to talk about their market losses. If you ever listen to folks discussing their stock or mutual-fund portfolio performance, they all appear to be making tons of money and discovering unique and incredibly lucrative opportunities. It would seem that everybody and his cousin is growing wealthy in the stock market. Even in down markets, cocktail-party braggarts tell anyone who will listen, "My portfolio hasn't been affected *at all* because I made such smart choices." Hearing this sort of talk makes us feel foolish that our portfolios have suffered so much in down markets. The problem, of course, is that everyone takes a hit in a market downturn, protestations to the contrary notwithstanding. Although the market treated the investment community more than graciously during the years before this century's crash, even the tech bubble doled out some hard lessons:

- Eighty-nine percent of all mutual funds underperformed the S&P 500 from 1990 through 2000.[2]
- The average mistake rate in stock picking for professional analysts is probably about 40 percent.
- Between 1985 and 2000, "the average mutual fund gained 15 percent annually, but the average mutual fund investor gained only 10 percent. Fully one-third of investors' available return was lost by switching from one fund to another. . . ."[3]

So market statistics, as opposed to market talk, suggest that while some investors may be making money, most underperform the market and many lose money on a regular basis, even in bull markets. Every investor must cope with these losses, and how we deal with mistakes and loss may shape our future in or out of the market.

What drives most investors off course is the sudden onset of a correction or a bear market. A significant decline in a bull market evokes a myriad of emotional reactions, from anxiety to panic, despair, self-blame, and anger, just as a significant advance in a bear market engenders relief, hope, and even euphoria. What underlies these ephemeral psychological states is usually an intense feeling of uncertainty stimulated by our inability to organize what is happening in the market into some coherent ideas to guide our actions. Not knowing whether or how to act, there is always the fear that, as T. S. Eliot wrote,

> *What might have been is an abstraction*
> *Remaining a perpetual possibility*
> *Only in a world of speculation.*[4]

Investors fear holding their position because a correction in a bull market may turn out to be the beginning of a bear market; and they fear selling because of capital losses, transaction costs, and concern about missing the resumption of the bullish trend. Should we "buy cheap" and double up on our stockholdings, or should we dump the lot? The fact that a correction and a rebound can happen at dizzying speed makes life even more confusing, creating concern that decisions must be made with split-second timing to be effective.

CORRECTIONS

In his book *Trader Vic—Methods of a Wall Street Master*, Vic Sperandeo quotes Robert Rhea's *The Dow Theory*, suggesting that corrections are analogous to release valves on a boiler system. They provide an escape route for the excess buildup of hopes and expectations so that severe internal pressures do not destroy the market.[5]

Whatever factors may precipitate a correction, the primary question is whether the drop in prices will turn out to be the first leg down in a bear market or merely a short interruption in a major upward trend. Hindsight is always very accurate. If the market drops 5 percent to 15 percent and resumes its upward momentum, we look back and call it a correction; if the market attempts to rally and fails, then retreats a total of 25 percent to 30 percent, we call it a cyclical bear market; and if the market continues its free fall 45 percent to 50 percent over a prolonged period, we call it a secular bear market.

Corrections, as opposed to most bear markets, tend to occur as steep and sudden declines in market averages and individual stock prices; but the volume levels in correction phases tend to decrease as the market drops. Bear markets, in general, are slower to develop and are marked by increasing volume as the decline continues. Bear markets usually produce fear; corrections typically evoke anxiety. As I pointed out in Chapter Two, fear is a state of worry directed at a recognizable danger that can be realistically assessed and countered with rational actions. Anxiety, on the other hand, is a diffuse tension state that not only fails to generate rational actions, but frequently elicits the illusion of excessive danger, thus leading to irrational responses.[6] The suddenness and steepness of most corrections are the primary culprits in creating high anxiety, which can be magnified when juxtaposed with the hopeful, complacent state enjoyed just before corrections occur.

This type of anxiety propels us to sell stocks at a point that all too often turns out to be the bottom of a correction. We would actually be better off experiencing fear over the possibility of a correction leading to a bear market. Then at least we would have the capacity to wait judiciously for a bear market correction (an upward move) before selling. We know historically that investors are always given a second chance to exit stocks after the first leg down in a bear market. But anxiety magnifies the sense of danger or, worse, causes some investors to irrationally deny the danger.

PREDICTING CORRECTIONS

Anticipation typically does not help, either. As far as I know, no one has ever accurately predicted, over any ten-year period, whether a correction is a temporary retreat or the first leg of a bear market. Most advisers have tried to accomplish this feat by keeping track of a plethora of statistics. These are culled from a variety of areas, including technical indicators (price and volume measures, advance–decline line), monetary policy (changes in interest rates, money supply, free reserves), fundamentals (P/E ratios, price to sales, book value, debt levels, dividend yields, stock offerings, and buybacks), smart money trades (insider trading, short selling, money-manager buying versus retail buying), contrary indicators (news comments, investor sentiment poles, put-call ratios), the state of the economy, political factors, and the psychology of market participants. These data are available to all investors, large and small. Most of them can be found in weekly or daily publications such as *Barron's, Investor's Business Daily,* and *The Wall Street Journal.*

The fact that all this information is becoming readily available in real time means that market events unfold with increasing quickness. But even the most sophisticated computer models are not yet smart enough to weigh all the variables correctly. In addition, the fact that all this data must eventually be interpreted by human beings, who are influenced by their own beliefs and psychology, makes predicting corrections more art (or luck) than science. Even market gurus who appear prescient and omnipotent on occasion are dead wrong the remainder of the time.

Luckily for people whose livelihood depends on predicting market moves, the psychology of the market augurs for very short memories. For example, pessimistic advisers predicted a cyclical bear market for most of the 1990s. Despite their cataclysmic pronouncements, the aging bull market managed to fool most of the pundits and reach new heights until March 2000. Whenever we experience a correction, however, the doomsayers are featured in every business publication, reminding us of their recent predictions. What they fail to mention, of course, are their incorrect prognostications for the previous five or six years.

What are we to make of this phenomenon? Warren Buffett, perhaps the most successful investor of the past century, offers a history lesson in his 1994 Berkshire Hathaway annual report: "Coke," he said, "went public in 1919 at $40 per share. By the end of 1920 the market, coldly reevaluating Coke's future prospects, had battered the stock down by more than 50 percent, to $19.50. At year end 1993, that single share, with dividends reinvested, was worth more than $2.1 million." Buffett went on to quote Ben Graham as saying, "In the short-run, the market is a voting machine—reflecting a voter-registration test that requires only money, not intelligence or emotional stability—but in the long-run, the market is a weighing machine."

While I may be biased by training, I believe emotional stability is the primary force in preventing disaster during a correction. For the investor caught up in the anxiety of a correction or bear market, however, judicious actions are difficult to formulate, let alone execute. That's primarily because anxiety upsets our sense of self. And for most of us, the idea of having to wait seventy-four years for the market's "weighing machine" to devalue one share of Coke by 50 percent and eventually elevate its appraisal to $2.1 million won't do much to help keep our anxiety in check.

Consider, for example, the panic that followed the crash of the technology bubble in March 2000. It was still palpable three years later, and it was a humbling experience for most investors. Paper losses exceeded $7 trillion; the record ten-year economic expansion collapsed into recession; the Nasdaq 100 retreated nearly 83 percent from its highs; and many technology stocks retreated 80 percent to 90 percent from their 2000 highs. Because of the speed and intensity of the crash, monetary loss was devastating, comparable to the crash of 1929. During this troubling period, I received many calls from journalists wanting to know, beyond monetary loss, what all this meant for our collective psychological state. Based on conversations with distraught investors during the new century's first crash, my short answer is that we still have a lot to learn. My longer answers follow.

OUR FANTASIES OF MR. MARKET

Before most of us commit money to a stock, assuming we're doing our research, we delve into a company's management, products, and services, financials, technical trading patterns, and analyst reports. For many investors, this research produces objective data that help determine buy-sell decisions. But our decisions, as we now know, are based on more than objective data. Every investment is accompanied by fantasies, conscious or unconscious, that embody our deepest experiences of being in the world.

Some of these fantasies relate to the ostensibly objective data we've collected. For example, we may believe that some new technology will change the way our culture does business; we may believe that a CEO is the smartest manager we've ever met, someone capable of leading his or her company to tremendous market share in his or her industry; or our financial analysis may lead us to conclude we've brilliantly discovered an undervalued investment opportunity.

Other fantasies revolve around how we use the market to sustain our sense of self, our self-esteem, confidence, vitality, security, initiative, and wholeness. We are hard wired to need and seek out attachments and experiences that provide the psychological ingredients that maintain and foster the growth of our sense of self. As discussed in chapter two, most of these attachments involve relationships with other people. But institutions, ideas, books, nature, and even the stock market can serve the same function.

Think of the times you buy a stock and it immediately appreciates. Even if the transitory increase has nothing to do with the reasons you bought the stock, you feel smart and competent. Everyone who invested in the dot-coms before March 2000 felt like a brilliant investor to be admired and applauded for his stock-picking savvy. Those who believed in Henry Blodget or Mary Meeker and were guided by their analysis of some of the Internet stocks felt bolstered and uplifted by their imagined connection with these gurus. Their logic was as follows: "You're smart, you understand how to value these new economy stocks, and I follow you, so I'm smart, too." Those investors who decided fundamental analysis was passé and joined to trade stocks according to candlesticks, resistance and support levels, oscillators, and other complex technical formulas felt like kindred spirits.

It seemed marvelous at the time, and we look back with nostalgia, because we all felt so sustained, so good about ourselves. The process of investing in that environment performed an internal psychological function, helping to sustain, expand, and enhance our sense of self. These functions are different for everyone because they are subjectively perceived. In reality Mr. Market could care less whether our stocks go up or down. It is the fantasies created and identities defined in our investing activities that serve as the sustaining functions.

PRESERVING YOUR SENSE OF SELF
IN A DOWN MARKET

Of course all of this sustenance changed with horrendous speed after March 2000. All of a sudden, the daily (if not hourly) ritual of checking our stocks on the net with delightful surreptitiousness at work became agonizing and depressing. For we not only lose objective things like money when the market crashes, turns bearish, or severely corrects, we also lose the sustaining functions that the investing process provides. Even if our new market wealth earmarked for that new house or those college-tuition bills for our children was only on paper, it had become part of our being, and now it had vanished. With it, our self-esteem was pummeled, our capacity to calm ourselves down was diminished, our motivation was sapped, our confidence was shaken, and our vitality ebbed.

In addition, during many corrections and bear markets, an external sociopolitical crisis intensifies our sense of lost hope or battered fantasy. In 2001 we were not only in a recession, but many portfolios had been cut in half, more than a million jobs had been lost, and we were living in the aftermath of a traumatic attack on innocent citizens that eviscerated our sense of physical security. These real-world occurrences left most investors feeling vulnerable in several ways:

- Our sense of well-being had become more shaky.
- Our self-esteem was no longer as resistant to the stress of everyday life.

- Our sense of feeling like the same persons we were before September 11, our identity in time and space, became less stable.
- Our sense of feeling relatively independent and efficacious—our sense of being able to have an impact—lessened.
- Our sense of optimism and hope had given way to a more pessimistic and despairing outlook.
- Our sense of inner cohesion had given way to an inner disorganization, imparting a certain senselessness to the world.
- Our sense of psychological activity felt more frozen, with a kind of emotional paralysis impairing our mental activities.

With the emergence of these vulnerabilities, many reacted with a heightened sense of vigilance and alertness. This hyper-vigilance phenomenon occurs not only in everyday tasks of going to work, traveling, or entering crowded venues, but also in our investing activities. For example, we start watching our portfolio too closely, worrying about every downtick in a stock, reacting to anxiety by selling core holdings without thinking it through. When combined with our vulnerable state, hyper-vigilance creates very short-term investing orientations because the emotional impact of immediate events becomes overweighted. And in a reflexive way, this short-term orientation feeds on itself to create a more pessimistic market outlook.

THIS IS WHAT MARKET BOTTOMS LOOK LIKE

All of these market-related vulnerabilities are common at market bottoms. Because all of us are motivated to make rational sense of our emotional reactions, we tend to attribute them to external events. For example, psychologists talk about the World Trade Center explosion evoking post-traumatic stress syndrome. While generally true, the fact remains that at nearly every market bottom we observe similar emotions, with or without a traumatic event. When a market bottom is accompanied by an external trauma, it serves as a beacon that attracts explanations for our psychological state.

The moment when we feel most vulnerable to political and economic events generally signals the nadir of the bear market. But because investors have been traumatically silenced by their psychological vulnerabilities and because cognitive and emotional distortions are common at market bottoms, there is little motivation to think long term about our portfolios. Survival in the present takes precedence over everything. Yet it is exactly at those moments that the market offers us some of the best buying opportunities of a lifetime. Ironically we are then most likely to institute emergency measures in response to our psychological injury to compensate for the lost sustaining functions.

For example, when we feel anxious and lose the capacity to calm ourselves down, we might frantically seek out others to serve that function. We repeatedly call brokers, company management, and other investors, and we pursue scattered rumors on the stock message boards. When our vitality ebbs and we feel empty and depleted, we are most inclined to seek out stimulating activities, hoping to overcome the deadness that has set in. We might trade too often in an attempt to make up for losses. Some may use drugs or alcohol as a stimulant. Others may engage in high-risk activities. But no matter what the idiosyncratic response, the common theme to behavior in the wake of a down market is less determined by the external loss per se than by its impact on our self-experience.

Down markets affect each of us differently, depending on the relative strength of our sense of self. Think, for example, of two people whose boss criticizes them. One is able to allow the criticism to bounce off her with the realization that the boss is having a bad day; the other allows the criticism to eat away at her for the whole day, feeling immobilized and unable to accomplish any meaningful work. Both reactions are determined by how solidly we have internalized our self-sustaining functions. When less has been internalized, we will need more external compensation.

Most investing mistakes occur in our attempts to compensate for the loss of self-sustaining functions. That's why well-known investor Barton Biggs commented that "the mature, diligent, intelligent investment manager enhances his potential for better investment performance only through greater self-understanding."[7] Too many times in down markets we lose sight of this axiom and, with it, our self-understanding. Distracted by anxiety, we too often try to solve our dilemmas by solving the wrong problems because we address them on a behavioral (external) rather than psychological (internal) level. To solve investing problems stemming from market losses, we need to focus on the subjective experience of the investor. Consider the following example.

John repeatedly bought stocks that were recommended to him by friends, including some well-known money managers. In each case after he invested, the stock plummeted, usually a market phenomenon more than a fundamental problem with the recommended companies. John was consulting me because he wondered why he kept making the same mistake over and over. He knew that he shouldn't invest on rumors or recommendations without doing his own research. But the pattern continued despite this knowledge.

John was well aware of the pertinent rules against his investment behavior. Knowing the rules didn't help because rules approach the problem on a behavioral level. They didn't address John's subjective experience in buying these stocks. When I asked John what came to his mind when he thinks about buying on his friends' recommendations, he replied, "These guys are pros, they know what they're doing, and they don't go around telling everyone what they're buying." So it quickly became clear that John read into these tips that the money managers felt he was special.

John was having difficulty regulating his self-esteem as an investor in the absence of others thinking he was a unique and special person. When he bought on their recommendations, he was enhancing his self-esteem, but ultimately at the cost of his independence and net worth. Unconsciously the self-sustaining function being offered by these "special" recommendations was more important at that time than making money. In an up market, the recommended stocks probably would have appreciated in value, allowing John to feel both special and brilliant. In a down market, the frenetic pursuit of self-enhancing functions becomes decoupled from sound investing. That's why it becomes extremely important in down markets to understand how psychology affects investment decision-making.

PSYCHOLOGICAL TRAPS

When we desperately pursue emerging measures to shore up our sense of self, we often yield to psychological traps. Just when we need emotional stability the most, since it's the primary force preventing disaster during a correction or bear market, those traps steer us away from it. While there are numerous psychological traps for investors during any correction, the following three are perhaps the most common distractions:

The Primacy of Negative News. It is a psychological axiom that human beings pay much more attention to negative than positive news. We seem to share a perverse but ingrained fascination with suffering, loss, catastrophe, and the ills of others. Sometimes it is merely out of guilt, as when we stare at a handicapped person, not wanting to think "better you than me." Sometimes the fascination has its roots in complex feelings of jealousy, envy, and fear of loss. That's why media headlines emphasize disasters and often feature market commentators who are most fond of predicting gloom and doom. Our penchant for negative news, combined with our tendency to place the highest value on most recent information, leaves us vulnerable to undue emotion-based pessimism. This phenomenon prevails not only for broad market corrections, but even more so for corrections in individual stocks.

Rumors and Gossip. Because we tend to perceive any correction as a crisis, we have a natural defense of retreating to herds for protection, just as our evolutionary history teaches. As the goddess Athena suggested about herds:

> *Someone may tell you something*
> *Or you may catch a rumor straight from Zeus,*
> *Rumor that carries news to men like nothing else.*[8]

Herd mentality, fostered by corrections, promotes rumors and inaccurate information. Even the most rational investor is subject to their influence if the messages are repeated often enough in disparate contexts. Those who read the Internet stock message boards can witness firsthand how inaccurate information becomes "truth" in a matter of minutes. Only those who perceive themselves as outsiders, individuals who don't quite fit in with the current system and have come to terms with that status, seem able to resist capitulating to the rumors and gossip fed on by the herd.

Scapegoating. Every correction seems marked by a psychological need to blame someone. Both the suddenness of its onset and the anxiety it engenders leave investors temporarily feeling like the small child who, while running into the kitchen, bumps into a table and is furious at either the table for being there or the parent who put it there: "My broker should have told me," or "The CEO knew this was going to happen," or "The analyst's timing was dead wrong," or "It was only a stock promotion." As Zeus stated in *The Odyssey,*

> *Ah how shameless—the way these mortals blame the gods.*
> *From us alone, they say, come all their miseries, yes,*
> *But they themselves, with their own reckless ways,*
> *Compound their pains beyond their proper share.*[9]

Psychological scapegoating absorbs time and energy that should be directed to understanding the fundamentals of our own stocks and the market's monetary, valuation, and psychological dynamics. It allows investors to get caught up in frivolous and self-destructive activities, the worst being class-action lawsuits typically benefiting no one but the attorneys.

THE TRAUMA OF SHORT-TERM LOSSES

Even when we're not facing a correction or bear market, losing money can be traumatic to almost every investor. This doesn't mean you need to rush to a therapist or seek crisis counseling every time you lose money in the market. Short-term market losses become a problem only when we don't deal with this trauma, when we bury our feelings and carry on as if nothing has happened. This form of denial causes us, paradoxically, to become *more* vulnerable to our emotions, and that in and of itself can precipitate more mistakes. By working through our feelings from market losses, we can gain superior clarity, learn what emotions to anticipate next time we lose money, and discover what we need to do to regain our balance and focus.

THE PSYCHOLOGICAL MECHANISM OF TRAUMA

Because trauma has become such a prominent part of our culture—natural and man-made disasters, sexual and physical abuse, war-related atrocities, and terrorism—it may sound petty to include stock-market losses in this category. But if we define trauma as a real occurrence in the world, with a subjective impact that "changes our feelings and perceptions about ourselves in an intolerable way,"[10] then trauma is not properly confined to profound personal or geo-political catastrophes. It can result from any external event that, sub-jectively, shatters us to the point where the normal reorganization of our sense of self becomes temporarily or permanently impossible.[11] Thus trauma is always caused by a combination of external events mediated by subjective internal meanings attributed to the events. The notion of trauma has become increasingly important as our mar-kets have become more volatile, investors have become more active, and individuals have accumulated and lost fortunes in short periods of time.

Because the idiosyncratic meaning we give an event is what changes our self experience, events that seem minor to observers can be trau-matic to the individual experiencing the event. For example, monetary loss for some becomes traumatic not only because of the important, realistic consequences of loss of purchasing power, but because indi-viduals attribute subjective meanings to money—self-esteem, power, recognition, authority, creativity, status, and control.

To feel cohesive, good about ourselves, whole, alive, and vital with stable self-esteem and without undue anxiety and depression, we must, consciously or unconsciously, be surrounded by the empathic respon-siveness of others from birth to death. This may sound obvious, but it happens to be one of the more fascinating and important empirical and clinical discoveries of the past two decades. It is one of the con-cepts that challenges the very foundation of classical Western cultural thinking. It is in stark contrast to the old Freudian idea of independence as a pillar of mental health. We don't notice this in our daily lives because, paradoxically, it's when we are surrounded by the empathy of others that we most strongly feel a sense of our own independence. However, research indicates that certain people are more vulnerable to trauma than others. If we did not grow up in an atmosphere with sufficient empathic responsiveness to facilitate healthy self-development, or if our lives don't provide us with enough empathy today, our sense of self is likely to feel overburdened.

Ordinary minor losses in the market are not traumatic except to the extreme perfectionist. But for most of us, especially those who prided themselves on their great investment skills in the go-go '90s, the sustained losses in technology stocks since March 2000 could understandably amount to trauma, whether or not recognized contemporaneously. Those of us who thought we had equaled Peter Lynch had to watch as our much-hyped portfolio of hot stocks like Amazon.com, Priceline, Enron, and Worldcom came tumbling to earth. This forced us to cope with material loss, including lost dreams of early retirement and generous inheritance gifts. But more important, it also forced us to reevaluate our skills and beliefs about ourselves and to cope with those realizations. Perhaps the hardest dream to relinquish was the fantasy of being investors of genius who could sit at home and virtually print money just by calling our brokers or clicking our mouses.

This sudden, unexpected loss in the market, accompanied by loss of the normal experiences that supported and sustained the structure and cohesion of our sense of self, understandably resulted in emotional trauma for many investors. It was typically characterized by a constellation of symptoms. These include a number of aberrations:

Losing Touch with Our Self. Our investor personality no longer feels familiar; it's almost like a stranger to us now. We feel an almost zombie-like detachment, as if watching ourselves from afar and not really participating in our own investment activities. What seemed like second nature becomes foreign. This sense of being out of touch forces us to think carefully about investment strategies that formerly seemed intuitive. Alan, a longtime friend and investor, put it this way: "I used to have an intuitive sense of what I was doing each day in the market;

trading was natural. But now my thinking is labored and deliberate. I constantly second-guess myself, which only hurts my performance."

Disengagement. We no longer feel emotionally engaged in the investment process. We are devoid of feelings, surprisingly lacking in strong emotional reactions to market events. One investor told me, "I've just lost interest in the market. I don't understand it. I've always been so passionate about investing. Maybe I should take some time off."

Cognitive Deterioration. Those of us who previously maintained superior concentration and almost instant recall of facts and figures now have amnesia for the usual details. Our former acute memory feels like mush, and the capacity to rattle off years of statistics about the market or individual companies now requires Herculean efforts and written notes. As one investor put it, "I had the same facility with stock-market statistics as some kids have with numbers from the backs of baseball cards. Now it's like I had a lobotomy performed. My brain just feels empty, and I can't even remember yesterday's numbers."

Reliving Experiences of Loss. We continually relive the circumstances around a sudden loss. Some of us may frequently lie in bed at night reworking each minute detail of the scenario that led to the loss. We become preoccupied with the ways it could have turned out differently, if only we could have altered one tiny variable in the picture. Dreams and recurrent nightmares that concretize the event in images seem never-ending.

For example, one active investor reported a series of dreams that all had the same theme: He got into his car to go to work, was driving his usual route, when suddenly a large truck crossed his path. He jammed on the brakes and woke up before the crash, immediately recognizing the theme as "the same thing that happened to me in the market, and probably what makes me so hyper-alert these days." Hyper-alertness to the details of the loss makes the next attempt to trade or to invest seem exquisitely painful. We may also find that each new investment becomes a painful reminder of past losses. We become suspicious of any new investment possibilities and those who recommend them, almost to the point of paranoia. As one investor related, "I felt paralyzed by my tie to the past. Each component of my mistake was blown way out of proportion whenever I started to make a new investment. I couldn't get away from reliving the past."

Rage. To one degree or another, those of us who felt traumatized by our investment losses experienced an unrelenting rage and need for revenge following the trauma. Some express this rage by firing their brokers, posting libelous statements on the Internet, filing shareholder suits, or engaging in angry soliloquies at annual shareholders' meetings. These and other reactions generally reflect what appears to be a chronic discontent with the world. No matter how much others try to assuage the trauma, the rage remains palpable until the traumatic period is over. Buy and sell decisions reflect this rage in the way stocks are sold without regard for the investor's knowledge of the fundamentals of the company. It is as if by selling a stock one has attained the needed revenge against the company. And frequently competitors' stocks are bought with equal disregard for the fundamentals.

Hypochondriacal and Real Symptoms. The symptoms of trauma can also include health-related fears or actual illness. Somatic symptoms are common: tension headaches, stomach upset, chronic indigestion, minor aches and pains, irritation, hyperactivity, and shortness of breath. Panic attacks can also occur. With hypochondriacal symptoms, it is as if, instead of mind and body functioning as a whole, our sense of self breaks down into bits and pieces. We begin to worry about our individual body parts in much the same way a parent would worry about and try to comfort a small child who was under stress.

If you experience any of these symptoms following a precipitous decline in the markets or in your individual stocks, the important thing to recognize is that you need to complete the mourning process. You will get back to normal and feel like your old self only when the mourning process is complete. Until then your emotions will be sending you signals to do just what you should *not* be doing to bring your portfolio back to life.

THE MOURNING PROCESS

In his book *Only the Paranoid Survive*, Intel Chairman Andrew Grove commented on loss in another context—that of downsizing in today's corporate world:

> The sad news is, nobody owes you a career. Your career is literally your business. You own it as a sole proprietor. You have one employee: yourself. You are in competition with millions of similar businesses: millions of other employees all over the world. You need to accept ownership of your career, your skills, and the timing of your moves. It is your responsibility to protect this personal business of yours from harm and to position it to benefit from the changes in the environment. Nobody else can do it for you.[12]

The same is true of your investments. They are your responsibility, and yours alone, and they will suffer if you take too long to recover from the trauma of losses. Confronting a market loss creates a psychological crisis not so different from the one evoked by downsizing. In Grove's language, it creates a *personal* "strategic inflection point," a time when the opportunity for change must be grasped quickly. Although he doesn't use these words, a strategic inflection point for an individual is a crisis—a turning point at which we have the potential to achieve new growth or decline beyond all hope of quick recovery.

Most investors suffering a significant loss in the market experience variations on phases of mourning different only by degree from those experienced following the loss of a loved one. While we can separate these stages for discussion purposes, they are often more fluid and less distinctive.

Disbelief. When suddenly confronted by the reality of loss, we feel disbelief: "I can't believe this. How did I let it happen? I knew something was building, but I didn't do anything about it. I should have sold when the stock was at $50." At this stage, our feelings are dominated by apprehension and anxiety and a need to do something. But at the same time we feel frozen, unsure what to do next. While there may be some denial of the reality of loss, many of us demonstrate an oppositional quality. We respond to a perceived attack on our judgment and investing skill with aggression. We hunt for scapegoats—the broker who recommended the stock, the analyst whose projected earnings were inaccurate, or the friend or relative who offered the hot tip. What we are reacting to in this phase is not only the prospect of monetary loss, but, more important, loss of self-esteem and an important bond to the market, a fund manager, or company management. Eventually we will attempt to restore our damaged self-esteem, which leads to the beginnings of a second stage in the mourning process.

Faulty Attempts to Restore Self-Esteem. An injury to our sense of self precipitates emergency measures to reestablish self-esteem through abortive attempts to reconnect to those who provided sustenance before the loss. These attempts are usually abortive at this stage because our anxiety predisposes us to more unworkable styles of restoring contact, much like the child who uses strong emotion to elicit attention from others. Some investors react with frantic phone calls to company management, financial advisers, or brokers. Management perceives the emotional states accompanying these calls as whiny, entitled, demanding, and hostile; and they typically evoke cold, defensive responses. When rejected by their admired others, these investors often try to mobilize a community of like-minded other angry investors on the Internet. Message-board attacks on the company proliferate, and investors' fragmented selves begin to be held together by unfounded rumors and innuendo that serve to restore their sense of power and control while simultaneously evoking needed responses from others. When caught up in these reactive states, we also tend to relive in detail the memories of how we got into the stock, what management told us about the prospects for the company, the exact wording of press releases, and so on. This phenomenon is analogous to the grieving individual who dwells on memories of a lost friend or relative.

Temporary Fragmentation. Because these emergency measures are unlikely to restore self-esteem in the wake of market trauma, the investor's self remains shaky and unstable. If the loss is severe enough, we may experience temporary depression, anxiety, insomnia, physical symptoms, or simply feelings of emptiness and lack of motivation. The temporary nature of these symptoms does little to reduce their intensity while being experienced. It is crucial in this stage that we let family, friends, and peers provide emotional support. This is when we are most at risk for emotionally reacting to our loss in the market and compounding our errors. If we don't get vital support, our emotions can push us into overtrading, engaging in high-risk investments to make up for losses, arrogant grandiosity, unwarranted anger, or, for the unprincipled few, dishonest practices.

Beginning Recovery. At some point we must cease our frantic search for attunement and begin to accept the reality of our investing errors. It is at this point that we begin to realize, "I have no one to blame but myself." There are still hurdles to overcome in healing from our losses. The mourning process may be disrupted by our peers who can't get beyond their anger or, in egregious cases, by law firms that swoop in to mobilize class-action suits, refocusing the blame once again on the company and its management rather than allowing investors to continue their own soul-searching. To recover from our market wounds, we must try to examine our losses without strong emotion and to learn from them. Once we understand the logical reasons for our losses (even if just the truism that investing is risky), then we can begin the process of understanding our errors, restoring our confidence, and believing that we can invest profitably again. This is when we begin to believe that we can choose the next stock without repeating our mistakes. During this time we may also turn to admired others, whether through books of our favorite authors or talking about the investment world with people we admire. In this way we can borrow strength from them and further integrate their functions into our own functioning. Because this is a natural progression, it explains why sales of classic investment books increase dramatically during a bear market.

Final Recovery. Once our sense of self becomes stronger, when we have regained the needed functions that were lost, then we should start to feel motivated again to engage actively in the capital markets.

George Hagman, whose writing influenced this chapter, discusses the end of the mourning process: "There is a joyful reinvestment of the restored self in new experiences and initiatives. There is an experience of greater (emotional) stability, renewed vitality and self cohesion . . . [and] the self state has returned to its pre-loss conditions."[13] At this point the investor is able to return to the market with a sense of hopefulness and excitement that motivates the search for new companies or funds without the lingering depression, pessimism, and fear that characterizes investment trauma.

Successful mourning requires that we receive support and empathy from those around us. This is difficult for individual investors because loss of money is usually followed by some attempt to hide the devastation from oneself and one's family or friends. It is even more difficult in the professional community, where there is little tolerance for errors, and one year's poor performance often leads to public humiliation or job loss. However, it is just this change in jobs that may bring the money manager or analyst into contact with a new and supportive group of investors who are attuned and responsive. This change often facilitates the mourning process and enables market professionals to have a new and positive beginning, often in less time than afforded the individual investor.

TAKING ADVANTAGE
OF MARKET BOTTOMS

Most of us wear the scars of confronting investment trauma and portfolio disruption from market declines. Yet all investors know that one of the best ways to make money is to take advantage of market bottoms. To accomplish this we must go through the stages of investment-trauma recovery, begin to shift our attention from the behavioral level of our actions in the market to understanding how we subjectively experience ourselves, and start to shift our psychological outlook on three levels.

First, we must find ways to revive our lowered self-esteem. This requires us to get past the paralyzing sense of shame accompanying our investing failures. The reality is that we are indeed responsible for those failures; but only through the process of overcoming our shame are we able to review our mistakes, understand them, and regain enough confidence to find ways to avoid repeating them. Part of the process is understanding that our sense of shame evokes a need to hide our mistakes from others and ourselves. It encourages us to focus on a sense of badness that accompanies our humiliation. We need to accept the fact that no one in the stock market escapes losses. Those who tell you otherwise are lying. Bringing yourself to the point where you can accept and discuss your losses automatically decouples the shame from the mistakes and clears the way for resumption of purposeful investment strategies.

Second, we must regain our sense of efficacy. In other words, we must have the confidence that we are the authors of our actions. When feeling vulnerable, we assume that we are at the mercy of the market, that we have no control over our fate. To act in a contrarian way when the market reaches its bottom requires that we resume our belief that we can in fact affect our financial future by investing intelligently in the market. The best way to accomplish this psychological retooling is to sit down and formulate a strategy for going forward with whatever monies remain available for investment. If this feels impossible, then more time and effort is still needed for healing through the soothing, calming, and orienting functions of family, friends, or advisers.

Third, reengaging the market at its low requires overcoming a sense of detachment and numbness. Exposed by the harsh reality of investment losses, our vulnerabilities predispose us to a certain detachment from the market. This "I don't care anymore" attitude prevents the excitement and enthusiasm necessary to play the stock-market game. At this point we need to find something in the market that excites and motivates us, whether a new technology, a new management team, an encouraging broker, or an intellectual challenge to understand a financial report. Any investing plan is not absorbed from without; it is discovered from within.

Ask yourself the following questions to help with the shift from trauma to recovery:

- *What comes to my mind when the market is going against me?* This is a way to come to grips with the impact of the external situation (the down market) on our self-experience and the accompanying self-sustaining functions. In other words, what is the internal loss? Are we losing our ability to regulate our self-esteem in the absence of the market's confirming validation? When we focus on our losses, does it make us feel stupid, wonder how we made so many mistakes, kick ourselves for not selling earlier? Are we losing our internal belief in someone we looked up to? ("I knew I shouldn't have trusted that analyst.") Are we losing a role that was affirming? ("I can no longer be a good provider for my family.") Knowing what self-sustaining function is being affected leads to the next question.

- *What have I done in the past to restore myself when this has happened?* This question should help direct us to similar affirming feelings experienced in the past when we were able to marshal the resources we needed for recovery. For some the trigger may be positive feedback from others who appreciated our investment strategies, which may allow us to think about our other strengths, like being a good mother or father, well respected at work, or thought of as special by clients. Once we allow these other areas to become more recognized, we may no longer need "gurus" to confirm our specialness.

- *Despite my mistakes, what have I done right in this market?* The answers to this question should highlight pockets of strength that can be used to reformulate a constructive approach to investing. For example, Laura spent many months researching a company before she made a large investment in the stock. After waiting several years, the stock increased nearly 2,000 percent, but she failed to sell before the market crashed around her, wiping out most of her paper gains. She became extremely self-critical, which made her hesitant to make any further investments. But when she focused on what she had done right in the market, she realized she had done a superb job of researching the company she invested in. The company performed exactly as she predicted it would. Even though she failed to sell at the correct time, the realization that she had performed superior research restored her confidence in making the next investment. It also allowed her to examine her mistake of letting her sense of competence become too grandiose and ignoring warning signals from the market. This acknowledgment should help her avoid making the same mistake again.

- *What kind of cognitive planning can I do now?* Cognitive planning allows us to decenter from our emotions and put our intellectual capacities to work on the process of recovering from a psychological injury. Rather than being frozen in a bear market or retreating to an "I don't care anymore" mode until the market recovers, we can begin to examine ways to get back in the game. What should we be selling to be prepared for the next upturn? How much cash should we have on hand for new buying? What industries will lead the next recovery? Which stocks in those industries should we be prepared to buy and at what price? What new choices do we have to play this down market that we haven't thought about before? This type of disciplined examination should help revive our lost confidence and generate new motivation to reengage in the market.

GETTING BACK ON TRACK: PRACTICAL CONSIDERATIONS

Many summers ago my oldest son spent four glorious weeks hiking in the Talkeetna Mountains of Alaska with the National Outdoor Leadership School. In addition to the risks inherent in being out of touch with civilization for a month, the primary danger on his adventure was a chance encounter with grizzly bears. These creatures generally prefer to avoid human contact. But when surprised by unwary hikers, their reactions may be unpredictable and even life-threatening. To avoid surprises, the hikers were taught to continually recite "Hey, bear!" as they trekked through the Alaskan wilderness. The loud chanting was designed to warn bears of approaching humans and thus prevent unsuspecting encounters. Although the Hey Bear defensive strategy was not designed to eliminate the possibility of stumbling across a grizzly, it provided a comfortable Margin of Safety for the group.[14]

The concept of Margin of Safety is also useful in planning our actions in a correction, bear market, or any uncertain and volatile market periods. In fact Ben Graham, who co-authored what many regard as the most influential investment book ever written, *The Intelligent Investor*, considered it to be one of the central concepts of investing. Margin of Safety within the investment wilderness refers to structuring our investment decisions so that the odds favor profit over loss. To achieve a Margin of Safety, your answers to the following questions should help free up unknown strengths and put them to work in reentering the market:

• Do you know ahead of time what you will sell and what you will hold in a correction? Waiting for the correction to end will put you behind the curve for sorting out your portfolio.

• Can you treat all corrections as opportunities to increase holdings in your favorite stocks? For individual investors this means following a rule of buying only half to three-quarters of what you want to own and then waiting for a pullback to buy the remaining position.

• Can you ignore yearly relative performance? You should not worry about outperforming the market or other investors on a short-term basis. Even extended periods of underperformance make no difference as long as your stocks perform in a way that meets your long-term investment goals.

• Can you treat the increasing noise in the media about devastating corrections as a contrary indicator? Try to maintain the courage of your conviction that the best time to be a contrarian is at turning points in the market.

TEN

Interpersonal Investing

Psychologists have spent years proving that our identities, self-esteem, sense of competence, and even our subjective feelings of independence all depend on the state of our connection to other human beings. Connecting to others is also vital to the development and productive use of our skills and talents. It comes as no surprise, then, that my numerous interviews with both professional and individual investors suggest that the exceptional ones who consistently outperform the market do their best work in the presence of others. Contrary to popular belief, these interpersonal arrangements do not lead to groupthink; they actually protect us against it. Ironically the more alone we are, the more susceptible we become to the siren call of the herd.

When people share ambitions, values, and ideas, their investing skills and results improve. Particularly when investors develop a small network of like-minded others with whom to share information, successes, and failures, they make fewer mistakes. And when investors create a cohesive group atmosphere, it protects them against the isolation and loneliness that can make us so vulnerable to herd mentality. While there are some truly exceptional investors who manage to outperform the market alone, for the rest of us investing side by side with a small group of colleagues or friends seems to provide a special psychological glue that helps hold our sense of self together in the face of Mr. Market's capricious behavior and often dysfunctional responses.

OUR RELATIONSHIP WITH MR. MARKET

Ben Graham was the first investor I'm aware of to attribute human characteristics to an organized securities market. In *The Intelligent Investor*, Graham relates the following parable:

> Imagine that in some private business you own a small share that cost you $1,000. One of your partners, named Mr. Market, is very obliging indeed. Every day he tells you what he thinks your interest is worth and furthermore offers either to buy you out or to sell you an additional interest on that basis. Sometimes his idea of value appears plausible and justified by business developments and prospects as you know them. Often, on the other hand, Mr. Market lets his enthusiasm or his fears run away with him, and the value he proposes seems to you a little short of silly.
>
> . . . You may be happy to sell out to him when he quotes you a ridiculously high price, and equally happy to buy from him when his price is low. But the rest of the time, you will be wiser to form your own ideas of the value of your holdings, based on full reports from the company about its operations and financial position.[1]

We know, however, that most investment decisions are based on more than company financials and business developments. My premise throughout this book is that investors' perceptions of the market are shaped by more than just "objective" data, since all company and market information must be filtered through lenses we each use to organize the data into some meaningful interpretation that can be translated into action. These organizing lenses and translations are determined by our psychological structures—those "cognitive and emotional blueprints" that function (mostly unconsciously) to assimilate the data and subjectively make sense out of them.

If you accept this premise, it follows that our investment behavior is determined by both our psychological organizing principles (our emotional beliefs and convictions) and the external context (Mr. Market) that pulls for the use of a particular organizing principle. And as all investors know from painful experience, Mr. Market is adept at evoking a variety of emotional convictions, pushing our buttons and sometimes forcing us to adopt exactly the wrong organizing lens at the worst possible moment. When we have colleagues to talk with, someone we test out our organizing patterns with, it's harder for Mr. Market to manipulate us. And when we invest alone, it's more difficult for us to maintain our identities in the face of Mr. Market's wild gyrations, which mix stunning disappointments with base flattery.

Therefore, we are left to fill in all the uncertainties with our own fantasies and longstanding emotional convictions. In psychological jargon, this process is called transference. Transference is defined as the ways in which our experience of a person, place, or situation is shaped by the lenses or emotional convictions that have accumulated during a lifetime and that, through their expression in fantasy, help to structure our understanding and perception of that person or situation. To clarify the concept, consider how your experiences can shape your reaction to people's names, even if you don't know them. Transference plays similar tricks in the market, where it functions as an organizing activity for interpreting market events according to the blueprints of our subjective world.[2] Transference always feels rational, logical, and reality-based, but it actually involves a confusing combination of idiosyncratic emotions evoked by a situation that is similar to, but not exactly the same as, a past experience.

Transference to Mr. Market is fueled by two factors. The first is ambiguity. Whenever we have incomplete information, we rely more heavily on our own internal organizing lenses, feelings, thoughts, and fantasies as a guide for making meaning. And in a complex arena like the stock market, we can never hope to have complete information unless we possess a crystal ball with godlike powers. The information we glean about publicly traded companies is by its very nature ambiguous. We never know all of the relevant facts, and we're never as up-to-date as company insiders about what's going on.

The second factor that encourages transference reactions to Mr. Market is the inconsistency of his attunement to our needs. Because Mr. Market sometimes appears to be completely in sync with us, completely understanding of our needs and thoughts, it becomes all too easy for us to assume the market will *always* be in tune with us in this way. We get fooled because whenever there is a long bull market and our portfolio is performing well, there is a tendency to feel that all of our successful fantasies attached to the market will be fulfilled. We start to believe we really do understand the market and that it reciprocates with empathic validation of our most longed-for fantasies.

When the bull market enters a correction phase or slumps into a bear market, suddenly failing miserably to respond empathically to our needs, our hopeful expectations are driven underground. We protect ourselves by not mobilizing hope, and instead we rekindle defenses that preserve our threatened sense of self. For example, consider an employee who perceives his boss's behavior as critical. If the employee found a way to resolve a difficult problem, his expectation of criticism could put a dent in his enthusiasm when presenting his proposed solution to his boss. A reserved approach that downplays the importance of his plan reduces the anticipated blow from another failure to have his work appreciated and validated. Toward the end of the technology crash, many analysts reacted in a similar self-protective way by keeping their earnings estimates unrealistically low. Their defensive reactions represent emotional convictions elicited by the dysfunctional Mr. Market. It is only by recognizing these defensive reactions that we can prevent them from skewing our investment decisions.

TRANSFERENCE AND MR. MARKET

The instability, dysfunction, ambiguity, and lack of attunement of Mr. Market pulls for strong transference reactions. Particularly because he often does just the opposite of what investors expect, without offering any consistent reality that large groups of investors can agree on, he presents a plethora of situations that lend themselves to idiosyncratic interpretation by each investor's unique organizing principles. The market consistently mobilizes investor fantasy, both positive and negative. And because we all experience transference fantasy as objective, investment actions can *feel* extremely right no matter how completely and expensively wrong they turn out to be.

There is perhaps nothing as difficult to overcome as the need to take an investment action that *feels right* but is actually patently wrong. I remember one investor who called to tell me that a questionable technology was about to be used by a large multinational company in its oil-exploration activities. When I asked Stan where he had heard the rumor, he told me that it was not rumor, that he had heard about the development directly from the CEO. I reminded him that the large company in question had publicly stated it would be staying with its own technology, and I had no reason to believe it would change its position without a public announcement. But Stan was adamant that his information was correct and said he planned to buy a lot more stock in the company near term. I was unable to convince him to refrain from his purchase because he was convinced he was "on target all the way on this one." Needless to say, the multinational never did use the third-party innovative technology, and I never heard from Stan again.

When the market cooperates at times and confirms our investment decisions, our expectations for making money (and all the emotions that money represents) are heightened. When the market is going up, it evokes similar positive experiences in our life that assume center stage in our decision-making processes. We find it difficult at those times to resonate with any negative consequences of a bull market. But Mr. Market is extremely fickle and invariably finds ways to disappoint investors. The letdown heightens the defensive, fearful side of the transference, and we become fearful that our needs will be disappointed and rejected once again. As increased fear emerges into the foreground of our perceptions, cynicism and pessimism color our emotional convictions. We start to rely on this fearful and pessimistic lens to filter data coming out of the market. While protecting us against the perils of rekindling hope too quickly, it also biases us to notice only negative news when making market decisions. Pessimistic and fearfully tinted lenses easily become rigidified when they are attached to investors with slightly depressive personalities. These investors experience a heightened vulnerability to the prevailing negative herd mentality, and we often see them turn into perpetual bears, missing out on the next run up that may signal an emerging bull market.

TRANSFERENCE FANTASIES

We often become aware of our transferences through their expression in fantasy and dreams. One way to think about fantasies is as concrete images that dramatize our emotional experience and, as Stolorow and Atwood have suggested, "confer . . . on . . . [an] experience a sense of reality and validity that otherwise would be absent."[3] Thus fantasies often portray the state of our sense of self as it is represented in images. Dreaming about becoming lost on our way to a familiar place, for example, may represent a temporary state of disorganization in our sense of self. Dreaming that the walls of a sturdy house develop cracks often may represent symbolically a sudden threat to the structural integrity of our sense of self. Grandiose fantasies about what kind of house we would buy with our millions of dollars can be used to offset a severe invalidation of our experience of efficacy in the face of an investment failure. Obviously these sorts of dreams or fantasies have many alternative or deeper idiosyncratic meanings, but they often give us insight or at least a clue about our current emotional state. According to this theory, fantasies are heightened when our emotional experiences are not validated. Whenever you experience your fantasies becoming more intense than usual, it should serve as a signal. The message is not to try fulfilling the fantasy but to work at finding ways to strengthen your sense of self.

Let's say, for example, that an investor, Carrie, is excited about the prospects of a small company, the United Widget Corporation, and excitedly buys the stock. Mr. Market, fickle as ever, fails to validate Carrie's decision, and the stock initially drops. In the face of this disappointment, but without reviewing the fundamentals of the company, Carrie begins to mobilize fantasies about what an incredible buying opportunity now exists because Unique Widget in all likelihood is secretly poised to take over a big chunk of the $600 billion widget market. Solely on the basis of these grandiose fantasies, she buys a large block of additional shares. Her fantasy both dramatizes and confirms what the market had failed to validate as well as depicting what Carrie needed for the validation to take place.

In this example, Carrie may in fact be correct about her additional purchase, or she may be devastatingly wrong. For now we don't know because she never took a second look at the company's fundamentals. Assuming there was no fundamental change in the company's operating or financial position or real-world prospects, and the company's growth potential remained solid, Carrie may have been taking advan-

tage of a short-term market fluctuation. The problem with her decision was its basis, or lack of one, since it was motivated by a reactive
fantasy in the context of Mr. Market's invalidating response to her initial purchase. In this all-too-frequent scenario, the grandiose fantasy
validates the investor's pride in her original decision and prevents her
from seeing or even looking for any glitches in the company's business.
Of course, if United Widget prospers, her fantasy will have enhanced
what turns out to be positive motivation, so long as the fantasy is kept
within reality-based parameters and our investor stays away from the
undercapitalized and mismanaged Amalgamated Widget.

In some instances the validity of an investor's perceptions can come
under continuous attacks from those trying to drive a stock price down
or even to drive a company out of business. Consider the volume of
statements and innuendos on Internet message boards about company
insiders supposedly dumping their shares. No matter how fictitious
and manipulative, they still evoke intensely negative fantasies divorced
from reality and yet readily believable. Always consider the source.

Let's turn now to three other major interpersonal transferences that
occur in the market. In no particular order of magnitude, these stumbling blocks are the transference to management, to financial advisers
and brokers, and to short-sellers.

TRANSFERENCE TO MANAGEMENT

Many decisions to buy and sell stocks are quite properly based in part
on our assessment of management. But these assessments are by
nature perceptions, so they are fraught with all the ambiguities, uncertainties, and difficulties that characterize the relationship between Mr.
Investor and Mr. Market. In general there is both a tendency to look
up to management as admired others and a desire to have that admiration validated by competent guidance of the company's performance. The fear, of course, is that management will fail, remobilizing all
those past market disappointments in the investor's life. Where management does err and fail to live up to expectations, we discern a number of common transference reactions.

For example, many investors who feel humiliated and invalidated in
their decision-making counter these feelings with intense anger and

vindictiveness directed against the perceived source of their disappointment. I remember performing some consulting services for a company whose management ended up rejecting my recommendations. I found myself feeling dismissed and invalidated. My first reaction (which I kept to myself without acting on it) was "This is an incompetent management; I think all the shareholders in this company ought to sell their stock and get into a company that's run more competently." I initially wished to punish the current management, not so much on the basis of rational beliefs as out of a frustrated wish for retribution for their failure to agree with me. Instead, of course, I settled down and tried to put myself in their shoes, to discern the world from their perspective, thus gaining a more complete understanding of the reasons behind their decision. Unfortunately many people have difficulty allowing themselves to experience a full range of reactions without acting on them. When that happens, the type of negative reaction I first experienced can lead to premature selling and, at the extreme, frivolous, vexatious shareholder lawsuits that too often only enrich the lawyers at the expense of our companies and our economy.

Management often evokes anger by its failure to appreciate the transference bond that investors form with the company. This transference bond to management—the positive expectations—is disrupted by any glitch in the company's progress. These disruptions can create a sense of humiliation as they remobilize in the investor a repetition of past failures and disappointments. Silence or attempts to mask the reasons for poor performance or failure provoke continued revengeful fantasies because they exclude investors from the "life" of the company. If management had a better understanding of these transference bonds, perhaps they would be encouraged to provide interested investors with a more forthright explanation of the company's problems in a way that allows the investor to feel involved in management's efforts to solve those problems. Ideally allowing investors to feel like participants in the ongoing restoration process would foster their tolerance for these glitches while strengthening their bonds with the company. The importance of strengthening this bond is heightened in situations where the company is confronted by organized attacks by groups that are betting on the company's downfall, particularly when they resort to tactics designed to dramatically disrupt share-holder–management relationships by destroying management's credibility with long-term investors.

TRANSFERENCE TO ANALYSTS AND BROKERS

How we respond to the companies in our portfolio is often colored by our relationships with brokers and analysts. While there are numerous factors involved in what is clearly an underappreciated and complex relationship, one of the most important is the transference toward brokers. Most investors look to their brokers to clear up all the ambiguity and provide all the attunement that would make for perfect investing. To some extent we all seek out relationships with others that will somehow make up for what we perceive as lacking in ourselves. This demand that brokers or analysts be omnipotent puts an unusual burden on the relationship and often leads to disappointments, as brokers and analysts are acutely aware. However, when brokers are able to appreciate and respond to transference as needs being expressed rather than abject devaluation, their nondefensive acceptance can increase self-cohesion in the investor and functionality in the relationship.

For example, as the Nasdaq began to crash in March 2000, an acquaintance of mine waited anxiously but passively as he watched his heavily weighted technology portfolio collapse daily. He became increasingly panicked about his retirement plans and increasingly angry with his broker for "getting me to invest in all those overpriced technology stocks." Of course, John did not consider them overvalued when he loaded up on them and enjoyed their initial flights. In John's transference, his broker became the incompetent, untrustworthy, and uncaring "other" who was causing him so many difficulties.

When John called his broker in a rage, blaming him for what was happening to his portfolio, Mr. Broker did not respond in a defensive or argumentative way with lame excuses. He understood psychologically how let down and disappointed his client must have felt. As John calmed down, his broker also invited him to come in to go over the portfolio to make a plan for which companies they would sell and which looked like keepers that would survive the meltdown. John was surprised to find himself feeling much less panicked and less angry at his broker and more interested in becoming actively involved in making plans for managing the crash. As the connection with his broker was restored, his sense of self felt stronger, which allowed him to tolerate intense emotions without becoming disorganized and angry.

The nature of an investor's transference to his broker, financial planner, or adviser partially determines how he will react to unexpected happenings in the market. The quality of an investor's transference to his broker partially determines the level of risk that the investor can assume. This is why transference to professionals in the market becomes so important for maintaining our equilibrium in the face of Mr. Market's mercurial actions.

TRANSFERENCE TO SHORT-SELLERS

Legitimate short selling has a useful purpose in the stock market. It corrects the excesses and allows investors to make judgments about industry cycles and fundamentals. In fact specialists could not function without the capacity to short stocks. But shorting is often used as an emotionally manipulative device, where short-sellers not only bet against the success of a company, but do their best through rumor and innuendo to discredit management and others associated with a company. This is a predatory process subtly carried out by a small minority of investors with the conscious or unconscious intent of influencing stock prices through manipulating investors' emotions. Because the process relies on deceit and misdirection, it is difficult to uncover and often impossible to prove, accounting for the lack of effective regulatory control. For example, longs are required to file a Schedule 13-D with the SEC if they beneficially own 5 percent or more of any class of outstanding equity securities in a public company, but the shorts have no equivalent reporting requirement.

It is important to understand the emotional impact that the minority of unscrupulous short-sellers have on legitimate investors. By recognizing the psychological forces at work, investors have a better chance of protecting themselves against acting out of irrational emotion on which these shorts thrive.

As investors, we are motivated by a variety of emotions. Perhaps the most powerful one is hope—the hope that our selection of stocks will provide the means to achieve cherished ambitions and ideals or the ability to correct deficiencies in our lives. And as investors, we fear that any stock we select and put our hopes in will repeat previous disappointments or trauma (losses) experienced earlier in life. Each of these two dimensions has unique meaning for every investor, but I want to focus for the moment on how short-sellers, or anyone trying to manipulate stock prices in either direction, can use the media and other means to elicit our dread of repeating earlier feelings of emotional vulnerability. By understanding this process, you will be better prepared to filter useful information from disinformation and manipulation.

The Creation of Misunderstanding. Most investors perform considerable due diligence before committing their money to a stock. It is our cognitive understanding of the company's product, services, and management, our organizing and ordering of the available data, that gives us the sense of confidence to face the risk of losing our money. When we feel confident in our understanding, we experience a self-affirming, self-enhancing emotion. This understanding strengthens our sense of self and allows us to remain invested long term in our chosen companies. But to some degree we all have remnants of a childhood fear that we might have misconstrued or misinterpreted a situation. This is why it is so important, particularly in higher risk small- and micro-cap investing, for company management to continually make themselves available and be up front with investors. As long as our sense of self feels strong, and as long as we feel as though we have a solid understanding of our companies, we can tolerate a wide variety of daunting, fretful emotions about the companies we follow. Without a strong sense of self, those emotions would be intolerable when our stocks decline, and we would tend to sell out at just the wrong time.

One of the first ploys of market participants attempting to manipulate retail investors' emotions is to cultivate their misunderstanding about their companies. For starters, reports are published with emotionally tinged language and highly pejorative connotations. For example, "its been *reported* that *highly questionable* relationships exist with the *apparently unknown* investment bankers. . . ." Reported by whom? What questionable relationships? Who says they are questionable? Why does it matter if they are unknown? These are all reasonable questions. But the herd rarely challenges the distortions and negative hype. Instead they buy into the demeaning and inflammatory connotations that are designed to create confusion and misunderstanding in a contextual absence of facts tacitly or otherwise supporting the author's pejorative biases and pecuniary objectives.

When investors feel they can no longer trust what they thought they understood about their stock, a number of interesting psychological phenomena take place. The containment of strong emotion becomes impossible, and the normal self-doubt characterizing speculative investments is no longer tolerated. Psychological defenses are mobilized, paranoia mounts, and the cohesiveness of our sense of self (along with our confidence in our decisions) begins to break down. As a result, the successful creation of misunderstanding leads to enough self-doubt to make it increasingly difficult to tolerate the risk, and vulnerable investors are increasingly prone to exit an important position at exactly the wrong time.

Ad Hominem Arguments. An ad hominem argument is a statement designed to destroy the validity of a proposition, product, technology, or service by attacking a person's character rather than addressing the flaws in the product or the company's business plan. For example, a CEO is criticized or attacked because a large shareholder had been involved in an unrelated shady deal ten years ago. By implication the CEO might be dishonest also. This is a case of guilt by association. Or an "alert" is posted on an Internet message board (under an assumed name, of course) about the CFO's employment more than five years ago at a company that went into bankruptcy, not mentioning that the company tanked years after the CFO's departure. By implication the CFO had a direct responsibility for the bankruptcy and will repeat his mistakes in his current position.

One of the requirements for maintaining a cohesive sense of self is the perceived connection with available others who can be admired, looked up to, and felt to be a source of strength and empowerment. In fact many investors remain with a company through difficult times because they respect its management and have faith in their abilities.

Idealization of others is also an important safeguard against painful tensions and narcissistic vulnerability. This is one reason why investors become so frustrated and angry when they think management has let them down. By calculating ways to destroy the credibility of company management, people who stand to gain from the company's demise attempt to weaken investors' connections to their idealized others. Psychologically this disruption tends to temporarily short-circuit the integrity of the investor's sense of self, leading to a drop in self-esteem and vitality, and thus limiting his staying power in the stocks of troubled companies.

Contagious Affect. It is a fact of life that emotions can be contagious. Whenever our sense of self weakens, a psychological regression takes place in which cognitive functioning no longer remains at a logical, rational level. Rather than maintaining our usual cognitive sophistication when making reasoned judgments, we begin to associate words and concepts with their emotional connotations. For example, the word *red* no longer denotes a color along a spectrum; it connotes danger or a certain geopolitical orientation.

When the media wittingly or unwittingly relies on short-sellers for their headlines "du jour"—those sound bites that sell newspapers or attract viewers—they choose emotionally laden topics designed to appeal to investors' emotions, usually suspicion and paranoia. For example, if a struggling company resorts to a Reg-S stock offering, company detractors can enlist the media to point out the numerous underhanded stock deals that occurred in what is in actuality a legal and legitimate mode of financing. Media commentaries rarely include an analysis of the specific deal under discussion to determine its merits, or the fact that the particular financing was obtained at market rates rather than at the usual discount, or the fact that the loopholes that led to abuses in the Reg-S market were closed years ago. The seeming intent and likely impact of the inflammatory language is to evoke in investors an internal response aligned with the author's pejorative analogy, since emotions are contagious. This type of subtly biased (positive or negative) writing has been referred to in the literature as "journalism of illusion," and more recently by Robert Samuelson, a contributing editor of *Newsweek*, as "junk journalism."

The World as Attacker. Whenever our self-cohesion is threatened by anxiety, misunderstanding, or blatant attacks on our judgments, capacities, or character, we become emotionally vulnerable. Our sensitivities become heightened. Sights, sounds, smells, offhand comments, or rumors that we typically ignore become very disturbing. We are more prone to experience others as attackers because the easiest way to master the stimuli to which we have become so sensitive is to organize it in a paranoid way. This is the reason why people who use emotionally manipulative devices can disrupt financing arrangements and relationships so easily. The investment bankers that companies rely on for raising capital become just as caught up in the generated paranoia as the average investor. They are also just as vulnerable to herd mentality. When the rest of the world (or a highly strident subgroup) is on the attack against a company, the rest of the bankers are saying to themselves, "If Merrill Lynch or Salomon Smith Barney hasn't jumped for the company's business, why should we?"

The Negative Use of the Obvious. Many concepts in the investment world that are routinely taken for granted can be easily manipulated to appear anomalous. For example, a common ploy when discussing development-stage companies is to point out that the company has never reported any meaningful sales or earnings. One could argue that these comments either reflect very little experience with development-stage companies or that someone is attempting to turn the obvious into a frightening revelation. Statements of this nature contribute to the naive impression that we should never recommend or invest in emerging-growth companies that have yet to grow to the profitability stage. As a fan of development-stage companies, I have observed them for many years but have yet to see a single one produce significant revenues and earnings in the early stages. Even though this is all-but-axiomatic, the negative use of the obvious can still give investors a psychological feeling of estrangement when they're most vulnerable: "How could I be so stupid to invest in a company with no earnings or revenues?" People seeking to exploit that vulnerability know how to distort some of the most common-sense facts of life to foster a sense of enfeeblement in their targets' sense of self, often succeeding in making investors feel exposed to such an "obvious" mistake.

The Illusion of Objectivity. Those attempting to manipulate investor emotion set themselves up to become the admired, omnipotent, and reliable purveyor of objective information to others. Playing on the notion that companies sometimes exaggerate the benefits of their products or services, these individuals display an unshakable self-confidence in their statements and express their "knowledge" with absolute certainty. They usually back up their revelations with erroneous or out-of-context statements from ostensibly reputable studies that just happen to be available to investors with the good sense to inquire. These tactics are especially effective on investors whose self-esteem has been temporarily weakened during periods of emotional upheaval. Like cult leaders, these "experts" find ways to surface at just the right time to "objectively" point out hidden weaknesses in our companies and secret flaws in managements' personalities, behavior, and judgment.

As they say in Economics 101, "buyer beware." With an understanding of these transferences to the market, to brokers and analysts, management, and the press, your interpersonal investing can become the antidote to avoidable mistakes in the market as well as the prescription for a more rational approach to investment decision-making.

TRANSFERENCES OF CREATIVITY

Kohut has pointed out that during periods of intense creativity, many artists and writers develop a relationship with another person that is analogous to the transference relationships that evolve between patient and therapist in the consulting room.[4] Within the therapeutic setting, transferences are defined as the rekindling in the patient of early and often unfulfilled needs in the hope that they will now be fulfilled by the therapist. All transferences are influenced by hopes, fears, and expectations that we bring into our current relationships. Some transferences are common in everyday life, particularly our yearning for an attachment to someone who provides functions that strengthen our sense of self, functions that can be critical during periods of draining creative work. A fair amount of attention has been paid to these relationships with writers and artists (James Joyce and James Stephens, Pablo Picasso and Georges Braque, Sigmund Freud and Wilhelm

Fliess are prominent examples).[5] Their occurrence and role in the investment world has generally been overlooked.

One example of this sort of relationship is the twinship bond. Twinship relationships help us to feel sustained by being in the presence of investors who are like us. Within a twinship relationship we feel the reassurance that comes from our connection to a like other. According to an account by Roger Lowenstein[6] in *Buffett: The Making of an American Capitalist,* Buffett and his partner Charlie Munger seem to have this sort of relationship. Lowenstein quotes Buffett's daughter as saying the two were "clones," "walking with the same foot forward and even bearing a slight resemblance." As Lowenstein describes it, "the two of them had a peculiar symbiosis and, as in a good marriage, an aura of inevitability."

Janet Lowe, in her biography of Munger, also appreciated this creative transference between Buffett and Munger: "In Munger, Buffett found someone who shared his values and goals and to whom he could talk on a sophisticated level."[7] And Munger himself once stated, "You know the cliché that opposites attract? Well, opposites don't attract. Everybody engaged in complicated work needs colleagues. Just the discipline of having to put your thoughts in order with somebody else is a very useful thing."[8]

It is also clear from Lowenstein's account that Buffett's extraordinary capacity for pursuing his work was dependent for many years on his wife's background presence and sustaining emotional support: "Even on a normal day, Warren's face would light—a touching betrayal of his feeling, when Susie entered the room. She would run her fingers through his hair, fix his tie, sit on his lap, and hug him. She sustained him."[9] Such sustaining relationships are always part of creative transference.

Creative work under conditions of risk often demands these types of bonds to support our sense of self. Twinship partners are often able, almost unconsciously, to support each other through difficult periods, like the lonely stretches when the market goes against them. Interestingly twinship relationships, when they exist successfully, tend to operate in the background without the participants acknowledging or necessarily realizing that important functions are being supported.

In my experience the good enough investor needs the support of a partner to perform at peak efficiency. The partner may be a business associate, a friend, a spouse, or a sibling. All that matters is that they share an essential sameness and provide critical emotional support for the often lonely work of investing.

When two people are connected by their sense of we-ness, or essential alikeness, an interesting phenomenon takes place. Each tends to enhance the skills and talents of the other. For investors this means that each partner's efficacious capacities occur in the context of a shared human connection that helps both partners recognize his or her own organizing patterns and expand them.

Consider Julia, an investor who generally functioned alone in the investing world. She had a long-term perspective, thoroughly researched her companies, and then made large bets on those few she thought had the best overall prospects. Through her investing, she met a shorter-term player, Mary, and they began what turned into a multiyear dialogue about their different stocks and styles of investing. In many ways Julia and Mary were very different, but they forged an underlying bond through their essential alikeness. They had similar worldviews, philosophies about life, and beliefs about what characteristics went into making a good investor. As the relationship grew, they were able to discuss mistakes, exchange investing ideas, and "hold" each other through stressful periods in the market, thus preventing many mistakes.

In the course of the relationship, Julia began to expand her investing lens to discern the value of short-term trading with a small amount of her funds. Trading side by side with short-term-oriented partner Mary enabled her to expand her organizing patterns and emotional convictions, and she developed a skill in short-term trading that was previously undeveloped and that enhanced her overall market performance. Similarly the short-term investor Mary expanded her investing repertoire to include a longer-term perspective, and she began to earmark a larger portion of her funds for long-term investing. Through continual telephone contact, which occurred several times a week, they were each able to expand their market perspective to include the other's organizing patterns to enhance their own investing style.

THE VALUE OF MENTORS

Investing in an interpersonal context also means developing relation-ships with admired others, whether through their writings, discus-sions, or other activities. Connecting with a looked-up-to person's stature, strength, and calmness, as psychologist Jim Gorney has described it, "enables the unique shape of an individual's talents and skills to crystallize ultimately in the . . . workplace and the world."[10] The investment literature is replete with references to heroes. Warren Buffett had Ben Graham and Philip Fisher; Peter Lynch had his teachers at Wharton and Boston College; traders have Jesse Livermore; technicians have Martin Pring; John Templeton has his spiritual heroes; mutual-fund investors have John Bogle. The list is infinite. In fact much of the training for the investment profession occurs through the apprenticeship model. Seth Klarman, author of *Margin of Safety* and president of the Baupost Group, a private money-management firm, confides that "I was extremely fortunate in my first real job to have the opportunity to work alongside Michael Price and the late Max L. Heine at Mutual Shares Corporation. . . . My learning in the two years working with Max and Mike probably eclipses what I learned in the subsequent two years at Harvard Business School."[11]

In a review of Robert Hagstrom's *The Warren Buffett Way*, Joe Queenan is critical of the "Aw Shucks School of Great Investors" (specifically Lynch and Buffett) for suggesting that anyone can be successful if he just follows certain down-to-earth principles. Queenan's criticism is indeed valid. Ordinary investors generally do not have the same access Buffett had to the likes of the *Washington Post*'s Katharine Graham, whose stock Buffett owned. But the fact is, in times of stress, well-defined heroes and idealized experiences are among the best sources of self-sustenance. If you feel attached to an admired other (or his or her writings), a sudden disruption in the market will send you scurrying to reread your favorite author, call your favorite newsletter writer, or seek guidance from an admired broker. In the process you're more likely to get settled down and usu-ally prevent major mistakes. How many times does a call to a newsletter hotline soothe the anxiety of a distraught investor? While the apprenticeship model is not available to all investors, building up a library of your investment heroes' writing provides an often-overlooked form of support for individual investors.

Establishing connections with admired others also supports our capacity for self-soothing so that anxiety in the wake of difficult market environments or mistaken investment decisions does not lead to further complicating actions. As Barton Biggs once suggested, "It may seem corny, but when the market or a stock goes against you, it always seems to help to have someone else to complain and commiserate with."[12] One of the most important margins of safety in my own investing has been the development of a small group of admired investors whose opinion I respect. Their support has been invaluable, especially in difficult market environments. This is also why some of the best mutual-fund companies use co-managers to run their funds, and why investors are frequently hungry to read books by their favorite gurus.

MIRRORING

Another style of relationship that buoys the self-esteem needed for rational investing is a mirroring connection with others. We always feel a bit vulnerable when buying or selling stocks because the market may not validate our decisions. A mirroring relationship provides those validating, affirming experiences that strengthen and sustain our ability to continue to make investment decisions through good times and bad times. When a member of an investment club tells his fellow member, "You made a real good call on that last stock pick" or "Even though the stock didn't move, I think your fundamental reasoning was right on," it prevents those humiliating, incompetent, and gun-shy emotions that inevitably complicate our next investment decision. Mirroring relationships are not the "pat on the back, you did good" kind of support and sympathy you might imagine. Rather they are relationships in which we feel a sincere acceptance and confirmation of our personhood in the context of the task at hand. Particularly for investors who are not working in institutions, where there is more opportunity for affirmation (although often discouraged by the culture), individual investors need this kind of support to avoid the dangerous and common practice of using the stock market (rather than their peers) as a mirror for their self-esteem.

Consider a doctor who had been investing alone for years, with performance continually lagging behind the major indexes. Most of Harry's mistakes occurred because he had difficulty buying a stock even after spending weeks researching the company, talking to management, and following its trading pattern. As Harry explained, "I always think I have to buy it at exactly the right time because if the stock goes down after I buy it, I feel so badly about myself that I often sell just to restore my self-esteem." Harry depended on the market to maintain and enhance his self-esteem, always a dangerous addiction in the market.

At an investment conference, however, our doctor–investor met several conferees who had a similar interest in small-cap investing and asked him to join their loosely knit group of investors. While not a formal investing club, the group did occasionally meet, although most of their contact was via telephone and e-mail. Within the group, Harry was appreciated for his thorough research and "offbeat" ideas. Even when some of his stock choices failed to perform in the short run, his colleagues encouraged him to stick with his choices because of the solid research underlying them. Harry began to feel that his stock-picking methods were being validated, and as he confessed, "Since the others seem to respect my work, I've even started to buy my own picks without procrastinating." His mistakes subsided, and his performance began to improve with his confidence as he became a valuable member of the group.

I have heard investors repeatedly tell similar stories, not only in the retail world, but in the institutional world. When interviewing institutional analysts, for example, I obtained considerable anecdotal evidence that the analysts who felt respected and appreciated by the chief of equity research tended to have much more confidence in their decisions than those who, for whatever reason, felt they lacked their boss's affirmation. For the most part, their performance tracked their confidence levels.

Investors need relationships that not only provide opportunities for connecting with looked-up-to others, mirroring others, and others who share similar beliefs and investing styles, we also need relationships with supportive others who question our choices, opinions, and decisions. These are supportively adversarial relationships. The Buffett–Munger partnership reflects this sort of connection. Munger questioned Buffett's allegiance to the Graham philosophy as a sole means for valuting stocks, and according to Buffett, Munger was responsible in part for Buffett's expanding and revising his views on valuations.[13] The good enough investor needs a cohort who can continually question his convictions, theories, and beliefs. The interaction helps to expand our perspectives without forcing us to abandon them.

GOING IT ALONE

But what about investors who insist on going it alone? Some people insist that they perform better when uninfluenced by others. Indeed there are some very successful "isolated" investors. In my experience, however, those who are successful investing alone are really not alone because there is always the representation of another person present. A good example of this quasi-aloneness outside the investing field is the hermit who is surrounded by meaningful representations from the past, which prevent him from feeling emotionally isolated. Think of the comfort some folks receive from being surrounded by books, music, or nature. Or think of the comfort some elderly people experience in relating their memories to only slightly bored younger relatives. The small percentage of people who buy and sell stocks alone do so without feeling isolated. They thoroughly enjoy the investing process and are sustained by their research, systems, books, and internal connections to others.

These investors have more than a wish to do it alone. They have the ability to function well when alone, and they frequently value solitude as a prerequisite for doing their best work. They generally surround themselves with a nonhuman environment represented by symbols that provide comfort, motivation, tension modulation, and confidence. These symbols, be they trading systems, books, or a particular spatial setting, are usually connected with meaningful others from their past. In my experience, investors who function in ostensible isolation invariably describe former mentors and teachers who seem to be invisibly and continually looking over their shoulders. Their offices are filled with important books from which they have learned their craft. And while not working with others directly, they tend to have a small cadre of investors with whom they compare notes on occasion.

RGK Kainer refers to these mentors as "figures who have gone before us, whose achievements guide, inspire, inform, and stimulate our own strivings, both consciously and unconsciously. For the strongly creative person, sustenance can come from the precursor who is idealized but is not necessarily part of one's actual life."[14] The paradox of the investor who functions alone is that, as Winnicott suggests in another context, he is "alone while someone else is present."[15] Someone else is always there in his mind, someone who silently serves validating, sharing, or guiding functions. Indeed the alone investor is not an isolated investor, but instead is psychologically immersed in a fulfilling environment. If you are one of this small minority, then actual support from others will be less important.

For most investors, however, the value of interpersonal investing cannot be overemphasized. An ongoing connection to a trusted other provides support in stressful times, expansion of our organizing lenses, validation of our own investing styles, and containment of both our grandiosity and our depression. These trusted relationships also promote a certain playfulness in the investing process, an invaluable intangible that enhances the creative use of our talents and skills and, ultimately, our prospects for sustained successful investing.

ELEVEN

The Good Enough Investor

As we conclude our journey into the psychological underpinnings of investment decision-making under conditions of risk, it is important to remember that cultural change, individual anxiety, and group panic, combined with Mr. Market's inherent unpredictability, will always prevent us from becoming perfect investors. New economic realities, novel pressures on our sense of self, and variations on herd mentality will continue to confront us with constant change, which may be the only immutable characteristic of the market. It is the nature of cultural, individual, and group change to foster investment errors. But the good news is we don't have to be infallible to succeed in the market. We just need to become good enough. Perhaps Warren Buffett, one of the few investors who seems to have understood this idea, captured it most succinctly with a well-known quote from Keynes: "I would rather be vaguely right than precisely wrong."[1]

Now that we're no longer burdened by perfection fantasies, we still need to figure out and then practice what it takes to become good enough or, in Keynes's words, "vaguely right." As you know by now, it's my basic premise that this more realistic goal requires each of us to focus on the psychological aspects of our individual investing style that make us as proficient as possible in the market. Understanding our own emotional convictions, our own way of interpreting reality, our flaws and biases, when to act on our emotions and intution, and when to put them aside is the royal, though rigorous, road to investing success.

Let's review the general rules of this road. Investors are most likely to succeed when they have developed a particular psychological framework that draws on their strengths and sidesteps their weaknesses in guiding their investing decisions. That framework includes:

- The capacity to be curious and puzzled
- The patience to investigate a company's potential
- The ability to imagine what could go wrong with our decisions
- Creating a good fit between our investing style and our personality
- The capacity to be an outsider
- The capacity not to know
- The capacity for self-reflective awareness
- The ability to decenter
- Emotional discipline
- The capacity for optimal restraint

To illustrate how these qualities of the good enough investor contribute to sound investment decisions, I want to conclude with a case study of a small company called Leading Brands (Nasdaq: LBIX). My assessment of Leading Brands offers a framework to clarify how our psychological characteristics interact with the financial elements of investment decision-making.

Leading Brands came to my attention when a PR firm claimed that this unknown small company in Canada would eventually become a large well-known North American phenomenon. I hear that kind of story every day and usually don't bother to skim the financials or even write down the stock symbol. In this case the company had a market cap of $13.5 million (based on 13.5 million shares outstanding and a market price of about $1.00), too small for a blip on anyone's radar screen. The company was in the bottling business and was based in Vancouver, British Columbia. I had already gone through a difficult experience with another Canadian beverage company, Clearly Canadian, and didn't want to repeat the experience. Admittedly, I was initially guilty of transference to the industry!

On the other hand, a quick glance at its chart indicated LBIX had been trading in the $1 range for the past nine months, so it probably wasn't going any lower if anything positive was happening. In addition, I was searching for undervalued non-technology companies in view of the difficult market that had befallen new economy stocks. It also occurred to me that, despite the recession, no one was going to stop consuming juices and other beverages. I was also curious: Why would a PR firm be so interested in a company with a $13.5 million market cap, especially since this particular PR firm had all the business it wanted? So I agreed to get in touch with the CEO and listen to his story.

THE CAPACITY TO BE CURIOUS AND PUZZLED

My reaction to the PR firm's heads up on Leading Brands reflects the first requirement on my list of components for the good enough investor—to be curious and puzzled. Forget the accepted wisdom about curiosity's effect on cats. Curiosity is part of what makes us human. But for most of us, it often falls prey to the general concerns of everyday life, particularly work. Our single-minded ways of seeing things and our unspoken theories about the world, while helping us fit into our surroundings, seem to have a way of keeping our creative puzzlement silently imprisoned in the deeper reaches of the mind. Perhaps that's why so many of us flounder with the latest technologies while our children or grandchildren gleefully experiment and solve problems using these contraptions, without so much as a glance at the directions.

John Bunyon supposedly said, "The dream will make a traveler of Thee." It will also make an investor of thee. As you walk the same path each day in your commute, try to notice and be puzzled about what's around you. Do you ever wonder who made the cell phone you use, or how it works? Who puts the bar labels on the junk mail you throw out, and what might you learn by opening the stuff before tossing it in the recycling bin? Why does one audio speaker sound better than another? Who makes it? What makes it better? What bicycle does your child ride? Why does he or she like it? How do the paintings at the museum get restored? Why do all baseball players but the pros use metal bats? What kind of machinery is used to make them? Which studios have produced your favorite films? Who is going to store all the data that corporations produce? What new forms of wireless services will make communications faster and easier?

This capacity to be curious and puzzled by our surroundings, be it art, science, business, nature, sports, music, or politics, is what produces creative ideas for new services and products. To be a proficient investor means recapturing your childhood curiosity about the world, the ostensibly innocent "Why is the sky blue?" sort of questions. A renewed sense of puzzlement about the world may well fuel some of your best investment ideas.

My first conversation with the CEO of Leading Brands, Ralph McRae, began with his asking whether I knew anything about the bottling and beverage industry. I told him that years ago I had been interested in Clearly Canadian and managed to acquire a little knowledge, but that the investment had been a disappointment. Ralph told me an interesting story from a number of years back, when Leading Brands had been essentially a shell company with $2 million in cash. Clearly Canadian was just starting out at the time and had approached this tiny shell with a proposed deal: Lend us $2 million, and we'll pay you $0.25 for every case of Clearly Canadian you sell. Clearly Canadian began doing well for a few years after the deal. Its management felt they were overpaying the shell and offered to buy them out of the contract. So Clearly Canadian paid this upstart shell $24 million to get out of the contract. Unrelated to the Leading Brands deal, Clearly Canadian then tanked, leaving the shell with a pot full of money. With that cash infusion, the shell decided to go into the bottling business. They built several bottling plants, and then, as often happens with startups, management nearly destroyed the business. Recognizing the company's potential, its lawyer, Ralph McRae, took it over. He discovered they owed the Canadian government a lot of taxes, which he was able to negotiate down. He then sold off two plants, paid off a lot of debt, downsized the company, and turned it around. He told me that he was publicly forecasting that LBIX would generate revenues in 2001 of about $45 million, with earnings of $0.14–$0.15 per share. Now Ralph had my attention, so in addition to what Ralph told me, I decided to look a little deeper.

THE PATIENCE TO INVESTIGATE
A COMPANY'S POTENTIAL

For me, researching a company's potential involves three concurrent processes: compiling and analyzing publicly available information to determine whether the data supports buying its stock, evaluating its management, and analyzing the role of my emotions in deciding whether to purchase the stock or hold the stock after a purchase. I'll take you through my research process for Leading Brands as an example of how I evaluate companies before buying (or selling) their stock.

I discovered that Leading Brands, a Nasdaq small cap company, had 16 million shares fully diluted and a public float of 8.5 million shares. It was the largest independent, fully integrated food and beverage distribution and brand management company in Canada, and it appeared poised for a major expansion into the U.S. The company's core business was the packaging, distribution, sales, merchandising, and brand management of juices, water, soft drinks, new age beverages, snack food, and confectionary products across Canada. In addition, its Quick, Inc. subsidiary was building an Internet-enabled consumer home replenishment system, as well as a unique business-to-business platform for the beverage industry. Here's a summary of the type of information I compiled about Leading Brands before accepting it as an investment opportunity:

- *Leading Brands's Products.* I discovered that Leading Brands's initial success came from its in-house beverage production capabilities, branded product lines, and distribution network covering all of Canada. On the beverage side of the business, LBIX's operations were on three fronts: First, they provided beverage packaging services (co-pack) to major branded beverage companies such as Coca-Cola, the Quaker-Oats Company of Canada, Ocean Spray International, PepsiCo, the Minute Maid Company, and Heinz. So there were a number of well-known companies that seemed to trust LBIX's services. Second, the company's private label program involved designing, developing, and formulating juices and other beverages for sale by chain stores under their private or controlled label programs. LBIX had entered into a joint venture with the Cliffstar Corporation of

Dunkirk, New York, to further expand this business across Canada and the Western U.S. This seemed like a promising route to new business. Third, Leading Brands had its own branded cocktail mixes, lemonade and iced teas, natural juices, and bottled water, which were marketed by the company's own sales force. LBIX was also the number two salted cracker company in Canada and the number five cookie company in the country, reselling for large mills in the U.S. This gave LBIX freight synergies and countered the seasonality of the beverage business.

- *Competitive Advantages.* Leading Brands had developed information technology and organizational systems that provided competitive advantages within its segment. Its proprietary Integrated Distribution System (IDS) allowed the company to move and track its products from the raw materials stage through the packaging, warehousing, and distribution phases with greater efficiency and less cost than its competitors, who were outsourcing each separate part of their business. Leading Brands also had the resources to help third-party suppliers design flavor profiles and packaging. These capabilities made them a one-stop shop for companies who wanted to coordinate their outsourced design, bottling, packaging, and distribution operations in markets dominated by Leading Brands. This capability plus the efficiencies of its IDS provided the company with what appeared to be a major competitive advantage. Its only real competitors in its niche market were Coca-Cola and Pepsi.

- *Facilities and Plants.* Leading Brands operated two beverage plants, together encompassing over 100,000 square feet and capable of producing over 18 million cases of beverages per year. Bottling could be done with glass and P.E.T. and HDPE plastics. They also had a separate snack food packaging plant with a capacity of approximately 6 million pounds per year. Major capital expenditures required for future growth had already been completed, and there appeared to be plenty of capacity available to accommodate expansion.

- *Sales and Marketing.* LBIX had an extensive sales, marketing, and distribution network that covered all of Canada. Their products were also distributed in seventeen states in the U.S., and they expected further U.S. expansion in the near term. The company's sales and merchandising team covered Western Canada, Ontario, and Quebec. The customer base was primarily chain grocery and drug stores, mass merchandisers, food service outlets, and convenience stores. They seemed to have a knack for working with their customers to continually develop innovative programs for effectively merchandising products and driving sales at the store level. Their IDS was also useful in retaining customers by ensuring rapid order processing and efficient order delivery.

- *Quick, Inc.—A Commitment to E-commerce.* Leading Brands had made a major commitment to e-commerce by acquiring Quick, Inc. and the domain name www.quick.com. The company had invested CD$10 million for the acquisition and site development, with the objective of providing an on-line purchasing service for home delivery of a broad range of grocery and other products within 24 hours. In January 2001, Leading Brands sold certain intellectual property and capital assets of Quick, Inc. to Northland Technologies, Inc. (NTI) in exchange for 12 million redeemable preferred shares in NTI. This was a financing transaction at its core but was structured as a sale and a put back for tax purposes. The operating business remained a wholly owned subsidiary of Leading Brands, but NTI acquired the hard assets. Leading Brands's objective was to re-acquire the assets within two years of the transaction. In October 2001, the company announced Quick's first use of its new fulfillment system for a business-to-business application. Management intended to establish Quick, Inc., with the help of NTI, as the fulfillment system of choice for the food and beverage industry. The company also expected this subsidiary to be profitable by spring or summer of 2002.

- *New Developments.* There were several recent events that seemed important to me in reaching my purchase decision. In November 2001, the company entered into a perpetual license agreement with Havana Iced Cappuccino North American Beverage Company of New Jersey for distribution of Havana Iced Cappuccino throughout Canada. Havana was one of the fastest-growing iced cappuccino products in the quickly expanding North American market for ready-to-drink iced coffee.

In January 2002, Leading Brands entered into a multi-year license agreement with the PopStraw Company of Michigan for the exclusive use of the PopStraw™ technology in Canada. The technology allowed consumers to enjoy beverages from plastic bottles with drinking straws that are already packaged inside and pop up when the package is opened. According to PopStraw, other beverage companies using the PopStraw feature had seen 10 percent to 14 percent increases in sales, even when product prices were increased to cover the added cost. At the time the license deal was announced, Leading Brands anticipated selling its first products incorporating the new technology within ninety days.

Also in January 2002, Leading Brands entered into a multi-year license agreement with Pez Candy, Inc. for the design, manufacture, and distribution of Pez Juice Drinks throughout the U.S. and Canada. The company planned to design a unique package to highlight the well-known brand attributes of Pez for a line of natural, preservative-free juice drinks targeted at eight-to-fourteen-year-olds. The new product would address what Leading Brands saw as a gap in the beverage market: a fun, healthful product that parents could buy for their kids and that kids would eagerly consume.

• *Management.* In May 2001, the company initiated a buy-back program for the repurchase of up to 10 percent of its issued and outstanding common shares from time to time in open market transactions. At the time I reviewed the fundamentals, LBIX had repurchased approximately 175,000 shares. To me, this reflected management's confidence that the company was worth more than it was given credit for in the market. Because the stock was thinly traded, the program also provided some liquidity for existing stockholders who wanted to sell shares without further depressing the stock price.

• *Financials (Expressed in U.S. Dollars).* For its fiscal year ended February 28, 2001 (fiscal 2001), the company reported revenues of $49.8 million, up 70 percent from $29.4 million in fiscal 2000. Net income for fiscal 2001 was $1.2 million or $0.09 per share, compared to a net loss of $608,000 or $0.10 per share in fiscal 2000. This was an extraordinary $1.8 million positive differential. For the first nine months of fiscal 2002, Leading Brands reported revenues of $33 million compared to $42 million for the first nine months of fiscal 2001. Net income for the first nine months of fiscal 2002 was $1.4 million or $0.10 per share, compared to net income of $604,911 or $0.05 per share in the corresponding prior period. Revenues for the third quarter of fiscal 2002 were $8.9 million compared to $11.4 million in the fiscal 2001 third quarter. I was concerned about the decrease in revenues but found out that it was the result of a change in the company's arrangements for distributing SoBe products in Canada after Pepsi bought out the distribution rights for those products. Excluding SoBe, revenue increased 11.1 percent over the corresponding prior period. Net income for the third quarter of fiscal 2002 was $54,312 or $0.01 per share versus a net loss of ($486,504) or ($0.04) per share in the same quarter of fiscal 2001. I expected the company to make up the revenue decline in fiscal 2002 through internal growth.

For the fiscal year ending February 28, 2002, I estimated revenues of about $40 million, with earnings in the range of $0.15 per share. For fiscal 2003, beginning in March 2002, I thought the company could reach $60 million in revenues and could earn up to $0.25 per share. With the bottom line improving at just under 70 percent per year and the forward P/E at only 4.3, I concluded LBIX was significantly undervalued.

I was also influenced by consistent improvement in the balance sheet. Current assets on November 30, 2001, the end of the company's third fiscal quarter, were $5.97 million, with current liabilities of $5.7 million. The core operating business was producing enough cash to offset the minimal working capital on the balance sheet, and management expected working capital to increase. Long-term debt was manageable at $2.4 million, representing 18 percent of the $13.6 million in shareholders' equity. On balance, the company seemed poised for sustainable growth, adding to my enthusiasm about Leading Brands despite my prior losses in its market sector.

RISKS: THE ABILITY TO IMAGINE
WHAT COULD GO WRONG

The next step in my process is to think through and imagine what could go wrong with the prospective investment. For Leading Brands, the major risks appeared to be minimal compared to most small cap stocks. But there were still a number of potential pitfalls. These included: the fickle nature of customer tastes, which could migrate away from the company's product lines; the uncertainties involved in raising capital on acceptable terms to finance expansion into U.S. markets or other initiatives; the possibility of contamination with bacteria in the bottling process, notwithstanding the company's excellent track record of close to 300 million bottles a year without any contamination problems; and a disruption of operations from a labor dispute, a plant fire, or other events beyond the company's control. I was also skeptical of their Internet business.

For most small cap companies, this list is much longer, and the chance of the horrible happening is considerably less remote. Help in identifying and assessing the risks of investing in a particular company can be found in the narrative section of its quarterly reports and particularly its most recent annual report. This is called "Management's Discussion and Analysis of Financial Condition and Results of Operations," often referred to (for obvious reasons) as "MD&A." Although SEC rules encourage public companies to include a full and forthright discussion of negative trends and business risks in their MD&A disclosure, the focus is often generic or near-term-oriented. Companies tend to do a much better job in a prospectus for the sale of new shares or the resale of shares from time to time by existing stockholders. In fact, during the dot-com IPO craze, the investment bankers would joke about the company's prospects by weighing the "Risk Factors" section of its prospectus, which commonly exceeded ten prominently featured pages. Too bad we didn't take those risks more seriously.

I considered the LBIX risks relatively low, but I still considered them seriously. For Leading Brands to successfully execute its business plan, the company would need to find ways to penetrate new geographic markets, primarily the U.S., where the competition was bigger and better financed than its rivals in Canada. Did they have the capacity to execute that strategy? On the psychological side, there were a number of questions that also needed answering. Did management have the psychological strength to stick with the company through thick and thin? Would they be able to attract and retain competent and effective marketers with relationships that could help the company expand into the U.S.? Would they be available to talk with me on the phone and be forthcoming when questioned? How would they handle mistakes, which would inevitably occur? Did they have an intuitive sense of how to carry out a realistic business plan? Could the CEO make a charismatic, yet realistically accurate, presentation to potential investors and investment bankers?

My concerns were satisfied by attending a group face-to-face meeting with Leading Brands's CEO. I came away from the meeting sharing some of the CEO's confidence that Leading Brands was one of the more innovative companies in the beverage industry, with a realistic plan for expansion into the U.S. I believed they could ramp up revenues and earnings quickly. After weighing the risks against all the positive indications from my operational, financial, and psychological analysis, I was convinced an investment in Leading Brands at the $1.00 range for its stock at that time was virtually a steal.

THE RIGHT FIT BETWEEN YOUR INVESTING STYLE AND PERSONALITY

But a steal for whom? It felt like a steal for me because investing in Leading Brands fit my personality. I get excited about small, unknown companies that are below everyone's radar and above the market's valuation. I enjoy getting to know management. I know they will make mistakes during their companies' growth period, and I know it will probably take longer than they expect for them to achieve anticipated growth.

With Leading Brands, I also liked the fact they had no analyst coverage and no institutional following because it provided an opportunity for me to buy what I considered an undervalued stock before the herd drove up the price. I thought the CEO was competent and had extraordinary vision, but I also knew he was entrepreneurial and likely to make decisions that were intuitive and fast—not the kind of guiding force that would attract analysts to cover his company in the wake of the technology market collapse. This reinforced my sense of its being the right fit for me. I believe the willingness to be strongly influenced by that sense of fit is one of the most important psychological characteristics of the good enough investor.

As part of achieving the right fit between investing style and personality, the good enough investor must find a particular market niche that meshes with his or her personality. It is nearly impossible to understand all segments of the market. Some of us understand technology, some understand retail, others focus on small caps or on IPOs, and some of us understand emerging markets. You must search out a market sector that provides a good enough fit between your personality and your investing style. This is like an athlete finding the right sport. Part of what made Michael Jordan a great basketball player was his fit with the sport, the way his personality, talents, and skills fulfilled all the requirements of the sport. His fit with baseball made him an average player. It's no different in the investment world. If you are only comfortable with numbers and charts, you will probably perform better doing technical analysis on established companies. If you have a particular capacity for assessing management, you might perform better analyzing micro-caps. If you work in and enjoy the insurance business, you have a unique advantage when investing in that segment of the market. As a good enough investor, you must find a niche in the market that blends with your personality and meets your psychological needs. Otherwise, we're prone to becoming general players in the market. Like a utility infielder in baseball, a general player in the market spends most of the time on the sidelines, sitting on the bench.

Once I've identified an investment prospect in a market niche that appeals to me, I enjoy talking to its management, not only to assess their competence but also their vision for the company. If management believes it will take three years to execute their business plan and the plan seems sound, I'd rather wait those three years without the stock moving and then achieve a 400 percent gain than achieve annual gains of 15 percent to 20 percent each year. I like to think I have a good feel for people, and I look for management teams that have staying power and a knack for working well together in an environment that encourages intuitive, emotional, inductive, and imaginative think-ing. This is exactly the kind of thinking that entrepreneurial CEOs use, and the kind of environment I found at Leading Brands.

Even when all these components of the right fit are in place, there is another important factor to consider—valuation. I search for stocks with a large discrepancy between their price and underlying value, and I look for catalysts that can alter the perception of a company's growth potential. In Leading Brands, all of these factors played a role in deciding it was the right fit for me. Their expansion into the U.S. and their contract with Pez could act as catalysts, their CEO was intuitive and visionary, and the stock had the potential for a substantial and sus-tainable gain according to my financial analysis.

In his book *Sacred Hoops*, Phil Jackson, the former coach of the Chicago Bulls, cites an ancient Zen teaching:

> *When a fish swims in the ocean, there is no limit to the water,*
> *no matter how far it swims.*
> *When a bird flies in the sky, there is no limit to the air,*
> *no matter how far it flies.*
> *However, no fish or bird has ever left its element since the*
> *beginning.*[2]

However smart you may be, once out of your element you can't expect to perform up to your potential. As Jackson notes, "you can dream all you want, but, bottom line, you've got to work with what you've got."[3]

Think back to the dot-com market at the end of the last century. We heard over and over that investors in Internet stocks were taking high risks, putting their hopes and savings in companies with no track record or profits, companies whose stocks were selling at huge multi-ples of revenues and at astronomical P/Es. What the critics failed to take into account was that successful Internet stock investing was pri-marily done by individual investors who had superior knowledge about the technologies they were investing in, by those who used the Internet to trade, and by those who had a personality type oriented to short-term trading. Technologists live in a fast-paced world and often have little patience for the type of analysis that we fundamental investors like to perform. For the most part, even with all the risks, they were extremely well suited to the type of investing they were doing.

There were also long-term investors with little affinity for technology or experience with the Internet who bought Internet IPOs in the secondary market shortly after the stocks had appreciated 100 percent to 200 percent above their initial offering price. These investors were generally not acting in sync with their personality or investing style. Perhaps that's why so many of them waited patiently while their stocks retreated 80 percent or more from their buy price. Despite the market's volatility at that time, they probably would have succeeded if they played to their strengths, focusing on sectors that are slower-moving, require fewer hours in front of a computer screen, and have histories of solid earnings growth for the past five or ten years.

THE CAPACITY TO BE AN OUTSIDER

The good enough investor must also learn to be an outsider. You must cultivate the ability to walk to the beat of a different drummer. Develop your own style and ignore how others invest or view the capital markets, even if it means underperforming now and then. In the mid-1920s, the well-known artist René Magritte painted a picture of a pipe. Beneath it on the canvas he wrote, "Ceci n'est pas une pipe" ("This is not a pipe"). His painting points out the importance of questioning what appears obvious at first glance. Both the media and investment gurus tend to view events and statistics in myopic black and white. The real world, of course, is much more complex, reflecting many interesting combinations of colors that defy simple explanations. By cultivating your outsider instincts, you can learn to question the obvious and begin to see something new in what others glibly take for granted.

During the mid-1990s, I consulted for an unusual director of equity research at Putnam Investments, Patrick O'Donnell. In building and expanding his analyst group, Patrick and I were interested in figuring out what psychological characteristics contributed to making a good analyst. In addition to interviewing each analyst candidate, we administered a battery of psychological tests that involved following the analysts' decision-making process for several years. It turned out that one of the most predictive factors in becoming a good analyst was think-ing of oneself as an outsider. This did not mean they lacked friends or failed to function in a group; rather, it meant they believed they didn't quite fit in with the crowd, and they valued their own beliefs and judgments over those of their peers.

I remember excitedly explaining Leading Brands to a colleague soon after I discovered it. He listened carefully and then told me he would never invest in a Canadian company, especially one that was close to Vancouver. He warned me about all the shenanigans that go on in Vancouver, criticized LBIX's small market cap, complained about the lack of any analyst coverage, and whined about the lack of significant sales in the U.S. At the end of the conversation, he politely told me how he thought he'd rather stick with his well-known compa-nies, like Tyco, Enron, Elan, Intel, and Microsoft, where he could get good analyst coverage. My colleague was not an outsider. He depended heavily on analysts' recommendations and was uninterested in doing his own research. When Enron, Tyco, and Elan collapsed, he blamed the analysts. If Leading Brands collapsed, I would have no one to blame except myself. As John Maynard Keynes once said, "Worldly wisdom teaches that it is better to fail conventionally than to succeed unconventionally."[4]

The problem with subordinating yourself to others' opinions is that it prevents you from developing and maintaining your own view of the market or of a company. Especially in times when the market goes against you, or when a company temporarily falters, there is a ten-dency to look to others to buttress your decision-making process. The industry is replete with analysts who only want to recommend stocks that other analysts are recommending. It is overpopulated by partici-pants who want to look, dress, and speak like everybody else. But the few outsiders who are secure enough to be different are the ones most likely to outperform the averages.

When Paul Johnson became the first analyst to write a buy recom-mendation on Cisco Systems in 1990, long before anyone had heard of the company, he was an outsider who believed in his own evaluation of both the company and the networking market trends. It took a while before others jumped on Paul's bandwagon. When they did, it became an insider mass movement rather than individual outsiders putting themselves on the line. The good enough investor must be willing to approach the market as an outsider with the same attitude you need when you're purchasing a home—careful research, limited dependence on a broker's information, comparison shopping, and a belief in your own perception of the house and how it might feel to live in it. As discussed in chapter ten, however, being an outsider also seems to require, somewhat paradoxically, an investing relationship with a trusted other who provides enough support to help you maintain your sense of self, and thus remain an outsider.

THE CAPACITY NOT TO KNOW

The good enough investor must cultivate the ability to act despite inescapable unknowns and ambiguity of the market. Successful investing involves analytic skills, time-consuming research, occasional luck, extensive reading, helpful personal contacts, good timing, an intuitive feel for an innovative product, psychological mindedness, and a host of other intangibles. While getting the facts and figures straight is important, we can never assemble or acquire all the information we would like before making a financial investment. So being a good enough investor means having the capacity to act when we know enough, while accepting that we can never know it all. Even when we know a lot about a company, there are just too many variables and unknowns to ever be able to invest with 100 percent certainty.

When I invested in Leading Brands, there was much I had yet to learn about the company and its market sector. Despite having read carefully all the public information available, I hadn't visited the bottling plants. Were they efficiently operated and clean and free of bacteria? I hadn't met any employees other than the CEO. Were their perceptions of management as positive as the picture presented by their CEO? Did the company really have the capacity to penetrate the U.S. market? After all, they had never really tried. Was their marketing ability effective enough to bring in more customers to grow the business? Would the popularity of their packaging and drink formulations withstand the fickle tastes of retail customers? How could I be so sure of my projections for $0.25 earnings per share and $60 million in revenue for the next year? While knowing management's background, did I really know them well enough to trust what they told me? Would the company be able to secure analyst coverage eventually or develop a major investment banking relationship? I had a good feel but still did not know the answers to these questions with any certainty. No matter how much I explored each of them, and no matter how many telephone calls seemed to confirm some of what I did know, I still had to make an initial investment decision in a partial vacuum.

To be a good enough investor requires the capacity to act while not knowing enough to feel overwhelmingly confident about our actions. But what enables us to act despite the ambiguity? My answer is that our sustained tolerance for ambiguity is absorbed in a reflective process that encourages a mental search for explanations and meanings. In other words, it is the enjoyment of these mental activities— the continual search for further data about Leading Brands, the continual questioning of my beliefs about the company, the repeated calls to management, and the discussion of my hypotheses with others I trusted—that prevents the premature organization of ambiguity into some definitive assumption that leads to direct, myopic action. In this sense the capacity not to know exists because we can enjoy the search for knowledge while accepting that we will never know all there is to know about any of our investments. This requires cultivating the ability to reflect, to search for explanations and meanings with an inquiring mind and intense curiosity, and a capacity to suspend judgment. It can become second nature when we enjoy the process for its own sake, rather than solely as a vehicle for making money.

Through this process you can develop a sustained tolerance for ambiguity. Sitting back and reflecting prevents you from jumping to conclusions and acting prematurely. You should enjoy the search for meaning while simultaneously knowing that complete understanding is an impossible goal. At some point during the process, the time for action will feel intuitively right.

SELF-REFLECTIVE AWARENESS

A first cousin to the capacity for tolerating ambiguity is the process of self-reflective awareness. We know from years of psychological research that as the ambiguity of an external stimulus increases, we are more likely to interpret and organize its meaning according to the emotional convictions that structure our subjective world. This phenomenon is familiar to every child who lies on the grass and perceives specific objects in the vague cloud formations wafting above. If the child is feeling afraid, he is much more likely to see scary animals and would-be heroes who try but fail to vanquish them. If he is feeling happy and content, he is more likely to discern less threatening images or at least feel comfortable coping with the threatening images. Almost by definition, investment decisions are made with incomplete external information that is at best ambiguous. Unless you are an insider, it is impossible to grasp all the internal nuances of a company's financials, services, products, and management, to say nothing of the vagaries of the market, institutional money managers' whims, or economic, political, and social factors that may affect a stock's price. Especially for small cap companies with little or no history of revenues or earnings, forecasts are often nothing more than projections of the forecaster's own subjective reactions to a company. And even in the large cap market, where analysts' views are often unwittingly biased by colleagues' recommendations and investment banking concerns, there is never enough objective data to make decisions that are not uncertain or ambiguous to some extent. In David Dreman's research, only 58 percent of consensus forecasts fell within a plus or minus 15 percent band, hardly a confidence-inducing number.

Because external data is so ambiguous, it follows that much of our "understanding" of our investments is shaped by our unconscious internal organizing patterns. The good enough investor learns to be aware of these patterns though a self-reflective process. Examples of some specific patterns that are common to investors were offered in chapter one. In considering an investment in Leading Brands, I was forced to deal with one of my own organizing patterns—my predisposition to see patience as a higher virtue than action. This emotional conviction is not uncommon, perhaps accounting for the financial adviser's maxim that if a stock is a good investment this month, it will also be a good investment next month. The problem with this philosophy is that it ignores the fact that entry prices do matter, and they matter significantly in low priced stocks. When I found myself hesitating to make an investment in LBIX at close to $1.00, I realized that my emotional conviction that emphasized patience had in the past cost me significant percentage moves in a number of stocks even when I was highly confident about them. In this case, all the facts suggested that with a forward P/E of 4 and a nine-month history of LBIX hovering in the $1.00 range, there was very little downside risk and no reason to be patient with an initial investment. Having learned to practice at least some of what I preach, I overcame my inertia and purchased shares in LBIX. Within several weeks, those shares appreciated 75 percent, and I still thought the stock was undervalued (LBIX eventually reached $4.00). So despite being very confident of my financial analysis of this company, my psychological reactions were holding me back, although thankfully not indefinitely.

It is our capacity to observe and comfortably reflect on our organizing patterns over time, as they emerge from repetitive investment decisions, that contributes to being a good enough investor. An increasing awareness of emotional convictions that subtly influence our stock picking systems, selling disciplines, and understanding of economic realities can only increase our success in the market.

One of the best methods for discovering your own organizing patterns is to conduct *psychological* post-mortems. After selling a stock, make it a point to review the personal reasons for buying and for selling the stock. I am not talking here about the traditional understanding, for example, of whether you understood the company, reviewed the fundamental numbers or the technical indicators, or misjudged management—although these factors are obviously important. Rather, I mean trying to comprehend our idiosyncratic conceptions—the subjective themes—that determine our actions.

For example, if you find after reviewing your sell decisions on several stocks that you hung on too long and watched the stock drop beyond where you should have allowed it to retreat, you should try to figure out what organizing principle underlies such behavior. When I asked one investor who frequently made this type of error what thoughts she had when watching her stocks drop precipitously, she focused on her intelligence as an investor: "Every time I buy a stock my intelligence is on the line, and the thing I hate most is admitting I made a bad choice, so I guess choosing not to sell prevents me from confronting the fact that I can't be a perfect investor." At my urging, she then went on to describe a childhood environment in which the best way to be connected to her parents was to be "perfect"—in her behavior, her grades, her athletic performances. It followed that her need for perfection, which she had never associated with investing, was nevertheless interfering with her ability to cut her losses quickly. Because this kind of emotional conviction tends to become deeply embedded in our investing mind-set, it is extremely important to discover not only their components, but also their implications for our investment philosophies.

DECENTERING

Once we discover our own organizing patterns, we have a much better shot at transcending them, not by abandoning them, but by widening our perspective. Organizing patterns provide a set of unspoken (mostly unconscious) rules for guiding action, but they are limited. For example, whether or not you believed in a new economic paradigm at the turn of the century, the investors who had the most difficulty in that market tended to share an organizing pattern that says growth and low unemployment rates lead to inflation. Their reluctance to see beyond that conviction can be traced to an inability or unwillingness to decenter.

Decentering is a learned process[5] in which we step back from emotional turmoil and begin to incorporate disparate opinions by asking how other viewpoints and theories could alter our perceptions, or what could be right or reasonable about others' views or convictions about a stock or management. This opens up our organizing patterns to other points of views and theories. One way of decentering is to participate in a silent dialogue with our "devil's advocates," those whose belief systems are antithetical to ours, with a view to expanding our emotional convictions. By widening our perspective and incorporating ideas beyond the limitations imposed by our own emotional convictions, we can attain a greater self-reflective awareness that can give us an advantage in the market. There is no complete truth about a stock, a company, or management; there is always more than one story on any stock, company, or management, depending on one's perspective. Decentering makes it possible to achieve a balance between our entrenched patterns of organization and the assimilation of new and more expansive "configurations of experience."[6]

We all know that market events and company developments can evoke strong emotional states. For example, when I first learned that Leading Brands had made a major commitment to e-commerce by acquiring Quick, Inc. and committing $10 million to develop an online purchasing platform for home delivery, I had a strong negative reaction to the idea of a business-to-consumer emphasis, even if the company did expect the operation to be profitable soon. But whenever we evaluate companies, we experience isolated emotional states that give us very different clues than we would discover by looking at a whole picture. If I had isolated the e-commerce operation, I never would have recommended or bought Leading Brands. The isolated view would have distorted the whole gestalt of the company and its management, which created a much different picture than the single e-commerce element. By decentering from my established emotional state, I managed to keep the big picture in focus.

EMOTIONAL DISCIPLINE

In the preface to Ben Graham's *The Intelligent Investor*, Warren Buffett wrote:

> To invest successfully over a lifetime does not require a
> stratospheric IQ, unusual business insights, or inside information.
> What's needed is a sound intellectual framework for making
> decisions and the ability to keep emotions from corroding
> the framework. This book precisely and clearly prescribes the
> proper framework. You must supply the emotional discipline.[7]

Buffett is not alone in recognizing the importance of emotional discipline in the investment process. Most of the icons in the investment business recognize that emotional discipline is important to investment success, especially because the primary thread woven through the larger picture of the market is constant change.

Despite this general recognition, however, no one has defined or even explained emotional discipline or how to achieve it. In the simplest terms, we know that it refers to keeping our emotions under control—subordinated to some higher cognitive capacity or technical system that prevents emotion from influencing our decisions. But as I have indicated throughout this book, it is not at all clear that leaving emotions totally out of your investment decisions will produce any better results than making decisions based solely on emotions. Nor is it clear how we can consciously regulate how much emotion to allow into investment decision-making, or what factors help investors remain rational during periods of stock market turmoil.

My research suggests that the capacity to deal with strong emotions or crises, to modulate tension states, is perhaps the most important contributor to emotional discipline in the investment world. If one of your companies issues an earnings report that is below expectations and the stock price begins to fall, it will inevitably create psychological tension. However idiosyncratic these tension states may be, you can react in several different ways. On the one hand, you can perceive the feeling state as an indication of impending psychological disorganization (or doom in the market) and therefore as a traumatic situation. On the other hand, you can perceive the strong emotional state as a signal of a change in our psychological equilibrium rather than impending psychological disaster.

For example, following my 75 percent paper gain in Leading Brands, the stock began to pull back. My gain dropped to 42 percent. A fellow investor in LBIX told me unequivocally he was going to sell: "You could sit around and wait another six months for it to recover to a seventy-five percent gain. Why not let it drop and then buy it back and you'll make twice as much?" The emotions he elicited should be quite familiar to most investors. Should I take my profit and move on, wait until the stock drops again and buy it back, or hold on for the long run? The question evokes anxiety either way. If I sell, the stock is sure to go up again. If I hold on, the stock is sure to drop back to my buy price, and I'll lose all my gains. If I react to the emotions as impending disaster, they will disrupt my decision; but if I can tolerate the emotions as a signal that I should step back, decenter, and calmly weigh the possibilities, I can at least make a decision in an emotionally disciplined way. I won't always be correct, but when emotional discipline plays a role in decisions, I will be correct more times than not.

In this case, nothing about the LBIX story had changed, and the reasons I bought the stock still appeared sound. In addition, I knew it was common for a stock that appreciates quickly to retrace a third to a half of its gains in the short run. When I added up the costs of trading and paying taxes on short-term gains compared to the profits I would make if LBIX stock increased significantly over time as I expected, there was absolutely no rational reason to sell the stock.

If you can tolerate emotions without experiencing them as traumatic, that is, without experiencing the feelings as disorganizing and disrupting your decision-making process, they will act as a signal to guide your behavior. Where investors have not internalized the capacity for tolerating strong affect, they tend to search for automatic self-regulating systems designed to take the emotion out of investment decision-making. These systems appeal to our yearning for a pure state of intellectual reasoning, free from conflicting emotions and clutter. As Warren Buffett once suggested about investors who use computerized systems with that objective, "They studied what was measurable rather than what was meaningful."[8] Emotional discipline is only possible if emotion is integrated into our decisions rather than isolated from them.

THE CAPACITY FOR OPTIMAL RESTRAINT

Optimal restraint is a term coined by Morton and Estelle Shane and used in the therapeutic literature to mean a "response that is neither in excess of what is needed or desired by the patient nor so withholding or so unspontaneous that it serves to derail the process."[9] Transposing this into the investment community, I have consistently observed two extremes of investors—those who are overly optimistic and those who tend to be highly skeptical and somewhat paranoid. At the extreme, the first group is characterized by a self-confident conviction that they can beat the market through superior stock picking without making any mistakes. At times this feeling leads to what I described in an earlier chapter as grandiosity—a sense of omnipotence and perfection that misleads investors into thinking anything they touch will automatically turn to gold. Behavioral finance writers have pointed out that experts tend to be overconfident in their predictions.

While unfortunately all too true, the overly optimistic investor group I am discussing here feels not so much overconfident as grandiose; they can defy gravity and magically take flight while mere mortals can only watch in awe.

This sense of grandiosity reached epidemic proportions in the frothy IPO market during the technology boom. We only have to dredge up the October 1999 P/Es[10] of some IPOs to recall how grandiose their investors had become: RealNetworks with a P/E of 1219 or DoubleClick with a P/E of 933, Yahoo! with its P/E of 1194 or Amazon at a P/E of 353. If nothing else, this reminds us that grandiosity is a relatively easy trap for the unwary.

With that in mind, I could barely contain myself when I bought and recommended LBIX at a P/E of 4. I had fantasies of the stock running immediately to $5 or $6. After all, that would have only been a forward P/E of 20. Super management, exceptional service, solid business practices, good PR—what more did this company need to "take off"? Perhaps if the year were 1999 rather than 2002, it would have obtained an outlandish valuation. While reality suggested that Leading Brands was a wonderful, undiscovered opportunity that probably had little downside risk, it was still a small Canadian company that had yet to prove itself in the U.S. Without the ability to capture market share throughout North America, it would never be a meaningful player in the industry. In fact, many colleagues told me that these pitfalls were enough to avoid the stock altogether.

Those who wanted no part of LBIX were at the other extreme of the continuum. They were generally suspicious of every investment, always looking for some reason to support their theory that proponents of an investment were trying to dupe them. At this extreme, investors create a system of thought that explains most positive comments about a stock as somehow deceptive, duplicitous, and purposely designed to pull the wool over their eyes. They now find friendly forums in the Internet chat rooms: "XYZ stock down $4 on good news. The stock is a dead duck and should be sold. I've never seen credibility go out the window so fast. CEO promised X vendors. I heard he doesn't even have any. Call him and ask the hipster." Without an excuse to find fault in the external world, these investors would have to confront their own internal confusion, sense of chaos, and paranoia. By creating an external event to fear, such as incompetent or corrupt management, they can organize their internal confusion and direct their internal anger toward an external target rather than having to believe they might be a bit paranoid.

Investors at both these extremes are unable to take market and company risk in stride as an occupational hazard. With optimal restraint, however, the good enough investor understands his or her own idiosyncratic emotional responses to risk and is able to restrain both an overly optimistic and overly pessimistic investment bias. He is both trusting and skeptical, which allows investment decisions to be made without complete information, but with an ongoing sense of questioning. Optimal restraint also allows him to exit an investment when new and substantiated information dictates admitting a mistake, and it allows him to buy more shares in a declining stock when new information indicates the herd is overreacting.

TOWARD SELF-UNDERSTANDING

Investing will test core aspects of your sense of self. I have highlighted the capacity to be curious and puzzled, the capacity not to know, the capability to find the right fit with your personality type, the faculty of self-reflective awareness, the ability to decenter, and the capacity for optimal restraint as forming the core of the good enough investor's psychological profile. If you can access these psychological conditions and become acquainted with your emotional assets and limitations, the markets will become an adventure for you, instead of a mystery, and you will have a good enough shot at enjoying a future of successful investing. There are four major steps that will help you on the road toward investing self-understanding.

First, your capacity to be curious and puzzled must initially be directed toward yourself. You must make a concerted effort to become familiar with your organizing lenses, those unspoken emotional convictions that (unconsciously) determine how you make sense of the world. Initially many of us find we can get in touch with our organizing lenses, but making the connection between these emotional patterns and our actions is more difficult. For example, since one of my organizing patterns is "patience offers more rewards than action," I

hesitated to buy LBIX at $1.00. I provided myself with all sorts of
excuses and rationalizations for not buying the stock immediately: I
didn't know enough about the company; maybe management wasn't as
good as I thought; I hadn't talked to their competitors; if the stock
hadn't moved for nine months, it wasn't about to move immediately,
so there was no hurry to buy. It took several days before I connected
my emotional conviction with my hesitation to buy the stock. If you
can become acquainted with the connections between your underlying
psychological assumptions and how they structure your actions, you
will gain an immediate competitive advantage over your fellow
investors.

Second, you must strive to develop a wider range of psychological
convictions. This doesn't mean ridding ourselves of our well-
embedded emotional conclusions or questioning their validity. It
means expanding them to create more flexible alternatives for making
sense out of the plethora of data we encounter each day in the market.
For example, if I can expand my conviction that "patience offers more
rewards than action" to include a conviction that "action in the context of relative knowledge is rewarding," it will enable me to make an
investment decision when I know enough, though less than everything, about a company and its management. Combining these convictions might also have allowed me to feel more confident about my
evaluation of LBIX and to have taken an initial position at a lower
entry price, thus providing more of a margin of safety. Expanding your
repertoire of emotional convictions occurs best in the context of a
relationship with others you trust who can help to supportively point
out alternatives to your decision-making process. It is only with the
help of others who can act as friendly adversaries that we can decenter
enough to observe and expand our organizing patterns.

Third, once you become familiar with your organizing patterns,
you must strive through self-reflective awareness to understand the
context from which they developed. Most organizing patterns have
their roots in our relationships with family and friends. The purpose
of understanding the historical development of our emotional convictions is threefold. Just as in psychotherapy, an understanding of our
past helps us to feel a sense of continuity through time and through
space, a sort of "aha, this is why I think and act the way I do." Feelings

of continuity strengthen our sense of self, and when our sense of self is strong, we are more capable of functioning as an outsider and reducing the influence of groupthink on our decisions. In addition, once we understand the origins of our organizing patterns, we are in a position to realize that however necessary they were in our family of origin, they may not be so automatically necessary in our current life, and therefore they are open to modification. Finally, the more we know about the history of our own reactions, the less likely we are to rationalize our investment decisions based upon what's happening in the market or what others are doing. We are much more likely to appreciate that our beliefs and actions alone will determine our success or failure in the market.

Fourth, we must begin to experiment with new emotional convictions and the behavior they promote. The first three steps add to our emotional discipline and capacity for optimal restraint. After taking those steps, we are in a better position to begin working constructively on altering our investment behavior. For example, when LBIX began to move up in price, I was able to buy additional shares without hesitation; and when it pulled back from its highs, I could once again add to my position without assuming that behavior would lead to disaster. Only time will tell whether Leading Brands proves to be a big winner in the long run. But even if it does not, the lessons learned in discovering and expanding my organizing patterns should pay dividends in future investments.

In a 1994 *Barron's* column, Gene Epstein quoted a 1918 statement by economist John Maurice Clark:

> The economist may attempt to ignore psychology, but it is sheer impossibility for him to ignore human nature. . . . If the economist borrows his conception of man from the psychologist, his constructive work may have some chance of remaining purely economic in character. But if he does not, he will not thereby avoid psychology. Rather he will force himself to make his own, and it will be bad psychology.

Investing success requires that we maintain a delicate balance between the external world of the market and our own internal emotional states when making financial decisions. It is relatively easy to teach yourself how to understand the external world, to analyze a balance sheet, read a 10-K or 10-Q, and use fundamental ratios to compare prospective investment opportunities. It is much more difficult to recognize the impact of your own subjectivity on success and failure in the market. If this book serves as a beacon to illuminate your initial foray into investigating the impact of your own psychology on your investment decision-making, it will have served its purpose. For as the world and the market become increasingly complex, an informed psychological sensitivity to your investing style and personality can radically alter your understanding and approach to the market and provide pleasure in achieving your financial goals.

THE INVESTMENT
PERSONALITY QUESTIONNAIRE*

1. My favorite source(s) of investment advice is
(rank in order of importance):
    a. TV/Radio
    b. Books
    c. Investment websites
    d. Family or friends
    e. Professional financial advisers
    f. Magazines or newspapers
    g. Stock message board on the Internet

2. How much time do you spend on investing activities?
    a. Two to five hours per week
    b. Two to five hours per month
    c. Two to five hours per year
    d. Most of my spare time
    e. As little as possible

3. I make most of my investment decisions:
    a. At home
    b. At the office
    c. While traveling
    d. In meetings with my financial adviser

4. I own (or have owned) the following investments
(rank in order all that apply, with 1 being the category that makes up the
majority of your portfolio):
    a. Individual stocks
    b. Bonds
    c. Mutual funds
    d. Real estate (excluding your home)
    e. Annuities

*If you would like to take the questionnaire online and receive feedback, you can
access it at www. investor.capitalinternational.ca. Click on planning and then on
investment personality. There is currently no fee for this service.

    f. Futures or options
    g. Guaranteed investment certificates
    h. Segregated funds

5. During the past year have you sent for either a mutual fund prospectus or a financial package on an individual company? (Check all that apply.)
    a. Yes, I have sent for either a mutual fund prospectus or financial package.
    b. I have also read the information I received.
    c. I have not sent for a mutual fund prospectus or financial package.

6. I subscribe to the following information (check all that apply):
    a. Investment newsletter(s)
    b. Business magazine
       (e.g., *Fortune, Forbes, Business Week*)
    c. Online service(s)
       (e.g., AOL, Earthlink, AT&T broadband)
    d. Business newspapers
       (e.g., *The Wall Street Journal, Barron's*)
    e. Popular financial magazines
       (e.g., *Smart Money, Worth, Kiplinger*)
    f. None of the above

7. I tend to sell investments because:
    a. My financial adviser recommends that I sell
    b. The reason I bought an investment changes
    c. I need the money
    d. The news headlines suggest the market is going down

8. If you were on a game show, which of the following questions could you answer?
    a. What is a bull market?
    b. What does ROE mean?
    c. What is a fund management fee?
    d. What is the TSE 300 Index?
    e. What is a growth and income fund?
    f. None of the above

9. I prefer to make investment transactions:
    a. Over the phone to my broker
    b. Using the Internet
    c. Through the mail
    d. Through my financial adviser

10. How would you characterize your investing style?
    a. Extremely conservative
    b. Somewhat conservative
    c. Willing to assume moderate risk
    d. Willing to assume a high level of risk

11. What would you estimate the average inflation rate has been during the past fifty years?
    a. 1 percent per year
    b. 3 percent per year
    c. 5 percent per year
    d. 7 percent per year
    e. 10 percent per year

12. If you were to use a financial adviser, which of the following characteristics in your relationship with the advisor would be most important to you? (Rank in order of importance.)
    a. Maximizing returns
    b. Protecting capital
    c. Trust
    d. Education
    e. Help in dealing with financial stress
    f. Confidentiality
    g. Investment knowledge
    h. Fee structure
    i. An ongoing relationship
    j. Other (please specify)

13. When I hear investment people talking about a "long term holding," they probably mean:
    a. One year
    b. Two to five years
    c. Six to ten years
    d. Until retirement
    e. Forever
    f. Don't know

14. If I bought a stock that went down 50 percent, I would:
    a. Sell it
    b. Buy more
    c. Hold on until I got even
    e. Consult a professional
    f. Contact the company
    g. Not know what to do

15. If I sell an investment, I would be most likely to:
   a. Buy another investment
   b. Put the money in a money-market fund
   c. Use the money to buy needed or wanted items
   d. Ask for advice
   e. Don't know what I would do

16. If I lost money on an investment, I would:
   a. Not tell anyone
   b. Discuss it with my family
   c. Ignore the loss
   d. Try to make it up as quickly as possible
   e. Talk it over with my financial adviser

17. You are on your way to a cocktail party. You know the group talks mainly about investing, and your portfolio is currently down. You would probably be thinking:
   a. I wish I weren't going to the party
   b. I'll avoid talking about investing
   c. I'll just talk about my winning investment picks
   d. I'll lie about how my portfolio is doing so I can at least fit in with the group
   e. I'll talk about my losses

18. In my family, the responsibility for finances falls to:
   a. Me
   b. My spouse or significant other
   c. My children
   d. My partner or spouse and me
   e. Other

19. While growing up, my family's attitude toward money could be characterized as:
   a. Money was discussed openly
   b. There was always tension surrounding money
   c. Money was never discussed
   d. Money was viewed as a distasteful subject

20. As a youngster, I felt that money was:
   a. A reward
   b. Something I had a right to have
   c. Something that had emotional meaning (power, self esteem, control)
   d. Something I should work to obtain
   e. I didn't really think about money as a kid

21. How I would you prefer to learn how to play tennis?
(Rank in order of importance.)
>   a. From a coach
>   b. From a book
>   c. From a video
>   d. From a friend
>   d. Through trial and error

22. I have been an investor for:
>   a. Zero to two years
>   b. Two to five years
>   c. Five to ten years
>   d. More than ten years

23. How would you react if you told a joke in front of a large audience and no one laughed? (Rank in order of importance.)
>   a. Blame the audience
>   b. Feel embarrassed
>   c. Ignore it and go on
>   d. Criticize myself
>   e. Wonder why they didn't think it was funny
>   f. I wouldn't dare to tell the joke in the first place

24. How do you handle a serious problem? (Rank in order of importance.)
>   a. Talk it over with friends
>   b. Listen to music or read
>   c. Take care of it myself
>   d. Consult a professional
>   e. Dismiss it as unimportant

25. How do you usually feel when the postman delivers a certified letter to your door? (Rank in order of importance.)
>   a. Anxious and tense
>   b. Excited
>   c. Curious
>   d. Neutral

26. I would be most comfortable with my portfolio if:
>   a. It increases at 15 percent per year
>   b. It loses money for three years and then gains 300 percent in the fourth year
>   c. I've never thought about it

27. When you experience a sudden and unexpected negative change, how do you generally react? (Rank in order of importance.)
    a. I discuss it only with family members
    b. I remain calm and rational
    c. I seek help from friends and colleagues
    d. I tough it out
    e. I use relaxation techniques
    f. I dismiss it as unimportant
    g. I temporarily panic

28. What do you think the next twenty-five years will bring to the world? (Rank in order of importance.)
    a. More peace
    b. Increasing danger
    c. More impersonality
    d. The destruction of the planet
    e. I have no idea about the next twenty-five years

29. If I had invited a houseful of guests for Thanksgiving dinner, in preparing the meal, I would:
    a. Follow a recipe
    b. Adapt a recipe to my own taste
    c. Experiment without directions
    d. Consult a friend
    e. Hire a caterer

30. Most people have experienced real or emotional losses in their life. I coped with the losses I have experienced by:
    a. Talking with someone
    b. Handling it myself
    c. Engaging in a soothing activity (yoga, listening to music, nature, etc.)
    d. Turning to religion
    e. I haven't experienced any significant losses

31. If someone I knew lost his or her job tomorrow, I would:
    a. Advise him or her to start a business
    b. Encourage him or her to explore alternative job possibilities
    c. Suggest he or she find another job in his or her field
    d. Advise him or her to take any available position to maintain his or her income
    e. Wouldn't know what to tell him or her to do

32. Other people tend to think of me as (check all that apply):
    a. A dreamer
    b. A practical person
    c. An adventurer
    d. A cautious person
    e. Independent
    f. Hopeful and optimistic
    g. Anxious and fearful
    h. Self-confident
    i. Other

33. If the stock market dropped 450 points, I would:
    a. Ignore it
    b. Feel worried
    c. Talk with friends about it
    d. Telephone my broker or financial adviser
    e. Assume it would recover shortly
    f. Sell everything

34. As a general rule, the years seem to pass:
    a. Slowly
    b. Quickly
    c. I never thought about it

35. If my plane was delayed more than an hour, I would:
    a. Try to find another flight
    b. Sit and read
    c. Call friends and family
    d. Insist on compensation from the airline
    e. Choose another airline for my next trip
    f. Begin pacing

36. If I worked for a large company and could choose my position, I would be:
    a. In charge of hiring
    b. The boss's right-hand man or woman
    c. The chief executive officer
    d. Middle management

37. If I were lost in a strange city, I would:
    a. Find my way by trial and error
    b. Ask directions
    c. Use a map
    d. Call someone on my cell phone

38. The subject of investing is:
    a. Fascinating
    b. Boring
    c. Challenging
    d. Something I don't want to deal with
    e. A topic I love to talk about with others
    f. A subject I don't have time for

39. If I were suddenly were given $1 million, I would feel:
    a. Overjoyed
    b. Anxious
    c. Guilty
    d. Depressed
    e. Don't know how I'd feel

40. Over the course of many years I have felt as though I:
    a. Walked to a different drummer than the
       rest of the world
    b. Fit in well with society
    c. Never gave it much thought

41. If I were conducting a research project, I would be most likely to:
    a. Look to others for guidance
    b. Put my own judgments and beliefs ahead of those in
       positions of authority
    c. Work comfortably with others
    d. I wouldn't want to do a research project

42. My biggest fear about investing is:
    a. Losing money
    b. Making a mistake
    c. Others finding out I failed
    d. Not having enough knowledge

43. When I buy a new VCR, I am more likely to figure out how it works by:
    a. Reading the directions
    b. Experimenting with it
    c. Asking a child to teach me how it works
    d. Calling technical support at the company

44. When making financial decisions, I am more comfortable with:
    a. As much information as possible
    b. A few significant facts
    c. Having someone else make the decision

45. Retirement is something I:
    a. Look forward to
    b. Don't think about
    c. Feel anxious about

46. When I go to bed at night, I generally feel:
    a. Satisfied with my day
    b. Relieved the day is over
    c. Worried
    d. Disappointed
    e. Concerned that I haven't had enough time in the day

47. In planning my vacation, I would (check all that apply):
    a. Make reservations in advance
    b. Make some reconnections in advance and play
       the rest by ear
    c. Book nothing in advance and find accommodations
       when I arrive
    d. Use a travel agent
    e. Make reservations online

48. If you decided to explore a new sport, which would you select?
(Rank in order of importance.)
    a. Adventure sports (e.g., mountain climbing, auto racing)
    b. Active sports (e.g., skiing, tennis, basketball)
    c. Leisure sports (e.g., golf, bowling, boating)
    d. Prefer to watch sports on television

49. If I were buying a new car, I would tend to make a choice based
primarily on:
    a. Research
    b. My intuition about the best car for me
    c. Advice from family and friends

50. When it comes to saving money, I:
    a. Tend to plan ahead for what I'll need in the near future
       (e.g., cars, vacations)
    b. Believe that living for the present is best
    c. Think that saving money for retirement is more
       important than my present needs

NOTES

INTRODUCTION: When Psychology Meets Finance

1. Dickinson, E. "Poem 1331." In Johnson, T.H. (ed.) (1961) *The Complete Poems of Emily Dickinson*. Boston: Little, Brown and Company.

2. Ellis, C. (1993) *Investment Policy*. Homewood, Ill.: Business One Irwin, p. 10.

3. Cited in Ignites.com. Jan. 21, 2000.

4. Dreman, D. (1979) *Contrarian Investment Strategy*. New York: Random House.

5. Ellis, C. (1993) *Investment Policy*. Homewood, Ill.: Business One Irwin.

6. Tversky, A., and D. E. Kahneman (1974) "Judgment Under Uncertainty: Heuristics and Biases." *Science*, 185, pp. 1124–1131.

7. Fischhoff, B. (1982) "Debiasing." In Kahneman, D., Slovic, P., and Tversky, A. (eds.), *Judgment Under Uncertainty: Heuristics and Biases*. Cambridge: Cambridge University Press.

8. Winnicott, D. (1953) "Transitional Objects and Transitional Phenomena." *International Journal of Psychoanalysis*, Vol. 34, Part 2.

ONE: Emotions in the Marketplace

1. Ellis, C. (1993) *Investment Policy*. Homewood, Ill.: Business One Irwin.

2. The clinician/researcher who coined the term *organizing lens* was Dr. Robert Stolorow. I highly recommend his work and that of his colleagues, an initial sampling of which can be found in Stolorow, R., Atwood, G., and Brandchaft, B. (1994) *The Intersubjective Perspective*. New York: Aronson.

3. Hunting, C. (1997) *The Experience of Art: Selected Essays and Interviews*. Orono, Maine: Puckerbrush Press, p. 154.

4. The term *emotional conviction* belongs to the Stolorow group of colleagues. It can be found in Orange, D., Atwood, G., and Stolorow, R. (1997) *Working Intersubjectively: Contextualism in Psychoanalytic Practice*. Hillside, N. J.: Analytic Press.

5. Stolorow, R., Atwood, G. E., and Brandschaft B. *The Intersubjective Perspective*. Northfield, N. J.: Jason Aronson.

6. Erikson, E. H. (1950) *Childhood and Society*. New York: Norton, p. 404.

7. Miller, M. H. (1986) "Behavioral Rationality in Finance: The Case of Dividends." In Hogarth, R. M., and Reder, M.W. (eds.), *Rational Choice: The Contrast Between Economics and Psychology*. Chicago: University of Chicago Press.

8. Dreman, D. (2001) "The Role of Psychology in Analysts' Estimates." *Journal of Psychology and Financial Markets*. Vol. 2, No. 2, pp. 66–68.

9. Damasio, A. (1994) *Descartes' Error: Emotion, Reason, and the Human Brain.* New York: Avon Books.

10. Stern, D. (1985) *The Interpersonal World of the Infant.* New York: Basic Books.

11. Dreman, D. (2000) *Contrary Investment Strategies: The Next Generation.* New York: Simon & Schuster.

12. Buffett, W. (2000) *The Essays of Warren Buffett: Lessons for Corporate America.* Cunningham, L. A. (ed.). New York: L. A. Cunningham, p. 168.

13. Ibid., p. 190.

14. Quoted in Buffett, W. (2000) *The Essays of Warren Buffett: Lessons for Corporate America.* Cunningham, L. A. (ed.). New York: L. A. Cunningham. p. 45.

15. For the use of this term in clinical work, see Erikson, E. (1964) "The Nature of Clinical Evidence." In *Insight and Responsibility.* New York: Norton.

16. Orange, D., Atwood, G.E., and Stolorow, R. (1997) *Working Intersubjectively.* Hillside, N.J.: Analytic Press, p. 25.

17. Ibid., p. 24.

18. Neuberger, R. (1997) *So Far, So Good. The First 94 Years.* New York: Wiley.

TWO: **Watching Out for Mr. Market**

1. This primer is based on the Self Psychological work of Heinz Kohut and his colleagues. Over the years I have been deeply immersed in teaching what has come to be called Self Psychology. In addition to being a very powerful therapeutic modality, I have found it particularly relevant to understanding the complexities of the psychology of investing. See particularly Kohut, H. (1981) *How Does Analysis Cure?* Chicago: University of Chicago Press. And Kohut, H. (1977) *The Restoration of the Self.* Chicago: University of Chicago Press.

2. Kohut, H. (1977) *The Restoration of the Self.* Chicago: University of Chicago Press.

3. Eiseley, L. (1970) *The Invisible Pyramid.* New York: Charles Scribner's Sons, p. 154.

4. Erikson, E. H. (1950) *Childhood and Society.* New York: Norton.

5. Gould, S. J. (1994) "The Evolution of Life on Earth." *Scientific American,* Oct. 1994.

6. Bernstein, P., personal communication.

7. Bullfinch, T. (1913) *Bullfinch's Mythology.* New York: Thomas Y. Crowell Co.

8. Tolpin, M. (1972) *The Daedalus Experience: A Developmental Vicissitude of the Grandiose Fantasy. The Annual of Psychanalysis.* Vol 2. New York: International Universities Press.

9. Goodspeed, B. (1978) "The World's Smartest Man Syndrome." *Journal of Portfolio Management,* Vol. 3, No. 4. Summer. New York: Institutional Investor, Inc.

10. Quoted in Kohut, H. (1966) "Forms and Transformations of Narcissism." *Journal of the American Psychoanalytic Association.* Vol. 14.

11. Tolpin, M. (1972) "The Daedalus Experience: A Developmental Vicissitude of the Grandiose Fantasy." *The Annual of Psychoanalysis.* Vol. 2. International Universities Press.

THREE: **Building Castles in the Sand**

1. Portions of this chapter first appeared in Lifson, L., and Geist, R. (1999) *The Psychology of Investing*. New York: Wiley.

2. Eiseley, L. (1969) *The Unexpected Universe*. New York: Harcourt, Brace, and World.

3. Jeffrey, R. (1984) "A New Paradigm For Risk." *Journal of Portfolio Management*. Vol. 11, No. 1.

4. Bernstein, P. (2000) "In Search of the Meaning of Risk." *Journal of Portfolio Management*. Spring.

5. For a more quantitative approach to the study of risk, which reaches a similar conclusion—that the meaning of risk is determined by subjective factors—see the brilliant work of Paul Slovic. A good introduction can be found in Slovic, P. (2000) *The Perception of Risk*. London: Earthscan Publications.

6. Personal communication.

7. Khan, M. (1974) "The Concept of Cumulative Trauma." In *The Privacy of the Self*. New York: International Universities Press.

8. Hawking, S. (1983) *Black Holes and Baby Universes and Other Essays*. New York: Bantam Books.

9. An important finding of behavioral finance—that we are much more likely to become risk seekers in the face of loss—suggests that there is probably a large discrepancy between our perceived capacity for risk and our actual behavior. See Kahneman, D., and Tversky, A. (1979) "Prospect Theory: An Analysis of Decision Under Risk." *Econometrica*, 47.

10. Morrison, A. (1984) "Shame and the Psychology of the Self." In Stephansky, P. and Goldberg, A. (eds.) *Kohut's Legacy*. Hillsdale, N.J.: Analytic Press.

11. Schachter, S., Hood, D. C., Gesin, W., Andressen, P., and Rennert, M. (1985) "Some Causes and Consequences of Dependence and Independence in the Stock Market." *Journal of Economic Behavior and Organization*, 6.

12. If you wish to take the questionnaire and receive feedback, you can access it at http://www.investor.capitalinternational.ca. At the time of this printing, there is no charge for the service. The questionnaire itself appears on pp. 283–291.

13. Barber, B., Odean, T. (2000) "Trading is Hazardous to Your Wealth: The Common Stock Performance of Individual Investors." *Journal of Finance*, 54.

14. The latest research coming out of Decision Research in Eugene, Oregon, supports this contention. See McGregor, D., Slovic, P., Dreman, D., and Bery, M. (2000) "Image, Affect, and Financial Judgment." *Journal of Psychology and Financial Markets*. Issue 1, pp. 104–110.

15. Buffett, W. (2000) *The Essays of Warren Buffett: Lessons from Corporate America*. Cunningham, L. A. (ed.). New York: L.A. Cunningham.

16. Ibid.

17. Shapiro, D. (1965) Neurotic Styles. New York: Basic Books.

18. Ibid.

19. Keynes, J. M. (1921) *A Treatise on Probability*. London: MacMillan.

20. Freud, S. (1927) The Future of an Illusion. New York: Liveright.

FOUR: **In the Company of Strangers**

1. MacKay (1848) *Extraordinary Popular Delusions and the Madness of Crowds*. New York: Harmony Books, 1980 edition.

2. LeBon, G. (1960) *The Crowd*. New York: Viking Press.

3. Winnicott, D. W. (1960) *Maturational Processes and the Facilitating Environment*. New York: International Universities Press.

4. Stolorow, R., and Atwood, G. E. (1992) *Context of Being: The Intersubjective Foundations of Psychological Life*. Hillside, N. J.: Analytic Press.

5. Ibid.

6. Kelley, K. (1998) *New Rules for the New Economy*. New York: Viking.

7. Dreman, D. (2001) *The Institute of Psychology and Markets Newsletter*. Vol. 1, No. 1.

8. Ibid.

9. I should point out, however, that there were many legitimate attempts to develop fundamental analytic tools for investing in the new economy. The most comprehensive one resulted in *The Gorilla Game* by Geoffrey Moore, Paul Johnson, and Tom Kippola (1998).

10. If you would like to keep track of valuation levels with the formula the Fed allegedly uses, all you need is your calculator. For a hypothetical example, take the forward twelve-month consensus S&P earnings estimate ($54.09), divide it by the ten-year treasury-bond yield (4.00) = 13.52 and multiply by 100 to get the fair value of the S&P = 1352. If the S&P were at 800, it would mean that the S&P was about 41 percent undervalued (800–1352 = 552/1352 = 40.8 %).

11. Erikson E. H. (1977) *Toys and Reasons*. New York: W.W. Norton, p. 64.

12. Nearing, H. (1992) *Loving and Leaving the Good Life*. Post Mills, Vt.: Chelsea Green Publishing Company, p. 17.

13. Slavin, M., and Kriegman, D. (1990) "On the Resistance to Self Psychology— Clues from Evolutionary Biology." Goldberg, A. (ed.). *Progress in Self Psychology*, Vol. 6. Hillside, N.J.: Analytic Press. See also Slavin, M., and Kriegman, D. (1992) *The Adaptive Design of the Human Psyche: Psychoanalysis, Evolutionary Biology, and the Therapeutic Process*. New York: Guilford.

14. I first heard this phrase in a conversation with Patrick O'Donnell, chief of equity research at Putnam Investments. Thus he deserves credit for its use.

15. Kelley, K. (1998) *New Rules for the New Economy*. New York: Viking, p. 5.

16. Ibid.

17. Winnicott, D. W. *The Maturational Processes and the Facilitating Environment*. New York: International Universities Press, p. 69.

18. Kohut, H. (1984) *How Does Analysis Cure?* Chicago: University of Chicago Press.

19. For a discussion of herding behavior among analysts, see Scharfstein, D., and Stein, J. (1990) "Herd Behavior and Investment." *American Economic Review*. Vol. 80, No. 3. Also see Olsen, R. (1996) "Implications of Earnings Behavior for Earnings Estimation, Risk Assessment, and Stock Returns. *Financial Analysts Journal*. July/August.

20. Tuchman, B. (1981) *Practicing History*. New York: Alfred A. Knopf, p. 248.

21. Levinson, D. and Atwood, G. E. (1999) "A Life of One's Own: A Case Study of the Loss and Restoration of the Sense of Personal Agency." Goldberg, A. *Progress in Self Psychology*. Vol. 15, pp. 163–81.

22. Stern, D. (1985) *The Interpersonal World of the Infant*. New York: Basic Books, p. 77.

23. Kohut, H. (1977) *The Restoration of the Self*. Chicago: University of Chicago Press.

FIVE: On Not Being Able to Wait

1. Langer, S. (1967) *Mind: An Essay on Human Feeling*. Baltimore: Johns Hopkins Press. Quoted in Goldberg, A. (1971) "On Waiting." *The International Journal of Psychoanalyis*, Vol. 52, No. 4.

2. Coleridge, S. (1927) *The Poems of Samuel Taylor Coleridge*. London: Oxford University Press.

3. WGBH/Frontline interview with Peter Lynch, 1998. www.pbs.org/wgbh/pages/frontline/shows/betting/pros/lynch.html.

4. Most calculators have a built-in formula for calculating net present value. But if yours doesn't, the following will work for you: $BV(1.0+G)^n = EV$, where BV = beginning value, G = growth rate, n = number of years, and EV = ending value.

5. Ellis, C. (2000) "Levels of the Game." *Journal of Portfolio Management*. Winter.

6. Eliot, T. S. (1943) "Burnt Norton." In *The Four Quartets*. New York: Harcourt, Brace, and World.

7. Buffett, W. (2000) *The Essays of Warren Buffett: Lesson for Corporate America*. Cunningham, L. A. (ed.). New York: L. A. Cunningham, p. 89.

8. Rotenberg, V. S. (1984) "Search Activity in the Context of Psychosomatic Disturbances of Brain Monoamine and RFM Sleep Function." *Pavlov Journal of Biological Science*. Vol. 19. Rotenberg, V. S. (1992) "Sleep and Memory 1: The Influence of Different Sleep Stages on Memory." *Neuroscience and Biobehavior Review*. Vol. 16. Rotenberg, V. S. (1993) "REM Sleep and Dreams as Mechanisms of Recovery of Search Activity." In Moffat, A., Kramer, M., and Hoffman, R. (eds.), *The Functions of Dreaming*. Albany: State University of New York Press.

9. Langer, op.cit.

10. Tomkins, S. (1992) *Affect, Imagery, Consciousness. Vol. 4: Cognition: Duplication and Transformation of Information*. New York: Springer.

11. Buffett, W. (2000) *The Essays of Warren Buffett: Lessons for Corporate America*, Cunningham, L. A. (ed.). New York: L. A. Cunningham, p. 208.

SIX: Letting Go

1. Notable exceptions are Justin Mamis's 1994 book *When to Sell for the '90s: Inside Strategies for Stock Market Profits*. Burlington, Vt: Fraser Publishing Company. And Donald Cassidy's 1997 book *It's When You Sell That Counts*. Chicago: Probus.

2. Gould, S. J. (1989) *Wonderful Life*. New York: W.W. Norton, pp. 320–21.

3. Erikson, E.H. (1950) *Childhood and Society*. New York: W.W. Norton.

4. Cassidy, D. (1999) "Why Is It So Difficult To Sell." In Lifson, L., and Geist, R. *The Psychology of Investing*. New York: Wiley, p. 37.

5. Gigerenzer, G. Todd, P.M., and the ABC Research Group (1999) *Simple Heuristics That Make Us Smart*. New York: Oxford University Press. Quoted in Boyd, M. (2001) "On Ignorance, Intuition, and Investing: A Bear Market Test of the Recognition Heuristic" in *The Journal of Psychology and Financial Markets*. Vol. 2, No. 3.

6. MacGregor, D., Slovic, P., Dreman, D., and Berry, M. (2000) "Imagery, Affect, and Financial Judgment." *The Journal of Psychology and Financial Markets*. Vol. 1, No. 2.

7. Black, F. (1986) "Noise." *Journal of Finance*. Vol. 41, No. 3.

8. Dreman, D. (2000) *Contrary Investment Strategies: The Next Generation*. New York: Simon & Schuster.

9. Buffett, W. (2000) *The Essays of Warren Buffett: Lessons for Corporate America*. Cunningham, L.A. (ed.). New York: L.A. Cunningham.

SEVEN: Talking with Management

1. Kohut, H. (1984) *How Does Analysis Cure?* Goldberg, A. (ed.). Chicago: University of Chicago Press, p. 82.

2. Schwaber, E. (1983) "Psychoanalytic Listening and Psychic Reality." *International Review of Psychoanalysis*. Vol. 10.

3. You will probably wonder how the Enron scandal might have played out differently if, following James Chanos's first suspicion of difficulties at the company, someone could have empathically explored with management what was going on at the company. Although I cannot prove it, based on other interviews, I believe the results could have been very different.

4. I want to thank Patrick O'Donnell, former chief of equity research at Putnam Investments, for helping to develop some of these questions.

EIGHT: Thinking Small

1. Cole, J. (1997) *Life List*. Camden, Maine: Down East Books, p. 155.

2. Holton, G. (1973) *Thematic Origins of Scientific Thought*. Cambridge, Mass.: Harvard University Press. Quoted in Erikson, E.H. (1977) *Toys and Reasons*. New York: W.W. Norton.

3. Einstein, A. (1973), Autobiographical notes. Schlipp, P.A. (ed.). *Einstein: Philosopher-Scientist*. New York: Harper Torch Books.

4. Graham, B. (1973) *The Intelligent Investor*. New York: Harper & Row.

5. Medwar, P. (1974) *The Hope of Progress*. New York: Doubleday. Quoted in Ferris, T. (1988) *Coming of Age in the Milky Way*. New York: William Morrow & Company.

6. For a deeper understanding of the concept of a "whole product," see Moore, G., Johnson, P., and Kippola, T. (1998) *The Gorilla Game*. New York: HarperCollins, Ch. 2.

7. Keynes, J. M. (1921) *A Treatise on Probability*. London: Macmillan.

8. Wilbur, R. (1969) "A Wood." *Walking to Sleep*. New York: Harcourt, Brace, Jovanovich.

9. *Stocks, Bonds, Bills, and Inflation.* 2002 Yearbook. Chicago, 2002.

10. Biggs, B. (1977) "Investment Strategy." In Ellis, C., and Vertin, J. (eds.), *Classics: An Investor's Anthology.* Homewood Ill.: Business One Irwin. p. 457.

NINE: Reacting to Loss in the Market

1. Fagles, R. (1996) *The Odyssey.* New York: Viking Penguin.

2. Ellis, C. (2000) "Levels of the Game." *Journal of Portfolio Management.* Winter, p. 12.

3. Ibid., p. 15.

4. Eliot, T. S. (1943) "Burnt Norton." In *The Four Quartets.* New York: Harcourt, Brace, and World.

5. Sporandeo, V. (1991) *Trader Vic—Methods of a Wall Street Master.* New York: John Wiley.

6. Erikson, E. H. (1950) *Childhood and Society.* New York: W.W. Norton, pp. 406–407.

7. Biggs, B. (1977) "Investment Strategy." In Ellis C., and Vertin, J. (eds.), *Classics: An Investor's Anthology.* Homewood, Ill.: Business One Irwin, p. 457.

8. Fagles, R., op. cit.

9. Fagles, R., op. cit.

10. Ulman, R., and Brothers, D. (1988) *The Shattered Self.* Hillside, N.J.: Analytic Press, p. 5.

11. Trauma, of course, is relative. From an objective vantage point, there is no comparison, for example, between the trauma suffered by those who lost loved ones in the terrorist attacks on September 11, 2001, and those who lost money and experienced a fragmented sense of self in the 2000 stock-market crash. But many investors described their experiences in the market as "traumatic," and it is this experience that I am trying to describe. For lack of a better term, I will call this investment trauma.

12. Grove, A. (1996) *Only the Paranoid Survive.* New York: Doubleday/Currency, p. 6.

13. Hagman, G. (1995) "Death of a Selfobject: Toward a Self Psychology of the Mourning Process. Progress in Self Psychology." In Goldberg, A. (ed.) (1995) *Progress in Self Psychology.* Hillside, N. J.: Analytic Press, p. 200.

14. The term Margin of Safety belongs to Ben Graham and was used to describe the difference between the price of a security and the intrinsic value of the underlying company. See Graham, B (1973) *The Intelligent Investor.* New York: Harper & Row.

TEN: Interpersonal Investing

1. Graham, B. (1973) *The Intelligent Investor.* New York: Harper & Row, p. 108.

2. Stolorow, R. (1984–1985) "Transference: The future of an illusion." *Annual of Psychoanlysis.* Vol. 12/13.

3. Stolorow, R., and Atwood, G. E. (1992) *Contexts of Being: The Intersubjective Foundations of Psychological Life.* Hillside, N. J.: Analytic Press, p. 61.

4.   Kohut, H. (1976) "Creativeness, Charisma, Group Psychology." In Ornstein, P. (ed.), *The Search for the Self*. New York: International Universities Press.

5.   Ibid.

6.   Lowenstein, R. (1995) *Buffett: The Making of an American Capitalist*. New York: Random House, p. 162.

7.   Lowe, J. (2000) *Damn Right: Behind the Scenes With Berkshire Hathaway Billionaire Charlie Munger*. New York: John Wiley, p. 7.

8.   Ibid., p. 7.

9.   Lowenstein, R., op.cit., p. 71.

10.   Gorney, J. (1998) "Twinship, Vitality, Pleasure." In Goldberg, A. (ed.) (1998) *Progress in Self Psychology*. Vol. 14.

11.   Klarman, S. (1991) *Margin of Safety*. New York: Harper Business. p. ix.

12.   Biggs, B. (1977) "Investment Strategy." In Ellis, C., and Vertin, J. (eds.) (1989) *Classics: An Investor's Anthology*. Homewood, Ill.: Business One Irwin, p. 458.

13.   See Lowenstein, R. (1995) and Lowe, J. (2000) above.

14.   Kainer, RGK. (1990) "The Therapist as Muse." In Goldberg, A. (ed.) *Progress in Self Psychology*. Vol. 6, 1990, p. 176.

15.   Winnicott, D. (1960) "The Capacity to be Alone." *The Maturational Processes and the Facilitating Environment*. New York: International Universities Press, p. 30.

ELEVEN: The Good Enough Investor

1.   Buffett, W. (2000) *The Essays of Warren Buffett: Lessons for Corporate America*. Cunningham, L. A. (ed.). New York: L. A. Cunningham. p. 185.

2.   Jackson, P. (1995) *Sacred Hoops*. New York: Hyperion, pp. 99–100.

3.   Ibid., p. 100.

4.   Keynes, J. M. (1936) *The General Theory of Employment, Interest, and Money*. New York: Harcourt, Brace.

5.   For a deeper understanding of decentering, which has its roots in intersubjectivity theory, see Orange, D., Atwood, G., Stolorow, R. (1997) *Working Intersubjectively*. Hillsdale, N.J.: The Analytic Press.

6.   Stolorow, R., and Atwood, G. (1992) *Contexts of Being: The Intersubjective Foundations of Psychological Life*. Hillside, N.J.: Analytic Press, p. 44.

7.   Graham, B. (1973) *The Intelligent Investor*. New York: Harper & Row, p. vii.

8.   Buffett, op. cit.

9.   Shane, M., and Shane, E. (1996) "Self Psychology in Search of the Optimal: A Consideration of Optimal Provision, Optimal Gratification and Optimal Restraint in the Clinical Situation." In Goldberg, A. (ed.), *Progress in Self Psychology*, Vol. 12. Hillsdale, N.J.: Analytic Press.

10.   Dreman, D. (2001) *The Institute of Psychology and Markets Newsletter*. Vol. 1, No. 1.

INDEX

ABOUT THE AUTHOR

Richard Geist is president of the Institute of Psychology and Investing, which provides consultation to brokerage firms, money managers, financial planners, small companies, and individuals. He received his undergraduate degree and his doctorate from Harvard University and is a clinical instructor in the Department of Psychiatry (Psychology) at Harvard Medical School. Geist is also a founding member and on the faculty at the Massachusetts Institute for Psychoanalysis. He is a codirector of Harvard Medical School's annual Congress on the Psychology of Investing and is an associate editor for the *Journal of Psychology and Financial Markets*. Dr. Geist also lectures extensively on the psychology of investing, and investing in the small-cap and micro-cap market.